IN THE NAME OF DEVELOPMENT

A Reflection on Nepal

Nanda R. Shrestha

University Press of America, Inc.
Lanham • New York • Oxford

Copyright © 1997 by
University Press of America,® Inc.
4720 Boston Way
Lanham, Maryland 20706

12 Hid's Copse Rd.
Cummor Hill, Oxford OX2 9JJ

Library of Congress Cataloging-in-Publication Data

Shrestha, Nanda R.
In the name of development : a reflection on Nepal / Nanda R.
Shrestha.
p.   cm.
Includes bibliographical references.
1. Poor--Nepal. 2. Economic development--Nepal. 3. Income
distribution--Nepal. 4. Nepal--Economic pollicy. 5. Nepal--Rural
conditions. 6. Social justice. I. Title.
HC425.Z9P677   1997 330.95496--dc21   97-12038 CIP

ISBN 0-7618-0758-6 (cloth: alk. ppr.)
ISBN 0-7618-0759-4 (pbk: alk. ppr.)

DEDICATED

To the memory of my parents,
Jog Man & Jog Maya,
who taught me
the meaning of dignity

and

to my wife, Pamela Lewis
and
son, Kiran Andrew,
who have taught me
the purpose of life.

✳

〜〜

TABLE OF CONTENTS

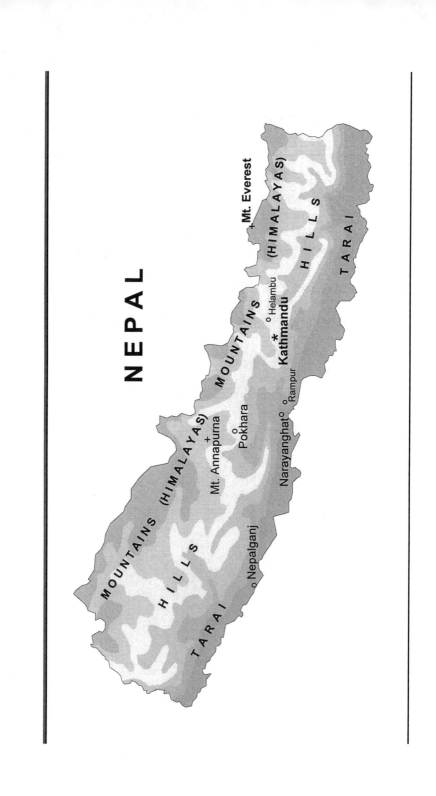

PREFACE

Dear Nanda,

Thank you for sending me "Enchanted by the Mantra of Bikas."
I found it fascinating, and it made me see that I and many other left
Marxists were also, in a way, dupes of bikas. We saw the horrors of
`underdevelopment' but only gradually came to the realization that the
standard ideas of `development,' right and left, don't have the answers. A really radical thinking of the whole `problematic' is urgently
needed.

Meanwhile, let me say that there is a yawning gap in your story
as set forth in this essay. You describe convincingly enough the
process by which you became enthralled to bikas, how you acquired
a colonial mindset, etc. But what is missing is any account of how you
managed to overcome it and criticize it from a polar opposite viewpoint. Not only is this a crucially important part of your intellectual/
political journey; even more important it should hold valuable lessons
for all of us who understand both the need and the difficulty of changing people's way of thinking.

I await the next installment of your story with great impatience!

All the best,

Paul M. Sweezy

This is the brief comment Paul Sweezy, a leading economist and co-editor of *Monthly Review*, wrote on an earlier version of Chapter 3. To
me, it is the second part of Paul's comment that is a challenge. While I
hope the real life stories, narrated in this book, reveal enough to inform
the readers of how development has brought undue suffering to countless
citizens, I cannot claim that I have overcome my colonial mindset. It is
still with me, and aches me like a lingering headache. Also challenging
to me is the poignant question that Paul seems to implicitly pose in his
comment: what can be done about the destructive course of contempo-

rary development? I also received a comment from Kellie Masterson, who once served as an editor at Westview Press. She wrote, "I find it disturbing that development can be so insidious," and then asked basically the same question as Paul. My search for an answer to their question has led me to offer some thoughts in the last chapter—but hesitatingly, I might add. While I have laid out some possible courses of action, I am not sure, to be frank, if there is any clear-cut, easy answer to the question. Although the roots of the problems facing today's underdeveloped societies may be universal because of their generally common colonial and neocolonial legacy, I see no universal solution. Common history does not necessarily produce common solutions.

Human history is a history of progress. So, in this respect, at least some level of development is inevitable. At the global level, consistent advancements of the forces of production have generated plenty of growth. Materially speaking, today's world is far more advanced than the world that existed before the industrial revolution. Paralleling this history of material growth, however, is the nagging persistence of poverty. That is, development has rarely been kind to the poor and downtrodden as it is invariably polarizing, both geographically and socially. History reveals that as Europe prospered, it left its colonies in a state of despair and underdevelopment (Amin, 1976; Baran, 1973; Frank, 1973; Rodney, 1974). The process continues. As the rich get richer, the poor are left by the wayside. As the center continues to grow and consume much of the resources, the periphery flounders. In other words, everywhere and throughout the history of economic growth, development has sharpened the lines that divide social classes as well as spatial economies, both at the local and global levels. Yet the appeal of development keeps surging.

In his discussion of the forces and relations of production, Karl Marx (1976) argued that advancements in the forces of production would have a revolutionary effect, ultimately liberating humanity from class-based exploitation. To him, modern technology was intrinsically "social" in character as it would push societies toward making people equal and interdependent. The production process would tend to make for a co-operative society. Technology thus had for Marx the qualities of a beneficent deity. Even Britain's colonial rule of India was viewed in positive light, for it was assumed to act as a channel of transferring British productive forces to India (or technology transfer as it is called today). As the logic went, this would not only result in "a social revolution," causing a breakdown of India's "barbarian egotism," but also eventually serve as an economic leveler. Referring to this presumed liberating role of colonialism, Marx (1959:480-81) expressed, "The question is: Can mankind fulfill its destiny without a fundamental revolution in the social state of Asia? If not, whatever may have been the crimes of England, she was the unconscious tool of history in bringing about that revolution." But contrary to Marx's vision, whatever technology England transferred to India was neither socially revolutionary nor economically progressive. As Feuer (1959:xvii) pointedly asserts, "In actual fact, however, modern technology has been among the principal forces working against socialism."

Almost a hundred years later in the postcolonial period, it is exactly this genre of Marxian vision that modernization theorists, including a staunchly anti-Marxist economist like Walter Rostow, projected about development. Of course, these theorists expressed their belief in their own lexicon with a capitalist bent. The angle was certainly different, but not the tone. They saw development as a mighty embodiment of modern technology and hence as a liberator of humanity from poverty across the world emerging from long colonial rule, the world that we today call "underdeveloped." Similar to the theory of Marx, the capitalist vision of modernization or development is a grand one that believes in the superiority and hence universality of the European mode of production in terms of its ability to free the people of these countries from their oppressive social systems by raising their economic standards. The underlying logic here is that foreign aid and foreign capital investment (e.g. technology transfer through multinational corporations) are two main agents of the diffusion of modernization principles from the West to the rest of the world. As such, they are seen as catalysts of development of the underdeveloped world.

The reality tells a different story, however. Irrespective of which periscope we use—whether Marxian or Rostowian—to assess the outcome of development, the picture is the same. Contemporary development in Nepal has been neither socially revolutionary nor economically progressive. Instead of acting as an economic leveler, it has been a polarizer. What has emerged is a gambling situation, one in which nobody wins unless somebody loses. So development has produced a trail of victims as the material growth of one segment of the population has been often achieved at the expense of another.

It is precisely this process of development victimization that forms the core of this book. To be specific, it is a narrative of development victims, a narrative based on their real life stories. Development victimization is not, however, confined to the poor and downtrodden; it encompasses a wide spectrum of people in society: rich and poor, peasants and prostitutes, dope dealers and development agents. In short, it affects both winners and losers. It is quite plausible to wonder how the winners could possibly be considered victims when they are the ones who have benefitted the most from development. This is certainly a valid question, especially given the fact that in our bifocal view the winners and losers are rarely equated with each other. They are often treated as two distinctly separate entities rather than as two interlinked but polar products of the same process.

In this book, I treat both winners and losers of development as being inseparable from each other. As Booker T. Washington (1986) implied in his autobiography, *Up From Slavery*, if you want to leave somebody in a ditch, you have to keep a constant watch on him. The point is that slavery, the ugliest social institution to ever terrorize humanity, exacts tolls from both the slave and slave owner. This does not mean that the toll the slave owner pays is comparable to the kind of physical and emotional dehumanization to which the slave is subjected. The tolls are vastly different—and any attempt to equate the two at the same par would be no less of a hideous crime than slavery itself. Nonetheless, the slave owner pays a price for his crime as he is bounded by the very slavery that he practices because he has to remain constantly watchful of the potential wrath and reprisals of his slaves.

So it is not just the poor who are victimized; the elites and educated too are victims of development. Surrounded by poverty and haunted by the looming shadow of rising social disparities resulting from development, they suffer from guilt as well as fear. It is not hard to detect a sense of disgust among many of the rich and elites about having to watch, day in and day out, their own kin and next-door neighbors going hungry while their plates overflow and bellies bloat. Furthermore, their obsession with material objects is so deeply entrenched that they even readily subordinate themselves to Westerners in order to bask in the glory that they bring to them.

The fact that the beneficiaries of development live like middlemen leaves them with little sense of true pride and dignity. While the ruling elites tightly control the domestic leverage of power, they hold no moral compass to guide the nation along a proud path of progress. As middlemen, the educated and elites of Nepal are directly tied to a feeble chain in their dealings and relations with Western masters who feed them. In fact, over the years I have personally come to know so many members of the Nepali intelligentsia who privately despise their subordination to whites, most of whom are junior to them in many respects, including education and overall qualifications. Boiling under the mask of their fake smiles is a deep sense of rage, one that is similar to the rage the black middle class in the United States feels (see Ellis Cose, 1993). It is all internalized and suppressed. Some are ashamed to admit it while others are afraid to even talk about it because of the fear of being labeled a rebel and thereby being excluded from the circle of Western aid. They don't want to give up their cozy material privileges derived from their association with Westerners. There is no doubt that they are troubled by their enormous identity crises as well as a sense of self-destructive emotional violence. Yet they are, to apply Orlando Patterson's (1994:117) phrase, "most postnational in their attitudes and behavior" as they are more concerned about their Western affiliation than their national affirmation and affection.

The educated and elites of Nepal are, therefore, the prisoners of the very material distance and demarcation they have created to separate themselves from the poor and downtrodden, those who are left bereft by development. Since the traditional bond of mutual dependence between the rich and poor has practically been broken, the discord and distrust between the two are growing deep. The elites are not only fearful of the deadly blow the poor may suddenly strike against the vital source of their material security rendering it asunder, but they also fear for their own physical safety. It is no coincidence that they have developed a barricade mentality, secluding themselves behind the security of iron gates and brick walls and even guards in some cases. Once almost entirely free of such fear, the affluent of Nepal today seek safety behind a barricade. Sure, these are intangible tolls to pay compared to the fear of daily survival the poor face, but still tolls that they cannot avoid paying in one form or another. The Promethean pain of development is bound to visit the rich sooner or later. When the poor fall, the rich will follow because their fate, as already pointed out, is mutually linked. This is the inevitable cycle of history. Development is after all more than just a matter of constructing roads and factories, fancy hotels and hospitals, huge dams and durbars (palaces), telephone lines and television networks. In the final analysis, development involves building (or destroying) mutually supportive human relations to uplift humanity, all humanity, not just a select few. Whether development can achieve such a collective goal of uplifting all humanity will ultimately depend on its ability to create a just society, a society where life is decommodified, where harmonious coexistence among all people and between people and nature is the norm, not mutual destruction in the name of individual progress.

My objective in this book is simple and straight forward: to give a voice to the victims whose cries have long been muted by the fiery rhetoric and empty slogans of development. To tell their stories in their own words as much as possible. To expose the insidious side of contemporary development, not so much in the form of some numbers detached from human feelings and pain, but in the form of real faces. After all, development is a human drama, a story of real people with real experiences, a story filled with personal tragedies and traumas, some directly inflicted upon them by the diverse forces of development and others simply cemented by these forces. Clearly, some of the tragic stories are unintended consequences of development. The outcome is the same, nonetheless, whether intended or not.

This book is based on years of personal experience and observations, both as a researcher and as somebody who grew up in Nepal. With my life deeply socialized and woven into the fabric of its culture, I am a product of Nepal. As a poor boy raised in Pokhara, I learned a lot about the hardships of life, as well as how to cope with them. And those lessons have stayed with me to this day (Chapter 3). As a peasant boy, I could not separate myself from the soil and from the forces of nature. As a young man, I learned to rebel against the king's autocratic rule, and roamed the hills and valleys throughout central Nepal, sometimes as a casual visitor and other times as a participant or representative in underground political activities. I visited many parts of the countryside, met many people, and tried to learn as much as I could about the way of life in rural Nepal. Once, back in the late 1960s, I even had a chance to teach at a middle school in a remote area called Jomsom, not too far from the Chinese (Tibet) border. So I am as much of an insider to Nepal as any resident Nepali can be.

There is no denying that all these outlooks and experiences, accumulated over many years, have profoundly colored my thinking and understanding of Nepali life and society as they have given me certain insights and consequently formed an integral part of my core belief system. The more these insights come alive from their deep slumber to guide my thoughts, the more I realize the destructive nature of contemporary development. As life softens with the passage of time, doubts about Westernized development that Nepal's ruling elites have been espousing for more than four decades become hardened. Given all of these elements, there is little doubt that I bring to this book an insider's view as filtered through the prism of my locally-crafted lenses.

Moreover, I intimately identify with the issues and people I write about because I am one of them (Chapter 3). To me, this book is not merely an outgrowth of some academic curiosity and exercise. I am, directly or indirectly, attached to the stories that fill the pages of this book. As a result, it is difficult for me to distance myself from their experiences and be a mere observer detached from their lives, or not to project my own sentiments and experiences on the screen in order to be able to carry the message of the silent voices which this book represents. These are the voices that epitomize the prevailing reality of development and dominant-subordinate relations between Westerners and Nepalis.

But, at the same time, I am an outsider, a distant observer, peeking in to discern the meaning of the puppet show that the Nepali intelligentsia is performing under the heavy shadow of development directed by Western agents and agencies. In 1972, when I was in my early twenties, I left Nepal (Chapter 3). Since then, I have lived in the United States that is now my home. My research endeavors have taken me back to Nepal several times, including two times in 1994. Each time I have spent months, going to villages and talking to countless villagers, both in group settings and individually. Although I have never encountered any problem fitting right in as if I had never left the country, there was always an outsider sitting inside me with his eyes and ears wide open. Since more than half of my life has been spent in the United States, it is hard not to see myself as an outsider, one who is quite removed from the day-to-day life in Nepal.

In addition, I have received almost all of my higher education in the United States. Although I have, in the past few years, grown extremely skeptical of the development role my adopted home country is playing in my previous home country, I must admit my theoretical education in the States has endowed me with a new set of lenses with which to view development. It has given me a tool to develop a different outlook on my past experiences and insights as well as on my ongoing research and field observations across the panoramic landscape of rural Nepal. It is fair to remark that, without this education, I would not have perhaps seen what I see now regarding the destructive nature of contemporary development. In other words, during every return since 1979 I have carried with me a pair of field glasses, one to view life in Nepal as an insider with rich personal experiences and another as an outsider well grounded in theoretical training.

It is precisely this insider-outsider perspective that serves as my methodological marker. In utilizing this perspective I have, as most readers will notice, oscillated between the use of first person and the use of third person, especially when addressing Nepali elites. As an insider, I am a member of the elite class, a self-made member. As such, I submerge myself among the elites, addressing them in first person. On the other hand, as an outsider, I address them in third person, thus distancing myself from their day-to-day role in Nepal's development process. Yet I am not a neutral observer—not by any means.

The insider-outsider approach is deliberate not only because I am both, but also because it allows me to echo the silent voices of development in a form that is generally free of the constraints imposed by a typical social science approach. Keeping in line with the spirit of both the research objective and methodological perspective of the book, I have tried to maintain an accessible language and a message that is simple and poignant, occasionally accented by some parables and metaphors. Direct quotes and citations are limited.

In the main, the present book, as already noted, is a narrative of development victims and their stories. While some readers may find such a methodological approach lacking in rigor or even question its scientific merit, others may see it as a refreshing pause in social science research. Regardless of their views, it is a simple book with a specific focus, and the readers, I hope, can at least hear the murmurs of the development victims' voices as well as touch their agony rather than treat it as playing victimhood. While development victims certainly form its nucleus, I make no attempt to play victimhood and place the blame squarely on Western development agents and agencies. It would be totally naive to absolve the domestic ruling elites from their deep-seated roles in development victimization, for they are full-time and active partners in this unholy process.

While the stories captured in this book are distinctly Nepali, their implications may reach far beyond the borders of Nepal as they reflect the broader reality of many other underdeveloped countries following a similar development trajectory. I make no claim to any theoretical formulation, however, for it contains none. Nor do I rely on any grand theoretical framework of development to define this book although, I must admit, my academic orientation has influenced the direction of its flow and the message of its contents. Whatever broad implications or theoretical connections it may have are largely a function of what I call historical commonalities most underdeveloped countries share despite their many regional and cultural diversities.

Writing this book has been a very difficult personal journey, not so much because of the arduous task involved but because of its contents and methodology. It has been a challenging exercise in self-reflection and soul-searching. Consequently, it has been personally very painful, yet revealing and rewarding. At times, I was overcome and confused and even embarrassed by the self-revelation of my own contradictory life. Yet thoughts came pouring out, like years of bottled-up pain rapidly bursting out in all directions, each vying for its own space and voice. So the book flows like a young mountain river without any predetermined course of thoughts rather than like a canal that is carefully engineered and dug up, that has a fixed path and destination. In light of this, let me caution that some readers may detect a few loose ends in the book. And some points are repeated. This is mainly due to its organizational structure. Since it is basically a collection of life stories with many parallels and overlaps, some repetition was inevitable or even unavoidable. While I have tried to minimize unnecessary repetition, some repeated points have been left alone in order to allow each chapter to have a life of its own. Almost every chapter stands on its own as it has its own character(s), complete with its own beginning and ending. As such, they can be read independent of each other, without losing the overall context of the book.

In preparing this book, I have received much help from many friends and family members. First of all, I owe my deepest gratitude to those who shared their stories with me, and to all the peasants who have, over the years, enriched my experience and understanding of Nepal. Needless to say, they are the primary subjects and guiding light of this book. They are the perennial spring of my inspiration. They are the ones who have helped me stay grounded in my roots, who have shaped my own life experiences. They are the ones who have nurtured and sustained my conscience. In addition, I am indebted to Mr. Ed Burgess for sharing his wide-ranging experiences in Nepal where he spent almost a decade, first as a Peace Corps Volunteer and later as a Peace Corps regional director. His comments were very helpful. Dr. John Metz, Dr. Dennis Conway, and Rev. Jon Magnuson spent many hours reading the manuscript and preparing their invaluable comments. I am also deeply thankful to Dr. Wilbur Smith for his insightful comments and to Dr. Ruth Sawh for her editorial help as well as thoughtful comments. Then there is Dr. Paul Sweezy who has for long been a quiet source of my inner strength. My wife, Pamela, my niece, Jamuna, and my brother, Min Bahadur, have always been there to cheer me up and to make sure that I keep marching forward no matter how hard the road may be. A slightly different version of Chapter 3 was first published in *South Asia Bulletin* (Vol. XIII, No. 1&2). I am grateful to its co-editors, Drs. Vasant Kaiwar and Sucheta Mazumdar, for permitting me to reproduce it here. Finally, I would like to acknowledge that this study was made possible by two major research grants from the National Science Foundation and one joint grant from the Ford and Rockefeller Foundations.

Nanda R. Shrestha
Tallahassee, Florida

1

NEPAL AT A GLANCE

Annapurna is a majestic massif situated in the central portion of the Himalayan range. Clad in snow all year around, it is one of the world's tallest and most popular peaks. Although mountain climbers have identified several annapurnas, to the natives of Nepal there is only one Annapurna: the one that is labeled Annapurna IV in mountaineering parlance. This Annapurna is situated directly to the north of Pokhara, a beautiful town in the central hills. Until the mid-1960s, Pokhara was a small, bucolic town with a population of perhaps 10,000 people; it was a major trading center in the central hills.

Today, Pokhara is completely spoiled by uncontrolled tourist and commercial growth. Yet the presence of Annapurna and its adjoining peak called Machhapuchhre (Fishtail mountain) keeps alive its allure as a major tourist spot in Nepal outside of the Kathmandu Valley. Then there is Phewa Tal, a lake nestled in the southern corner of Pokhara. On any clear day, one can see the reflection of the two peaks in the lake, floating away with its gentle ripples, in an enchanting motion. The scene is beyond description. Unfortunately, it is this very beauty that has become a curse as the lake area has now gained a dubious reputation as a hippie hub in Nepal. It is very polluted in every respect.

While the natural beauties of the two mountain peaks and Phewa Tal give Pokhara its distinct charm, it is Annapurna that writes its mystical melody, neatly framed in a folklore. Viewed from Pokhara, Mt. Annapurna uncannily resembles a human face, wearing a cap, with its head slightly tilted backward. To the inhabitants of Pokhara and its surrounding areas, Annapurna is more than a beautiful mountain. It is a legend, embroidered in an elegant folklore with a profound meaning for peasant life. Every winter this folklore came alive, almost as an annual ritual, either as a gleaming sign of hope or as a lurking threat of despair. To peasants, Annapurna is a self-descriptive word which means full of grains: *anna* (grains)+*purna* (full)=*annapurna*. So it is not merely a majestic mountain, towering above the valley of Pokhara. It actually stands as a mighty symbol of the much cherished dream of peasant life: to have a pantry filled with grains.

There lived in Pokhara, more than 25 years ago, an old peasant who loved to tell the folklore about Annapurna. That old peasant was my father. As the winter approached the end of its annual cycle in subtropical Nepal, he would periodically gaze at Annapurna, sifting through its messages—silent oracles for the new farming season. Pointing to the peak, he would say: "Look at Annapurna, son! Look at it carefully."

And I would dutifully stare at it for a moment or two. Then my father would ask, "What do you see, son?"

After the first few times, I had mastered the pattern. I knew exactly what he was directing me to focus on. "The cap of Annapurna is full of grains," I would reply if it looked fully covered with snow as if it was about to overflow. If not, I would say, "The cap looks empty."

"That is right; that's exactly right," he would say emphatically. "Annapurna is full of grains. This is going to be a good year, son!" he would proclaim proudly, with a deep sense of satisfaction. His eyes would gleam and face would light up. He was not just talking about his own fate and fortunes. What he meant was that farmers were going to have a good year, a bountiful harvest to insure their subsistence at least for a year, until the next planting season.

The cap wasn't always filled with snow, however. If the cap looked empty during the winter as it periodically did, my father would quietly look down at his feet and then cast his eyes at the peak, sadly muttering, "Son, not a very good year!" I could feel anxiety in his voice. Based on his years of observational experience, he could tell that a season of hardships was on its way to visit many peasants. So the winter cap of Annapurna was a natural barometer of either unfolding misery or relative prosperity for the peasants of Pokhara valley.

Back then, I never inquired about the logical basis of his folkloric belief, the predictive value of Annapurna's winter cap. To me, it was nothing more than a charming folklore, almost like a lullaby, routinely sung to little babies at bedtime. There was little realization that what was embedded in his folkloric calculation was the weather phenomenon, specifically precipitation, all based on many years of observation or what I today call "experiential knowledge." There was science involved in his method although there was no scientific formulation. That is, if the cap was filled with snow, that signified heavy winter precipitation in the mountains which nurtured the rivers flowing down to the valleys. It signaled good prospects for desirable weather conditions with plenty of moisture for the new farming season. Good weather conditions invariably translated into good harvests and hence relative food security for peasants. After all, for peasants, timely rains are their lifeline because in a predominantly agrarian society like Nepal with few irrigation facilities, life is closely entwined with the rhythm of nature and its grace. Simply put, life is a timeless reflection of nature, its bounty as well as periodic wrath.

That old peasant, my father, is long gone. And gone with him is the tradition of telling the folklore about majestic Annapurna to the children of Pokhara so they could keep it alive. I wonder how many peasants or fathers in Pokhara still remember this beautiful folklore and tell it to their children. Perhaps, very few! With the passage of every generation has come a silent passage of indigenous knowledge and its intrinsic value for self-reliant development. This is the first time since I left Pokhara in 1972 I have recaptured it in my mind. Yet it feels fresh as if my father told it to me just yesterday; it evokes the powerful images of natural beauty and simplicity that characterized the way of life in the past. As such, the folklore not only serves as a constant reminder of the lost past, but also of the vast emptiness that fills modern life, life in constant search for a definition, its true purpose and meaning in the midst of what can be called a development race.

While Annapurna has undergone little change in its physical manifestation, its winter cap looks awfully empty these days in terms of its social personification. For the Nepali poor, a betrayal seems to shroud the peasant dream, the dream of *anna+purna* (a pantry full of grain). Annapurna no longer transmits the prospect of hopes for peasants about peasant life. Few ever bother or take time to watch its cap today to see whether it is full or empty. In the face of Nepal's deepening amnesia about its own past and indigenous system, Annapurna has lost its folkloric mystique and power as a source of local knowledge.

Although couched in a traditional framework, this folkloric knowledge entailed a sound logical basis to predict the upcoming weather and by implication socioeconomic conditions for Pokhara's peasants, in fact, no less accurately than seasoned meteorologists equipped with scientific instruments. But such knowledge seems to command little meaning today as few see any value in its praxis and profound experiential roots. Most now deny, outright, the fact that folklores are not just curious tales of exotic traditions in far and distant places; they are an invaluable treasure of knowledge, deeply seeped in years of trial and error, that is often far more relevant to the local needs and resources than the highly touted algorithms and sophisticated science, blindly imported and imposed from the West.

What we are witnessing in today's Nepal is more than the death of a folklore, the folklore of Annapurna. A broader and frightening trend is under way. A rapid diffusion of Westernism is causing a global hemorrhage of the rich tradition of telling children folklores as a pedagogical vehicle of transmitting and preserving experiential knowledge generation after generation. The tradition is dying out, and tragically vanishing with it is an enormous trove of indigenous knowledge and wisdom "stored in the memories of elders, healers, midwives, farmers, fishermen and hunters" (Linden, 1991). Weaving their memories carefully into fascinating folklores, elders and healers, farmers and fishermen used to inculcate such knowledge in their children and grandchildren. But no more. Today, such traditions have become a mere relic of the past, occasionally dug up by curious cultural anthropologists and ethnographers. To paraphrase Eugene Linden (1991), as folklores spill into oblivion, so do the vast archives of irreplaceable knowledge and treatise contained in them, leaving humanity in danger of losing its past and jeopardizing its future.

So what does this little folklore reveal about contemporary Nepal and its future outlook?

The picture is self-revealing, and it is not too pretty. Like the dying folklore itself, the picture shows a growing decay of Nepal's overall socioeconomic condition. After four full decades of development efforts, Nepal has arrived at a critical crossroads of mounting hardships and declining prospects for a better future. Caught in the middle of its subsistent but self-sufficient past and rootless future is its bleak present. It is a society characterized by increasing class polarization, not only in terms of wealth but also with respect to class relations. Everywhere there is social disparity and disintegration.

A GEOGRAPHICAL PROFILE

Nepal is a small landlocked country sandwiched between two Asian giants—China and India. Its geographical position has been traditionally characterized as being analogous to "a yam caught between two rocks." Comprising about 55,000 square miles of land, Nepal is a highly mountainous country. Only 20 percent of its total land is considered lowland which is largely confined to the Tarai (plain) belt, stretching along the Nepal-India border. Other than land and forests, it has few natural resources of commercial value.

From the southern Tarai belt, the landform rises in successive hill and mountain ranges, including the majestic Himalayas. Beyond these Himalayas lies the Xizang (Tibet) plateau. This rise in elevation is punctuated by valleys nestled in mountain ranges, running in an east-west direction. Within this maze of mountains, hills, ridges, and low valleys some ecological and physiographic order can be discerned. Nepal is commonly divided into three broad physiographic regions based on elevation changes and ecological variations. They are: the Mountain (Himalayan) region, the Hill region, and the Tarai region. All three regions extend as continuous ecological belts, occasionally bisected by the country's drainage (river) systems.

The Mountain Region: The Mountain region is situated to the north of the Hill region, along the Chinese border. Its natural landscape includes some of the world's most famous peaks, including Mount Everest. Because of its inclement climatic and topographic conditions, extensive human habitation and economic activities are extremely arduous. As a result, the region is very sparsely inhabited, supporting merely 7.5 percent of Nepal's more than 20 million people. Whatever farming activity is found in this region is mostly concentrated in the low valleys and along the river basins. Pastoralism and trading are two common economic activities in the region (Furer-Haimendorf 1975).

The Hill Region: The Hill region lies to the south of the mountains, and includes the two famous valleys of Nepal: Kathmandu and Pokhara. In addition, there are other smaller intermontane valleys. Considered to be the political center and cultural hearth of Nepal, the hills have historically contained the largest population. Despite heavy outmigration over the past 30 years, the hills still comprise almost 46 percent of the total population. The hill landscape is both a natural and cultural mosaic, shaped by both geological and human forces. Sculptured into a massive complex of terraces, the hills are extensively cultivated. Although agriculture is the predominant economic activity in the hills, the region suffers from a chronic problem of food deficit.

The Tarai Region: In complete topographic and climatic contrast to the mountains and hills to its north, the Tarai is a lowland belt. It is the northern extension of the Gangetic Plain in India. The Tarai is formed and fed by the three major rivers of Nepal: Kosi, Gandaki, and Karnali. They all join the Ganges. Because of the fact that it contains the largest portion of the country's lowland areas, it is often called the granary of Nepal. In addition, it contains commercially exploitable forests which are being increasingly destroyed because of growing demands for timber and agricultural land. In terms of both farm and forest lands, the Tarai is the richest economic region in Nepal.

A POLITICAL PROFILE

Politically or in terms of the control of state apparatus, Nepal can be roughly divided into four phases: Shah rule, Rana rule, Shah rule, and the current multiparty system. Although the Shah dynasty has, since the inception of unified Nepal, served as the head of the state, they have not always been the most dominant force within the ruling class. While this class has historically been comprised of several factions and layers, one basic goal has been generally the same regardless of its clans—that is to serve their own vested interests rather than serve the masses and promote the national interests.

Shah Rule (1743-1846): Until the ascendance of Prithivi Narayan Shah to the throne of the principality of Gorkha on April 3, 1743, Nepal was a constellation of mini states, scattered mostly in the hills. Driven by his imperialistic vision and desire to protect Nepali territories from becoming incorporated into the British imperial orbit on the Indian subcontinent, the new king of Gorkha decided to embark on a war path to unify Nepal under one flag. His war campaign swept through several principalities with remarkable success. By 1769, he completed his conquest of the whole valley of Kathmandu that consisted of three kingdoms: Kathmandu, Bhadgaun (Bhaktapur), and Patan (Lalitpur). Then he shifted his capital to Kathmandu, thus laying the foundation of today's Nepal. Prithivi Narayan is commonly recognized as the initiator of the Shah dynasty that continues to serve as the head of the state to this day.

Even though the administrative apparatus was run by different feuding factions of the ruling nobility (or the ruling elite class such as the Thapa and Panday clans) at different times, the reigning Shah king remained at the apex of the elite class until the usurpation of power by Jang Bahadur Kunwar in 1846.

Rana Rule (1846-1950): Rana rule which began in 1846 was autocratic in every respect. When Jang Bahadur Kunwar (who later changed his last name to Rana) rose to become the first Rana premier of Nepal, the institution of Shah monarchy was reduced to a figurehead position. Jang Bahadur came to power through a coup called the *Kot Parba* (courtyard massacre). The entire Council of State, with the exception of Jang Bahadur, was wiped out during the Kot massacre. That is, Jang Bahadur had managed to achieve a feat that no previous ruling-faction leader had ever achieved: to render all competing factions of the ruling class powerless in one bloody palace intrigue. Once the Rana clan usurped all the power, they emerged as the sole axis of social, economic, and political power (Joshi and Rose, 1966).

It is no exaggeration that Rana rule was the most damaging era in the history of Nepal. They not only bled the country white virtually in every respect, they also undercut Nepal's self-reliant path of progress. Because their rule was dependent on British support and thrived under it, they readily subordinated Nepal's national interest and integrity to the British imperial design. They openly allowed Nepal to be a semi-colony, one of the primary suppliers of the most vital resource for the British imperial army: the able bodies willing to sacrifice themselves for the glory of England. While they were the law of the land and masters of the masses within the country, the Ranas were essentially lackeys to the British. They were more concerned about being decorated with meaningless honorary British medals for their servitude than serving the country. Almost in every aspect of life and living, they copied the British and hence laid the foundation for the emulation of Western values among the rest of the elites. The British were their primary patrons and guardians of their power. It is no surprise, therefore, that when the British left India in 1947, their rule crumbled in 1950 (for a detailed discussion, see Shrestha, 1990: Chapter 3).

Unfortunately, even almost half a century after they were deposed through a relatively popular revolution, the road that the Ranas paved for the emulation of Western ideas and values, for sacrificing national interests and integrity for personal material gains and glamour, and for depending on the West for handouts at the expense of self-reliance and self-sufficiency remains the main road, a road to self-destruction. That is to say, although the Rana rule has long ended, its legacy has not.

Shah Rule (1960-1990): Following the downfall of the Rana rule, Nepal underwent a period of what I call an administrative shuffling, all carried out by King Mahendra Bir Bikram Shah. Every few months, he would appoint a new prime minister to handle the administrative duties. Mahendra was in total control of power as he sat on its saddle with the bridle in his hands. The absolute power of the reigning Shah king was, once again, firmly restored. In 1959, Mahendra hesitatingly agreed to hold a countrywide general election to legitimize a party-based democratic system and have an elected government. As expected, the Nepali Congress party won the election overwhelmingly and appointed B. P. Koirala as the first elected Prime Minister and head of the government. Since Mahendra saw the democratic government as a threat to his own design of absolute Shah rule, he launched a palace coup in December 1960. He arrested and jailed Prime Minister Koirala. The parliament was dissolved and the party system declared illegal, thereby consolidating all the power in his own hands. The absolute power of monarchy, however, came to an end in 1990.

Multiparty System (1990-Present): Thirty years after Mahendra restored the absolute power of the Shah rule, the current king Birendra encountered a powerful revolt from the various segments of the populace. Failing to defuse the fury of the revolt and sensing a serious threat to the Shah dynasty as a monarchical institution, he agreed to dismantle the Panchayat system which his father, Mahendra, had carefully created and nurtured as his own one-party system, and institute in its place a multiparty system. This is how the party-based democratic system was revived in 1990. On paper, the Shah king now is a constitutional monarch, not an absolute arbiter of power.

AN ECONOMIC PROFILE

Economically, Nepal has been identified as a least-developed country. With a per capita income of less than $200, it has been consistently ranked as one of the five poorest countries in the world (World Bank, 1988). Lambers (1973:1) has aptly described it as a "supermountainous country which makes an ideal backdrop for documentaries on television. So it may seem to many of us, but its people have a life and economy of their own. A very simple one, it may seem, but geographical and institutional restrictions make it rather complicated."

Totally surrounded by India on three sides and China to its north, its landlocked position has made its economy somewhat unique, historically. Despite its geographical confinement, Nepal once had a self-sufficient, though subsistence, economy. It was characterized by what is generally referred to as the domestic mode of production. Most of the population produced for household consumption rather than for market exchange. As a self-generating economic system, it was able to produce almost all of the daily necessities. The external dependence was limited to such items as salt, kerosene, and spices, imported from India. Tibet also served as a source of salt, mainly land salt, which was preferred for human consumption (Regmi, 1971).

Today, the economic situation is totally different as external dependence has replaced relative self-sufficiency. Typified by the agrarian and semi-capitalist modes of production, Nepal, namely its ruling class, is almost completely dependent on foreign money—all in the name of development, of course. Underdevelopment and a rapidly growing population are two other prominent features of Nepal. As already noted, the total population of Nepal currently exceeds 20 million, with 90 percent of the households residing in rural areas (Sharma, 1989). In terms of employment structure, 90 percent of its population directly depends on the primary sector (CBS, 1992). While forestry, fishery, and pastoral herding are also included in this sector, farming is by far the most dominant component. It is, therefore, no wonder that Nepal is characterized as a typical agrarian society.

Being agrarian in nature is not the problem, however. What is notable is that while the country remains predominantly agriculture, its agrarian resource base is deteriorating. Land alienation is deepening in terms of both social access to land and per capita land availability. Socially, as discussed in chapter 4, peasants in increasing numbers are being disenfranchised from land, i.e., land that they used to cultivate on a sharecropping or rental basis. In the meantime, increasing population growth has placed additional pressure on land. More than 50 percent of the households own less than 0.5 hectare of land. Their average holding is merely 0.15 hectare. Another 16 percent owns between 0.5-1.0 hectare of land, the average holding being 0.75 hectare. This means more than 66 percent of the households have less than 1 hectare of land in their possession. This figure translates into less than 0.16 hectare per person because an average household consists of 6 persons. Basically, the amount of landholding is quite small to produce enough food in order to support the family for one whole year. The situation gets worse if and when the weather fails to cooperate.

In other words, while land remains the bedrock of Nepal's agrarian economy and hence the primary source of peasants' survival, they are facing a situation of growing land alienation. Alienated from the land, peasants become rootless. Rootlessness is a source of hopelessness. Detached from the way of life that provided some security of survival, but without any prospect for a better future, the present paints a terrifying picture for the majority of peasants. A situation like this creates immense uncertainties and a deep sense of fear among the peasants, especially when they cannot see other alternative sources of survival available to them. In sum, Nepal and Nepali peasants are not only faced with the situation of growing impoverishment, but also chased by the fear of being condemned to permanent degradation—both socially and economically. The threat to their survival and dignity is not imaginary; it is real.

2

LITTLE AMERICA
IN THE HEART OF NEPAL

The inability of the elites to adopt austerity at least until national development has taken place has encouraged a consumerist culture and placed before the masses the ideal of conspicuous consumption. The models of Prithivi Narayan or Mahatma Gandhi, with their philosophy of frugality with self-respect, is in irreconcilable conflict with the consumerist ideology of opulence without dignity, as espoused by the rulers from Rana times to this day.... A conflict such as this cannot be reconciled within the current economic thinking, and can only be resolved by a socio-political movement that can inculcate non-consumerist values. After all, followers of Gandhi did adopt frugality with dignity to defeat the mightiest empire of the day. It was basically a political victory of economic thinking which placed high value in having some form of control over the trade and consumption of necessities.

— Dipak Gyawali, 1994a:21

The Fort Durbar, that magnificent little America situated right in the heart of Kathmandu, the medieval city of Nepal, striving to ride the wave of modernity. A grand symbol of Western modernity, the social milieu within the compound of this Durbar is an American creation. There is no dispute about its status as a well-guarded preserve of the American contingency in Nepal.

The Fort Durbar is an old, elegant Rana palace surrounded by tall brick walls. In every sense of the word, it is a fort indeed, signifying Americans' security as well as social separation from the Nepalis. Its social position reminds me of an imaginative geography, a "comforting little piece of England," the British established in the hill stations of India. It was precisely this imaginative landscape of the hill stations that "...reflected and reinforced assumptions of social and racial differences, and in so doing naturalized the separation of rulers and ruled" (Kenny, 1995:695). That is, in the safe sanctuary of the hill stations the British were able to safely distance themselves from the racially "inferior, uncivilized" native inhabitants of the plains: the Indians. So one can see an uncanny parallel between the British invention of imperial geography and the contemporary American practice of using space as a social separator from the natives. To the Americans living in Nepal, the little America inside the Fort Durbar is an imaginative geography filled with many "comforting" images of America the beautiful. A little America away from America.

Standing at the Durbar's entrance gate with their watchful eyes are the Nepali sentries from the so-called hill martial tribes, generically known as the Gurkhas (Gorkhas) in the imperial parlance of the British raj. My understanding is that most of these guards are, in fact, ex-Gorkha mercenary soldiers who had served either in the British or Indian army. They are hired to protect this little America from the natives. With smiles glued on their faces, they stand at the gate, dutifully saluting every white face that enters the compound. Those guards do not even bother to check their IDs because their white faces are enough to serve as an unmistakable proof that they are legitimate and that they pose no threat to both American purity and security. Here color definitely sells and defines one's character as well as humanity. And those sentries... well, they see themselves as privileged to have the opportunity to serve the Americans. Whenever they talk about their employment, their faces gleam, exuding a sense of hollow pride.

Located right across from the king's palace, the Fort Durbar is a mini American colony, mostly inhabited by the diplomatic and development corps and their wives. In full display within this colony are American opulence, cultural glamour, and other value systems—all lively and vibrant. No, there is no emblem of the great bald American eagle hanging at the entrance gate. Yet there is no mistaking about the compound being a mini American colony, where Americans are seen constantly entering and exiting. No Nepali is allowed into the Durbar unless invited by an American, or given a pre-arranged pass, or employed within the compound. Walking into that compound is like walking into a well-maintained community recreation center in the

United States, equipped with sports facilities and other amenities such as snack bars and lunch menus. Also available are all kinds of American delicacies and drinks—hamburger, hot dog, pizza, french fries, ice cream, and what not. Americans frequent the Durbar to play sports or to simply enjoy the hearty American food as well as to socialize and gossip. They joke around among themselves as well as exchange jokes. Many times, Nepali people and their traditional practices end up becoming the butt of their favorite jokes. The Durbar is a true pastime activity hub! Inside it, Americans can feel right at home as if they never left America, basking in the glow of American comfort and luxury. Actually more so than in America as they are served by some of the most attentive Nepali servers (servants), always smiling and ever polite. At the snap of their fingers, Americans can get Nepali servers' immediate attention. I never saw any server complain or display "an attitude" no matter how rudely they were treated by some obnoxious Americans.

It is quite an experience to hang around in the compound of that little America and observe vividly the live drama of the power relations between the dominant and the subordinate, i.e., between the Americans (foreigners) and the Nepalis (natives). Although I never personally experienced the cruelty, brutality, or indignity of being subjugated to Western colonial rule, I could imagine a fantastic similarity between the dominant-dependent relations inside the Durbar and the numerous narratives of such relations under colonialism. That well-rehearsed drama was alive and fully acted out every time I entered that little American colony. There is no question that the little America inside the Fort Durbar stands tall as the bastion of not only American glory and glamour, but also its racial, social, and economic domination of Nepal and its citizens. Reverberating throughout the colony is a typical American plantation mentality and scene.

Whenever I went inside the Durbar, I saw two groups of Nepalis: one consisting of a large pool of servers doing various menial chores and running around from one finger snap to another like a tennis ball, and the other comprising a few well-to-do sports figures, namely some of Kathmandu's best tennis players, invited to play tennis with the Americans or give tennis lessons to their sons and daughters. While the latter group of sports figures appeared to carry a certain level of status as if they had been bestowed with honorary American citizenship, the servers were rarely acknowledged by the Americans and their spouses. Some of the Americans were outright snobbish toward the Nepali servers, treating them like a bunch of flunkies and house servants. Yet those Nepalis in the colony—both servers and sportsmen—appeared to display little sense of humiliation and anger. If they harbored any resentment or rage about their second class status on their own soil, one could not read it from their facial expressions. There was no open manifestation of any anger. They looked happy; many radiated an aura of superiority to other Nepalis that they had the enviable opportunity to work for the Americans, to be close to them. They acted as if they were the "chosen few" who made at least twice as much money for doing the same thing as other Nepalis employed in the domestic sector. I felt very uneasy about this tragic drama and the naked exhibition of the colonial culture and dominance, but I bit my tongue and swallowed my pride and bitterness and kept going back to that colony every time an American friend of mine, whom I had met in September 1979 during my return to Nepal, invited me. It was a very weird feeling, filled with irony and hypocrisy, rage and shame. Almost every time I walked out of the Durbar, I felt lost and confused. As a Nepali born and raised in Nepal, but grown accustomed to the American way of life, I could not quite figure out where I really belonged—inside the compound or outside with my fellow Nepalis.

Sometimes I deeply resented the whole idea of going to the Fort Durbar. It was really difficult for me to swallow my pride and dignity, something I never did before, not even when I was a young boy. I would rather go hungry for days than subject myself to somebody's pity and mistreatment. It was hard to overlook the fact that all those Nepalis were willingly playing a subservient role in that play of American power. It was painful to see my Nepali brethren always smiling even when they were treated like dogs as if they were indentured laborers or colonial servants. Furthermore, it was degrading to have to be reminded that I could not simply walk into the Durbar unless invited or accompanied by an American and that I was not welcome in certain quarters of my own country. It was very taxing to be a spectator, a compliant actor in that great colonial cultural drama, but I lacked the strength and courage to resist its temptation and allure. I went there willingly if for nothing else, at least to have a hamburger and a glass of cold beer. Even now it makes me feel very uneasy to be writing about it because the United States is my current home and I am a beneficiary of the material life it offers. Hypocrisy and irony aside, as a student of social realities and development issues, one who is submerged in both Nepali and American cultural values, I cannot ignore these observations and not express my thoughts and impressions of these realities. To ignore them would mean to deny my own heritage and inner conscience, as well as to denigrate Nepali humanity. After all, it is precisely these realities that reflect the fate of Nepal as well as its destiny.

Despite all my anguish and agony, I am glad that I had a chance to visit the Fort Durbar several times because that experience taught me a great deal about myself and about the nature of Nepal's development dependency and Nepali elites' subserviency to Americans and other Westerners, about the close ties between foreign aid and Western racism and its role in creating and recreating a colonized mindset among the natives.

What a stark contrast between the social scene inside the compound and the one outside—almost like day and night! It was amazing to realize that the distance between America and Nepal was only one step away, separated by a brick wall; it was simply a matter of whether one was inside or outside the Durbar. Inside it was America, "the world of civilization" as one American boasted. One step outside the Durbar, it was Nepal, the world of barbarism to apply the implied logic of that American's characterization of the Fort Durbar. Americans certainly know how to create little Americas wherever they go, little safe havens or the world of civilization and keep them off-limit to the natives except for a selected few.

One afternoon back in 1980, I was in the Fort Durbar with my American friend, Paul, who has a fantastic sense of humor and genuine concern for the rural people and culture of Nepal. Paul was at that time teaching rural development at a college in Nepal. He is a close friend, somebody I truly admire for his sincerity and no-nonsense style. He was my intellectual springboard during my field research in 1979-80. We were lounging around in the Durbar, drinking beer and chitchatting about various topics. Then he began to tell me a story about the nature of USAID development project in Nepal. It focused on native cows and the American bull.

It is commonly known that Nepali cows are normally quite small and don't yield much milk. So one day at a cocktail party, a couple of USAID development advisors thought about doing something about the low milk production of Nepali cows. Well, they decided to invite an American animal husbandry expert to evaluate the situation and make recommendations. An advisor was flown in at the rate of $250 a day plus accommodation in a five-star hotel in Kathmandu. After some cursory investigation and a visit to a nearby village, the expert concluded that USAID (United States Agency for International Development) should fly in a few American bulls to crossbreed local cows. Convinced of the logical soundness of his advice, the USAID development advisors made necessary arrangements to import American bulls. Not long after the expert's recommendation, the first American bull arrived in Nepal. It was taken to a village, and the villagers were invited to bring their cows for crossbreeding. Cows were herded to the enclosed area where the bull was stationed. Both the villagers and Americans, including the animal husbandry expert, gathered around, anxiously waiting for the bull to begin mating with the cows. It was a true spectacle.

They kept waiting and waiting and waiting, Paul continued. Hours passed by, but nothing was happening. The bull refused to buzz; it showed no interest in any of the cows in its newly established harem, not even sniffing around. Totally perplexed by the bull's defiant behavior, the advisors did not know what to do. The expert's face was turning quite red. It was getting late, and the Americans were running out of patience. With the sun fast approaching the western hills, the dusk was looming on the horizon. The air was filled with the murmurs of frustration, disappointment, and disbelief. Some villagers were laughing and cracking jokes as they found the whole experiment quite bemusing. As the crowd began to slowly thin out, the carnival-like atmosphere dissipated. In the midst of all this, one villager muttered to the Americans that there was a hermit, a sage in the village who was blessed with the ability to communicate with animals. "Really?" the Americans asked excitedly. "Yes, sir!" said the villager emphatically. Hearing this news the American advisors immediately ordered the villager to bring the hermit to the pasture to speak with the bull so they could find out why it was not doing the job that it was brought to do. They said they would pay the hermit a consultant's fee.

Paul added that feeling totally desperate and embarrassed by the bull's unusual lack of lust or haughty behavior, the American advisors were willing to try anything. They lost any sense of scientific "rationality" which they flaunt to condemn what they call Nepal's traditional value system. They suddenly appeared to believe that a person could actually speak with animals. Paul mentioned that on any other occasion, even a thought of such notion would have made them laugh, but not that day.

Anyway at the request of the villager the sage trekked down to the pasture and began to talk to the bull, standing motionless. In response, the bull all of a sudden began to shake its head and appeared somewhat agitated. The sage kept nodding his head as if he fully understood the bull's position. Visibly frantic and impatient, the advisors wanted to know what the bull had said. Looking calm and collected, the sage responded slowly: "Well... sirs, the bull...the bull asked me to tell..." "Tell what? What did the bull tell you? Go ahead tell us," the advisors interrupted the sage. "Well, the bull said that he did not come to Nepal to work; he came here to advise." The American advisors were all stunned by the hermit's words, and suddenly became dead silent, so silent that one could hear a leaf fall. They all hopped in their car and left hurriedly—without uttering a word. Not even a good-bye to the villagers who had been asked to come down to the pasture to watch the show, the breeding demonstration!

This story was actually supposed to be a joke, a light-hearted but poignant parody about American development advisors and the stupidity of their development thinking, a parody told by seasoned American advisors to the first-timers. It was a kind of initiation rite they performed to help the unseasoned attain their true advisorhood, fully blessed to carry out their American duty. Obviously told in various forms in various Asian countries, it was a fascinating parody. Even though both Paul and I had a hearty laugh over it, the joke was much too real to be drowned in a laughter. Etched in it was the true reality of the quixotic nature of development advising as well as the story of development advisors, not just American and other Western advisors, but domestic advisors as well.

That was the first time I had heard that joke. But it deeply stirred me. The more I reflected on it, the more I realized that it was not just an American bull tale and its failed experiment. Embedded in it was a much bigger picture, a disturbing picture, painted with the obvious symptoms of what may be called the "modernization project" or "development experiment" gone berserk. Yet there is no end to it; instead similar experiments are carried out throughout Nepal with the help of foreign aid. While the project's manifested forms may change from time to time and from place to place, its underlying process and mission do not. Instead of learning from mistakes, we repeat them as amply demonstrated by the absurdity of ongoing development policy patterned after the Western model of insatiable material pursuit.

A few weeks later Paul and I were both in Rampur, a small village in the central Tarai district of Chitwan situated along the Nepal-India border. He used to teach in Rampur, along with four other Americans, at the College of Animal and Agricultural Sciences that was financed by USAID. The USAID operation at the college had been contracted to Michigan State University. In my own case, I was in Rampur to launch my field research on frontier migration in Chitwan, where the very first planned land resettlement project was implemented in the mid-1950s, again with the help of the United States. My field research, funded by the Ford and Rockefeller Foundations, was being carried out in the villages surrounding Rampur.

As part of his USAID/Michigan State University contract to teach at the College, Paul had been given a nice three-bed room bungalow in Rampur for his residential use. There were several such quarters, all built for American advisors. Since his family lived in Kathmandu and he had the bungalow all to himself, he invited me to share it with him during the course of my fieldwork. I was more than elated to accept his generous offer, not only because I needed a place to stay, but also because his friendship was intellectually refreshing and stimulating. In addition, his company helped me deflect the loneliness that often accompanies field research, especially when it is long and carried out in places that are generally isolated. His field research experience in rural Malaysia and the Philippines also proved to be very helpful to my own field research endeavors. Despite his academic training as an anthropologist and mine as a geographer, our research interests overlapped. While in the field, I saw him as my intellectual compass to help me learn from his rich field research experience and avoid his mistakes. Paul's offer to share his quarters proved to be even more convenient when my wife, an American by birth, joined me in the field a couple of months later.

One morning, while sitting on his porch, sipping hot tea and enjoying the fresh morning breeze before the onslaught of pre-monsoon subtropical heat that arose like a burning inferno after about 10:00 o'clock, Paul told me another story, this time a real one, a story about an American advisor who had lived in Rampur a few years back. This fellow, Paul said, was a horseshoe game fanatic. The problem was no Nepali worker knew how to play the game, nor did they have any interest in it. But this did not deter the American advisor.

Determined to teach the game to the "unenlightened" Nepalis, deprived of the fine pleasures of life, he had them build a horseshoe pit. Often
in the afternoon, this American advisor rounded up the Nepali workers,
like a cowboy rounds up his herds of cattle at the end of the day, and
made them pitch horseshoes with him. Whether they wanted to play or
not, it did not matter. The American advisor derived much satisfaction
from the fact that he had been able to teach Nepali workers how to play
the game. He saw that as his important contribution to Rampur and its
citizens. But poor Nepali workers! That was no contribution to them; it
was a total nuisance. Yet they had no choice but to play the game to
keep the American advisor happy and entertained. Despite their feelings
of disgust about having to play the game, the Nepali workers had to
pretend that they truly enjoyed it as though that was the greatest gift of
life and civilization they had ever received from the Americans, and they
should feel honored to be playing a fine American sport with an American advisor. Furthermore, while playing the sport they had to put on
that ready-made, submissive smile on their faces, which they could flash
instantly to express their gratitude and pleasure for the opportunity to
serve the Americans—a clear manifestation of the colonial culture of
domination and subjugation, of the grossly unbalanced power relations
between the Americans and the Nepalis. A non-smiling or frowned face
is always viewed by Americans (Westerners) with suspicion, for such a
face conjures up in their minds an image of a creature that is ungrateful
to its master. Simply put, such a face is interpreted as a threat to their
sense of superiority as well as to their position of power.

Unlike the cocky American bull, those poor Nepali workers could
not dare to defy the advisor because their jobs were on the line,
especially when they were good-paying jobs and considered to be
"prestigious." They had to bury their pride and dignity in the very horseshoe pit that they had dug at the command of the American advisor.
They could not even go home, help around the house, and play with their
children after their duty was over for the day. They had to hang around
another hour or two, playing horseshoes with the white man until he was
completely satisfied. One possible way for them to avoid playing it was
to fake that they had to run errands for another American advisor or to
remain out of his sight, something that was not easy to do because the
compound was confined. The Nepali workers did not have much control
over their lives and space. This was true especially in a rural area like
Rampur where almost everybody lived within a shouting distance. In

essence, space performed a dubious task. In the relations of power and control, spatial proximity is a curse as it has a way of impinging on the freedom of those who rank low on the totem pole of power. While the Americans enjoyed the luxury of being able to easily seclude themselves into the comfort of their quarters whenever they wanted to avoid the natives, their Nepali workers had to be available anytime the Americans wanted them around, day or night. In their power relation with the Americans, not even their own homes could serve as a buffer zone to keep them from having to be on call 24 hours a day. This is what may be called the tyranny of spatial proximity, I suppose.

The story ends on an interesting note. The advisor's USAID contract expired. His sojourn in Rampur had come to an end. He had to return to his home institution (university) in the United States. As the main Nepali driver was getting ready to drive the horseshoe player to the airport some 20 miles away to catch a plane to Kathmandu, he instructed his fellow workers in Nepali—the American fellow never learned any Nepali during his two years' stay in Nepal—to entirely obliterate the horseshoe pit as if it were never built. He did not want to see any sign of its existence. He asked them to do it quietly but immediately, as soon as he left the compound. And the horseshoe pit was erased from the face of that little piece of earth. That was a form of their quiet protest against the American advisor's control over their lives. Since none of the Americans ever tried to understand Nepali workers, they rarely sensed the degree of resentment they harbored. Behind the veneer of their ever-smiling faces and obedient behaviors lay a deep reservoir of rage.

When the driver returned from the airport, he directly went to see if the horseshoe pit was erased. It certainly was erased. The American advisor's passionate civilizing mission, the fine pleasure of life, the horseshoe game that he had so carefully cultivated among the Nepali workers had suddenly bitten the hard dust of Rampur, in the hands of the very workers who played the game for two years. It vanished like the footprints of a canoe crossing a river, never to be seen again. There were only bitter memories buried under the pit. Finally, the driver was relieved of what he considered to be two years of torment; he was ecstatic. In my mind, I vividly pictured him relishing his moment of victory at last, a sense of power that he must have felt over the departed American, and screaming at the top of his voice: "Sala gayo!" (which can colloquially be translated to mean the s.o.b. is gone). Nepali workers felt a deep sigh of relief.

As revealed through the life stories depicted in this book, Nepal's development policy, regardless of its current claim and clamoring of sustainable development, is hardly about what is suitable and sustainable, what is practical and viable in the long run. Rather it is about what is grand and glamorous, about what pleases the Western donor agencies like the World Bank and USAID, the co-leaders of the pack, of course. It is about what those donor agencies want or think is good for Nepal and what deifies Western values and virtues irrespective of its cost to the general masses. So most of what passes for development among the Nepali is largely a monument to Western modernity as every development undertaking is framed within it. Many development projects are usually based on their visibility and status value, not on their real worthiness and public benefits.

Take, for example, the Arun-3 dam project in eastern Nepal, highly touted as an instrument of "development" and "progress," as an essential ingredient for "national capacity building" (Chatterjee, 1996; Gyawali, 1996). Although this project has fortunately been canceled because of persistent protests against its implementation, the World Bank had already approved its funding to the tune of about one billion US dollars, that is, about 25 percent of Nepal's gross national product (Most likely, the total cost would have been much higher by the time of its completion due to cost overruns and inflation). Had the Arun project been launched, Nepal would have certainly seen a high dam, but by no means high development to satisfy the needs of its hungry masses. Actually, it would have further eroded the country's economic base, for it was bound to uproot thousands of families and destroy local ecological resources as well as scarce crop land, all in the name of bogus development. Nepal does not need such a mega dam costing mega bucks to light up the villages and to power the country. Nor does Nepal need it to irrigate its farms. The same goals can be achieved at a much smaller scale, more efficiently and without drowning villages and draining scarce resources. The amount of power generated by the Arun project would have been two times larger than Nepal's total absorptive capacity (Gyawali, 1996:37).

Now, in the aftermath of Arun's demise comes the Mahakali dam project proposal in western Nepal, to be financed by a foreign loan and built in collaboration with India. Its monetary cost alone may amount to as much as one billion dollars. Its ecological and human costs (in terms of eviction) are also bound to run very high. Again, it is apparent that

Nepal has no need for this unsustainably expensive project. Yet the government is forging ahead with the project. In formally presenting it to the Parliament, the Water Resources Minister, Pashupati Shamsher Rana, claimed that "The Mahakali Treaty will open up the door for the speedy development of Nepal" (*Nepal Press Digest*, Sept. 16, 1996). The Parliament has already ratified the treaty (*Nepal Press Digest*, Sept. 23, 1996). Enamored by Western modernity and glamorous projects, the ruling class of Nepal has entirely lost their common sense that development is for the people and not a giant temple to house a technological god. The rulers never seem to learn any lesson about frugality and sustainability.

In a country like Nepal, development is rarely a cumulative process, evolving indigenously through its symbiotic interaction with the expanding base of local knowledge and resources. It is predefined and predetermined in accordance with the Westerners' assumption of superiority of their economic rationality, imbued with techno-fetishism. It is this overt emphasis on the presumed superiority of Western economic rationality that has led to the total devaluation of the local modes of life and economies, consequently breeding and nurturing the culture of dependency and dependent development in Nepal.

To be sure, in the past few years a bugle has been sounded within the development establishment, calling for the need to go beyond the Eurocentric universal and stress the local to recover the lost indigenous knowledge base. In fact, many international non-governmental organizations (NGOs) are at the forefront of this paradigm shift or new development orientation. In the wake of the downfall of communism in Eastern Europe and the Soviet Union and the subsequent triumph of free-market ideology, the international development establishment is vigorously promoting sustainable development, along with individual entrepreneurship or "the culture of self-help" and empowerment. But masked behind this new vocabulary and orientation of development is a great deal of fallacy and hidden agenda, not to mention gross contradictions and evasiveness. Simply put, this new slogan is one of the biggest development follies dumped on the poor and underdeveloped countries of the world by the World Bank and USAID. It would not be out of line to contend that this is the moral (or immoral) equivalent of the claim that colonialism was good for the colonies.

Why, one may ask, sustainable development for the poor and for "poor" countries? What does it really mean? Jeremy Seabrook notes that the whole notion of "sustainability" simply means maintaining the ideological fiction of industrial society, sparing it from potential worldwide ecological disasters. He goes on to argue that it means sustaining the privileges of the rich and powerful, not safeguarding the survival rights of those who depend on ecological resources (discussed in *Himal*, Nov/Dec., 1993:20). For instance, the United States, which shares only 5 percent of the world's population, consumes over 30 percent of the available resources. The degree of overbearing consumption of resources can be easily measured, based on per capita garbage production. An average person in the United States generates almost five times as much garbage as an average person in a country like Nepal.

In essence, what the advanced world is actually concerned about is its unlimited access and control of the world's resources. In theory, the fundamental premise of Western economics has been that wants are unlimited whereas resources are limited. In this sense, one primary objective of Economics is to manage or reconcile the antipodal tendencies between wants and resources. But, again, that is in theory. In practice, however, at least from a historical perspective, there is little evidence to suggest that capitalism's economic imperatives have ever treated resources as limited while its cultural norms continue to espouse unlimited wants. But, in recent years, there seems to have been some change in capitalist thinking, at least among its praetorian guards such as the World Bank. Simmering underneath their global policy outlook is a genuine fear that all these cheap resources may no longer be available at the same rate as before to maintain their sumptuous lifestyle. After all, if all the poor of the world, who constitute approximately 70 percent of the total population, were to raise their resource consumption to the same level as the wealthy citizens of industrial and postindustrial societies, the life expectancy of most natural resources, including those assumed to be renewable such as tropical forests, will be dramatically curtailed. Should this dreaded scenario materialize—a scenario that few can dispute—the global march of capitalism will suddenly come to a screeching halt.

While I do not personally foresee any immediate threat to resource depletion—at least not at the global level although it is already occurring at the local level in many countries—the long-term fear is real. It would not be farfetched to assert that the advanced world is already thinking of the future outlooks for the world's resources. As the lust for luxury soars, the cost of luxury will rise. Even more importantly, their so-called middle class and working class populations will experience hardships of unknown proportions as they will no longer be able to enjoy the fruits of cheap resources from previous colonies. When denied of what they have so far taken for granted or even considered to be their natural rights— material luxury—the middle and working class populations can turn into a source of massive discontent and act like an angry mob with a volcanic force. In the event that this happens, advanced countries will encounter waves of social chaos and unrest in their own backyards, thus posing a threat to their so-called democratic traditions.

In short, nature will finally exact its ultimate toll from capitalism for all those years of massive ecological ravaging and destruction it has caused. The mighty civilization of capitalism, rooted in the ever-increasing consumption of resources, will then be transformed into an aging dinosaur, facing the prospect of extinction, like all other past civilizations of the world. This is why sustainable development for the poor has become such an overriding issue for the international development establishment, headed by the World Bank and USAID. Taming or containing the materialistic use of natural resources by the poor has thus become the order of the day. For capitalism, depletion of global resources is a bad omen because without them it cannot flourish. Hence the mantra of sustainable development, the latest USAID and World Bank prescription for the economic ailment of underdeveloped countries around the globe. And Nepal is no exception in this global configuration of national development.

There is no dispute that sustainable development is a laudable concept and goal, especially when used in the manner espoused by Gandhi and Schumacher (1973) and many other advocates of "simple living." It is a potent vision of appropriate development for most countries. This is the best model for a country like Nepal with its limited resource endowment because it is both practical and attainable. But, in its present form, as promoted by the international development establishment, it is anything but Gandhian. The development establishment has misappropriated and circumvented Gandhi, turning him upside down. What is being peddled as sustainable development is hardly sustainable. It is a hoax, a cunning camouflage to protect the natural resource interests of advanced capitalist societies which continue to devour global resources at a rate that is absolutely unsustainable. Yet they shamelessly preach the mantra of sustainability. The truth is: sustainable development is not designed to assist the poor of countries like Nepal regardless of its stated objective.

The problem is not with the concept itself, but with the way it is being pushed and with the underlying motives of the agents and agencies touting it. There is a mammoth hypocrisy surrounding the model of sustainable development. One cannot help but be amazed by the fact that the World Bank and USAID, the most powerful twin advocates of material growth, are telling the poor to follow the path of sustainable development, preaching to them the virtues of natural resource conservation, but at the same time urging, and even forcing, them to grow more and more export crops and to expand commercialization. Furthermore, they are actively engaged in supporting corporate push to spread the cultural gospel of North-Atlantic consumerism across the globe. The brand names like Coca-Cola and Colgate are more readily recognized than the names of national heroes, not to mention the names of American pop and movie stars whose posters pop up everywhere, from private quarters to public parks.

These days, it is hard to find Nepali villages that remain unspoiled by Coca-Cola signs as even remote areas are infested with this patented logo. Famous tandoori chickens have yielded to KFC (Kentucky Fried Chickens) and the music of famed *gainays* (minstrels) to MTV. Beer, manufactured through joint ventures, has replaced *chhang* (local beer brewed from millet or rice) as a favorite drink, even during ceremonies and rituals. And TV antennas soar higher than the highest temples, forming an uniquely ugly skyline across the country's urban landscape (see Guha, 1996). In this Hindu kingdom, where Christian preaching was forbidden until recently, Christmas decoration and greetings have become chic. So, as Westernization penetrates every aspect of life, local traditions and values experience their gradual demise.

What we are witnessing with amazement or perhaps even distress is a cultural epidemic of consumerism sweeping across Nepal (and other underdeveloped countries). It is all part of the global tentacle of North-Atlantic consumerism. In an aptly entitled report, "How to sell more to those who think it's cool to be frugal," recently published in *The Wall Street Journal* (Sept. 30, 1996), Ellen Graham discusses the power of companies to extend the culture of consumerism even into the realm of frugality. In this culture, there is no room for frugality. As the logic dictates, to be frugal is to commit sin against the deity of consumerism which serves as the engine of capitalist drive across the globe. What ends up happening in this capitalist march is that as consumerism expands, poverty becomes not only an issue of economic deprivation, but also a source of social humiliation, for those who cannot afford to ride the waves of consumerism are invariably treated with contempt and disdain by those who have gained the most from Westernized development. In other words, the poor are forced into a situation where they either have to spend whatever little money or resources they have on senseless consumer objects rather than basic necessities in order to deflect total social humiliation or face the prospect of being teased and laughed at.

As succinctly expressed by Gyawali (1994a:21) in the opening quote of this chapter, the ruling elites of Nepal have failed to lead the way in setting the right tone for the kind of sustainable development the country needs to pursue to deal with poverty and other social ills. Their mindless pursuit of material life has sent the country reeling down the road of wasteful consumerism. While the elites extol the rhetoric of sustainable development, the Gandhian model of self-help, self-sufficiency, and sustainability remains a distant dream. To this day, one can't help but wonder if humiliating poverty would have been as widespread in Nepal and other South Asian countries and the poor completely denied their basic human dignity if the Gandhian model had prevailed over Nehru's policy of Westernized development. In the tussle between the two competing models, Nehru won, and now, some 40 years later, the poor are paying the price of his policy victory with their precarious lives haunted by misery and lost dignity.

Given this scenario, the question is: how can one conceivably pursue sustainable development under the rampage of reckless consumerism? It is beyond comprehension. To put it mildly, something is fundamentally incongruent about all of this.

Furthermore, the international development establishment's big push for privatization (free-market enterprising) is hardly conducive to the spirit of sustainable development. The inherent logic of free market suggests that greed is not only good but necessary to advance. Greed has little in common with basic human needs which constitute one of the central themes of sustainable development. It is, therefore, as difficult to reconcile between sustainable development and free market as it is to paint a human face on the ruthless pillars of capitalism. Uncontrolled entrepreneurship is a double-edged sword; it cuts both ways. While its profit motivation may propel some to find ways to increase production and make more money, it is questionable whether this paradigm can cure social ills and promote human progress. It is riddled with many internal contradictions. John Bellamy Foster (1995) characterizes it as a global "treadmill of production." Such a system not only constantly promotes more and more production, but also inherently creates a cut-throat world which cannot flourish unless it succeeds in trampling many along the way. To surmise from Broad's (1995) argument, the imperative of free market leads to a "bladerunner" society.

In addition, the international development establishment, as previously indicated, is preaching the culture of self-help and empowerment with a missionary zeal as if it is the newest gospel of development. One can almost see a cult-like mentality within the development establishment, with every one of its members chanting the same mantra. Of course, little is new about this gospel of self-help—certainly not in Nepal with a long past of self-reliance. For that matter, not much is new about sustainable development and entrepreneurship either. For most Nepalis they are all old hats, continuously recycled and worn many times over, inside out and upside down, patched up and passed down from one generation to another. Self-help was a way of life in Nepal. Almost everybody worked hard and shared work on many communal projects and activities. They routinely used to get things done, individually as well as in a group, whenever they needed something to be done. They had instituted a work-share system called *parma*, which involved sharing (exchanging) labor among villagers to get things done in a timely manner. This system was routinely used for farming, mostly during the times of planting and harvesting. Peasants or villagers did not rely on any outsiders, let alone foreigners.

Sustainability was deeply ingrained in Nepal's peasant ecology, a form of natural economy or the subsistence mode of production that was renewable and hence sustainable. It was an ecological system in which people formed an integral part of *prakriti* (nature or overall physical environment), not an agent of its destruction to make profits. It revolved around the triangular coexistence among the earth (land), domestic animals, and human beings, a form of relationship in which human beings protected the soil and derived from it the means of subsistence for themselves and for their domestic animals, and animals in turn supplemented food for people as well as fertilizer for the soil. In Nepal, therefore, sustainability was necessitated by the imperative of survival.

People regarded *prakriti* both as a force of destruction and a source of life (*prakriti mata* or mother earth). As a destructive force, they feared her, and precisely out of that sense of fear they revered her and remained constantly watchful of her wrath. They attached a specific meaning to virtually every act of *prakriti*—good or bad. They believed that their lack of reverence would arouse her anger, prompting her to strike back with a destructive force, at times rendering her human children hapless. That was not, however, a battle hymn of her anger against her own children; that was viewed as her reminder to them of their misdeeds and failures to insure her productive and reproductive viability. That is, peasants viewed natural disasters as a reaction to their own violence against nature, i.e., disenchantment and punishment for abdicating their ecological responsibilities. In order to express their repentance, peasants would perform rituals to honor the sanctity of her force. They would undertake measures to rectify the problem the best they could in order to avoid *prakriti mata's* future wrath.

As a source of life, we begged her for her bountiful harvests, for her warmth and grace. As human despair and tragedy mounted, begging intensified. We worshiped her, respecting the raw power of her fury as well as expecting the rewards of her bounty. That was Nepal's contribution to what may today be considered true or natural environmentalism, one in which there was balance and harmony—one might call it a reciprocity of grace and nurturing—between *prakriti* and the Nepali humanity. No doubt, we at times used, misused, and abused *prakriti*, but there was rarely any false pride framed in the human conquest over her bounty and raw force. Taming her force was not the primary goal of human existence; rather coexistence in harmony was the purpose of peasant life. We performed annual rites and ceremonies, praying to her during every planting season for a bountiful harvest, offering her thanks after every harvest, and asking for her forgiveness during natural disasters.

Prakriti was thus intrinsically intertwined with the viable survival of peasants, not a source of wealth and profits although land was often used as a social weapon by the landed class to solidify their economic position as well as wield their status and power. That is, while a few in society certainly secured their prosperity from *prakriti*, to most she was simply a mother with a preordained duty to insure her children's survival. And she, indeed, sustained countless of her human children and gave them a sense of dignity, something that today's development has denied to them. We watched very carefully for any sign of *prakriti's* pleasure (prospects for a good harvest and hence prosperity) and wrath (prospects for a poor harvest and hence hardship). Deeply carved in all of this were not just charming folklores and lullaby songs; there was, as revealed in the preface of this book, also profound practical knowledge built in those signs of nature and folklores, in those years of observations and oral traditions. Farming practices were, therefore, largely based on observational and cumulative knowledge, closely following the rhythmic cycle of nature.

Recounting of Nepal's peasant ecology and life does not necessarily imply that our lost past was all pure and pretty, paved for a smooth ride of progress, without any bumps and blemishes, and that it should be revived and resurrected in its previous form. Certainly it had many pitfalls. It was oppressive in some regards, particularly to women and others with little social power (see Chapter 5). The main point is that in the past the economic system or mode of life was definitely sustainable as it was rooted in the spirit of self-help and local resource base. Self-help was a national motto which Prithivi Narayan Shah, the founder of unified Nepal, popularized 250 years ago.

But, today, the story is very different. As indicated at the outset of Chapter 1, such sustainable economic practices and locally-based knowledge system are widely seen as a national shame. They are invariably branded as a principal hindrance to modernization and progress. As a result, the local knowledge system and economic practices have been relegated to a relic status to be occasionally investigated by a certain genre of cultural anthropologists as an object of curiosity and knowledge reconstruction. But it is rarely appropriated to be applied for the benefit of the masses whose sufferings continue to mount, all in the name of development.

Today's materialistic development emphasis claims as its core mission the alleviation of poverty and misery. While it sounds highly appealing on the surface, it has turned into a cruel joke. As Foster (1995) points out, the notion that development (i.e., increasing production) solves poverty is perhaps the biggest myth that the international development establishment has successfully propagated throughout the underdeveloped world (see Yapa, 1993). There is evidence to suggest that development—whether internally induced or externally generated—does increase national wealth. But poverty is rarely abated as it continues to sharpen its teeth against the poor, right in the midst of growing wealth. Nepal typically exemplifies the cliche that the rich get richer and the poor poorer. Since 1950 Nepal's per capita income has more than doubled, but so has its incidence of poverty and destitution, a parallel trajectory that has become the historical hallmark of capitalist development. That is, quite contrary to the passionate case made by the advocates of development, increased national wealth has done little to alleviate poverty (see Gyawali, 1994b).

Foster (1995) shows that today's capitalistic development has rendered countless peasants landless, thus compelling them to destroy nature in order to survive (also see Griffin, 1974; Brass, 1991). This observation also holds true in Nepal. Growing landlessness is at the root of the ecopolitical battles being waged by migrant peasants in the Tarai region of Nepal (Shrestha, 1990; Shrestha and Conway, 1996). As peasants become alienated from their lands in growing numbers, peasant ecologies come under increasing attack from the very peasants who used to serve as their stewards, who used to revere *prakriti* as a life-giving and life-nurturing force.

And about the Nepalis' entrepreneurial spirit? When defined in terms of hard work rather than solely in terms of profit-making activities, it was even more common. The Nepalis are born-entrepreneurs. As a people inhabiting a relatively harsh environment with a limited resource base, they had little choice but to be enterprising and to develop resiliency; it was almost like an instinctive survival imperative. Frugality was a living motto as they had to learn, from early on in their life cycle, how to negotiate with their environment. Entrepreneurship and self-help went hand in hand, thus sustaining peasant ecology. In such an ecological system, hard work was a way of life, often translated into the building and rebuilding of the soil, the bedrock of all peasant ecologies. Even today, the poor work twice as hard as the rich, exploring different avenues of survival. The survival skills and resiliency of Nepal's peasant ecology were put to a fire test in 1989 when it was subjected to an economic embargo by India. The urban economy of Kathmandu which has become heavily dependent on imports was paralyzed. Long queues were formed everywhere, virtually for everything. A sense of panic struck the capital as scarcity became a daily reminder of its utter dependence. But most peasants and their peasant ecology not yet fully chained to the highway and consumer culture emerged unscathed by what can be referred to as the "artificial" shortage, stemming from excessive import dependence (see Gyawali, 1994a).

In many corners of Nepal, peasants still see their survival and poverty closely entwined with the ecological fate of *prakriti*. So they were all there—sustainable development, entrepreneurial spirit, and self-help—all live and kicking, at least until the 1950s, when Nepal's virgin soil was impregnated and then hemorrhaged by the Western notion of development. But, today, they are all retreating like dogs defeated in a fight. Once known for its self-sufficiency, Nepal is now turning into a barren land, devoid of any pride of self-sufficiency and self-help. The whole process of development, both in theory and praxis, is little more than the ruling elites' concerted efforts to replicate the West by decorating the national economic and sociocultural landscapes with the images of material glory, the ultimate symbol of Western modernity.

Here is an ironic twist to the current focus on sustainable development. When Western development arrived in Nepal, the Nepalis were systematically encouraged to abort their sustainable practices and discard their tradition of self-help as embodied in the subsistence mode of production, communal cooperation, and co-existence. They were repeatedly told that such practices, when viewed through the microscope of Western economic rationality, were irrational and went against the grain of growth. Anybody who was not driven by profit motives, the central core of Western economics, was labeled traditional and hence anti-growth (more in Chapter 3).

It hurts to admit that, as a result of this persistent drive to inculcate the principle of Western economic rationality, so many Nepalis have, over the past four decades, lost the art of self-help as well as the science of sustainable development and self-reliant lifestyle. They have lost control of their indigenous knowledge base and support system. Now the same developed countries and their international development agencies, which once mocked and undermined our indigenous knowledge and sustainable system of production as archaic and primitive, are shamelessly preaching to Nepalis to practice sustainable development. This is bizarre! Once again, they are firmly in charge of our lives and destiny, telling us what to do and teaching us about our own traditional way of life. The history and logic of sustainable development would dictate that they learn it from us. But then, how can they learn it from us since we no longer practice it thanks to their development advice? It appears that those who write human history control human destiny (also see Said, 1993). Over the past four decades it is the West and its development agents that have been appropriating and writing over the history of Nepal's indigenous cultural knowledge and economic practices. It is no wonder that they have managed to firmly establish dominion over the elite minds of Nepal and subsequently control the course of its economic fate and destiny.

"Aphai boksi, aphai jhankri. " This is a Nepali proverb that describes a person playing a dual role: both a witch and exorcist. It is precisely this game of *boksi* (witch) and *jhankri* (exorcist) that Western agencies play to keep underdeveloped countries like Nepal totally spellbound. Like a *boksi*, they have invaded our bodies and souls, causing so much undue suffering and misery as well as transforming us into something that we are not. They have consumed us by eroding our traditional means of economic subsistence and survival. Like a *jhankri*, however, they try to look good by pretending to exorcise the demonic power of their own *boksi* role. Their prescription: more development to rectify the consistent failures of Westernized development to uplift the masses. I admit development in its *jhankri* mask has a magnetic appeal to a country like Nepal possessed by the *boksi*. But, unfortunately, the larger the *jhankri's* role, the more destructive the *boksi's* power.

Western countries' push for self-help in Nepal is deeply shrouded in the veil of hypocrisy. While the international development establishment (including omnipresent NGOs) preaches the virtues of self-help, it keeps Nepal under the tight grip of foreign aid dependency, vigorously funding and implementing various projects, all in the name of development and poverty alleviation. Instead of letting Nepal go its own way, offering it the opportunity and complete freedom to navigate its own course of destiny, the development agencies endlessly interfere in its development affairs. They continue to treat Nepal like a retarded child, thus further tightening the loop of its dependency on Western monies and material values.

If international development agencies mean what they say or if they want Nepal to become self-reliant, why don't they simply let Nepal loose and be free? These agencies know very well that foreign aid (which includes both loans and grants) is addictive, a form of social nicotine that disintegrates the tradition of both self-help and hard work (entrepreneurship). These are the same agencies that are opposed to government subsidies and other forms of social welfare for the poor. Yet they continue to perpetuate foreign aid, which rarely induces any notion of sustainability among the natives. This is particularly true among the national elites who control the domestic lever of power and set the development agenda. Since the elites are directly plugged into the pipeline of foreign money that Western international agencies are impatient to provide, they have few incentives to practice and promote self-help, to work hard to earn money, or to revive sustainable practices, especially when such practices mean abdicating their much-cherished material lifestyle.

The behavior and attitude of international development agents are little different from those of colonial agents who proclaimed to be the savior of the colonized. But again, they are both, in essence, the same agents and agencies with the same mindset, separated only by time and geopolitical contexts. Just like the colonial agents' claim that the colonized needed them or could not even rule themselves without their political acumen, today's development agents contend that a country like Nepal is unable to develop without their help. This is what they mean by "white man's burden," I suppose. One can't help but wonder whether it is a matter of guilt or capitalist imperative that the West can't leave the rest alone. It matters little, however, what the intent of their intervention is, for the outcome is essentially the same: more misery for the masses (more in Chapter 3).

Moreover, while Western development advisors act as cheer leaders of the self-help cultural parade, telling Nepalis to work hard, they live a life of obscene leisure and luxury as clearly exhibited inside the compound of that little America called the Fort Durbar. Unless churning out senseless reports—which are rarely read by anybody—and spending hours in meeting rooms are taken as hard work, few advisors are engaged in any real work that has some constructive meaning and value for the vast majority of the native masses. Little evidence exists to suggest that they practice self-help.

In reality they are parasitic freeloaders, the true beneficiaries of development, basking in the glory of fat pay checks drawn from what can be termed the institute of international welfarism alias foreign aid. They even receive allowances for housing, maid service, and their children's education at private schools, but pay no or little taxes on their income. It is no exaggeration that foreign aid is perhaps the biggest welfare scam in the arena of international development, holding under-developed countries hostage while fattening the already bulging coffers of the various interest groups within the development establishment—both at the national and international levels. Western development advisors generally draw their pay checks directly from the foreign loans given to Nepal. So while Nepal accumulates foreign debt, much of the money actually goes to development advisors.

To summarize, foreign aid keeps, on high pay rolls, some of the least useful Western advisors, most of whom would have a hard time finding a job in their home countries that amounted to anything better than a foreman or mid-level manager. Few are equipped with any meaningful practical experience or cultural and historical understanding of local conditions and realities. Nor do they have much theoretical grounding as related to Nepal's economy; it is mediocre at best. It is international welfarism *par excellence*. Yet it is these very welfare recipients who are waving the banner of self-help. Who said one has to be morally correct and consistent to preach?

Given this profile of entrenched hypocrisy and contradictions, is it any wonder that the ruling elites of Nepal, especially those within the intelligentsia and development establishment, have little regard for hard work and manual labor? Nor do they have any will power, desire, or need to adhere to the twin principles of self-help and sustainable development. As for the poor it is an entirely different story. Deprived of any reliable employment opportunities or productive resources, they find it difficult, no matter how hard they try, to be productive. The logic is simple: if people do not have land, they cannot grow crops. If they do not have jobs, they cannot work and produce. Most of them aren't lazy. They are deprived. They don't need any incentives or lessons on self-help; it is ingrained. They only need access to productive resources or jobs. Let them have these, and the vast majority will be self-reliant without any prodding. Yet they do not quit, not even the poorest of the poor. Even in the midst of despair and deprivation and despite the woeful conditions of employment and resource access, their search for ways to earn a living does not end.

Regardless of the frequently shifting paradigmatic frontiers of development, there is one constant. Grow or rot, that is the fundamental slogan of the ongoing development cult in Nepal. It is a simple motto, but a very destructive one. As history shows, under this capitalistic principle of "grow or rot" not everybody can grow, and many rot. It is like a gambling situation—nobody wins unless somebody loses. The playing field is not level. The dice is loaded and success predetermined. It has little mercy for those who are discarded and left behind; they are simply written off as hopeless cases who could not climb the trajectory of social and economic Darwinism. To wit, development is a historical imperative in the process of societal evolution. But the "grow or rot" logic of contemporary development, one which is defined and measured strictly in terms of material achievements and values, has created countless victims: victims of development. While some—a small segment of the Nepali population—have derived tremendous benefits, amassing wealth as well as social prestige, many have been left behind by the wayside. So, in the final analysis, the banquet of contemporary development is a banquet for the few whereas the majority are left at the end of the table, begging for a few leftover crumbs.

In the meantime, the little America continues to exist right in the nerve center of Nepal—Kathmandu—as a mighty exhibit of American power and material glory, giggling at the humiliated Nepali masses right outside the compound of the Fort Durbar. It symbolizes American supremacy over Nepal. Even more importantly, that little America thrives in the hearts and minds of Nepali elites as a daily reminder of their development mission and vision. To them, that is what development is or should be all about, an imaginative geography of material glory. What is disturbing is that the ruling elites, as Gyawali (1994b) points out, are so obsessively absorbed into the process of Westernization that they hardly seem to care about the slow obliteration of their own souls and sanity, of their own dignity and integrity.

In a recent letter to *The Tallahassee Democrat* (Sept. 30, 1996), Arjun Joshi remarked on the prevailing attitude of affluent Indians. "It is," stated Joshi, "pure fantasy, currently popular among the affluent Indians, to imagine that American corporations are primarily responsible for helping people in India fulfill their dreams and achieve happiness. Such fantasies allow this tiny affluent segment to escape their responsibilities in this matter." Had Mr. Joshi not made a pointed reference to India, anybody who is familiar with the contemporary condition of Nepal would have immediately equated this comment with the Nepali elites.

To conclude, the ruling elites of Nepal have abdicated their social responsibility to its citizens, as well as to safeguard its national identity. They seem to be hardly concerned about the degrading reality that the very image of that little America they are trying to invent through development undermines Nepal's nationhood. Nor are they mindful that it stands arrogantly right in the heart of Nepal not only as a towering geographical and cultural divide between Nepalis and Americans, but also as a shining social separator between the rich and poor, the powerful and powerless, and the dominant and dependent. Instead of using nationalism as a fundamental resource and powerful base for indigenous development and instead of taking a stance against the destructive forces of Western values, they have deliberately chosen to serve as middlemen, as the hawkers and peddlers of Westernization and its consumerist culture, so openly displayed inside the compound of that little America. All this in the name of development.

3

DEVELOPMENT ODYSSEY
OF A COLONIZED MIND

Colonial domination, because it is total and tends to oversimplify, very soon manages to disrupt in spectacular fashion the cultural life of a conquered people... Every effort is made to bring the colonized person to admit the inferiority of his culture which has been transformed into instinctive patterns of behavior, to recognize the unreality of his `nation,' and, in the last extreme, the confused and imperfect character of his own biological structure... [T]he intellectual throws himself in frenzied fashion into the frantic acquisition of the culture of the occupying power and takes every opportunity of unfavorably criticizing his own national culture...

— Frantz Fanon, 1963:236-37

Westerners may have physically left their old colonies in Africa and Asia, but they retained them not only as markets but also as locales on the ideological map over which they continued to rule morally and intellectually.

— Edward W. Said, 1993:25

Ever since the onset of Europe's colonial expansion into what is today aggregately referred to as underdeveloped countries—a process often euphemistically termed "discovery and exploration" by the European colonizers—there has been a colonial plan of one type or another for the colonized, occupying the world's tropical and subtropical realms. As the colonial plan continues to frame the current modes of thinking and development planning of these countries, it is useful first to briefly sketch out its design.

Although the colonial plan was invariably disguised as a policy of dual mandate—that is, developing the resources of the colonies both for Europe and for the colonies—there is little doubt that it was directly rooted in Europe's commitment to industrial advancements and modernization at any cost. As such, its ultimate goal was outright economic plunder of the colonies, and it revolved around the axis of both natural and human resource exploitation. Without such plunder, it would have been difficult for resource-poor Europe to be in a position to meet the insatiable raw material demands of its rapidly expanding factories and thereby emerge as the dominant power in the world. Since it was impossible in those days to exploit natural resources without exploiting native peoples as laborers, their subjugation became the first order of colonial business, a process which required their physical as well as psychological conquest. It is precisely this process that Davidson (1992) contends invariably led to their systematic destruction.

As Stevenson (1992:27-8) articulates, in order to execute this grand colonial plan, Europeans initially embarked on a war path, laying waste countless natives and destroying their sociocultural integrity. Powered by a predatory appetite, the war path entailed not only physical destruction of men, women, and children, but also the devastation of their material and natural economies. The war path created and recreated its own mechanisms of justification, and at the same time provided a basis for Europeans' collective feeling of superiority. It also promulgated a way of thought and psycho-linguistic vocabulary to reinforce the continuity of European superiority and dominance from generation to generation. In this sense, the war also developed into a cultural war. In short, it was a total war waged on all fronts: physical, economic, political, and cultural.

The war started with the coming of Europeans as divine agents, purportedly with a mission to "civilize" indigenous "savages." Equipped with such psycho-linguistic phrases and the Bible, the "civilizing mission" became a decisive linchpin of what Stevenson calls "the methodology of total war" and economic plunder. This methodology not only acted as a powerful weapon of psychological victory, endowing Europeans with a feeling of sociocultural superiority and with a noble and heroic sense of identity, but also justified imposing their savage measures on local "inferior barbarians" (Stevenson, 1992:28). All of this left indelible imprints on the minds of native peoples, specifically their elites. These are the imprints that continue to serve as the most dominant operational paradigm of development thinking and material life in today's underdeveloped world.

THE COLONIAL PLAN: A SKETCH

History is replete with accounts of wars, of the conquerors and of the conquered. While wars endow the winners with confidence, pride, a sense of superiority, and even personal wealth, they invariably bring the defeated humiliation and dehumanization, exploitation and oppression. Prior to Europe's colonial expansion, periodic wars between various clan groups, regional warlords, or principalities were common events across the globe. They were fought for territorial expansion as well as to access foreign resources, but few developed into the kind of "total wars" that Europeans waged against the natives.

As European colonial wars and conquests spread from one distant region to another, across vast oceans and continents, *a geography of European imperialism* was born; it was mapped out at a grand scale. This new geography was accompanied by new thinking in the field of cartography, clearly reflecting Europe's imperial ideology. Maps were produced with Europe at the top center, thus visually projecting both its centrality and dominion over the rest of the world, as well as reinforcing the image that Europeans (whites) were superior to the colonized. A mythical image such as this created through cartographic manipulation, initially by Contarini in 1506, became part of the social reality in the European psyche, as if it were divinely determined (*The Economist*, 1984). It is, therefore, scarcely surprising that such pseudo-scientific theories as social Darwinism and environmental determinism were later propounded as natural laws in order to rationalize this assumed racial superiority of Europeans (Blaut, 1993; Peet, 1985).

This new imperial geography was not merely a geography of global territorial conquests by Europeans; it was also a geography of racism, a geography of total control of "inferiors" by a "superior" race (Blaut, 1993). It was a geography of exploitation and violence against both humanity and nature. It represented a cultural map of the globe, displaying a distinct landscape filled with racial, environmental, and technological dichotomies and divides, a map on which Europeans occupied center stage while the rest of the human race was relegated to the periphery.

On this dichotomous cultural map of imperialism, economic Darwinism was presented in the form of what Gunnar Myrdal (1970) broadly termed the colonial theory of development. European colonizers, who constituted approximately 10 percent of the world's humanity, saw themselves as economically fully evolved with "rational" economic goals. They portrayed the colonized as cultureless heathens, incapable of responding rationally like the Europeans to economic opportunities in order to improve their material wealth. The concept of "economic man" was invented to describe Europeans, who could not see the indigenous peoples (and their economic systems) as simply different from their own. Within their special psycho-linguistic framework, natives were regarded as subhumans, constituted very differently from those of European stock, who somehow got frozen at the bottom in the process of Darwinian evolution, thus failing to reach the top of the human development scale. No matter how old in age, the colonized were invariably referred to as "boys" meaning not fully developed in terms of mental faculties, and were, therefore, viewed as only good for hard physical labor to serve European humanity and its economic interests (Fyfe, 1992). Moreover, the colonizers equated the colonized with "dogs"—a marvelous symbol of extreme docility as well as danger. When properly tamed, dogs symbolize ultimate obedience and servitude, but, when left untamed, they are the icon of dangerous beasts. As such, they could be physically tortured or terminated. This psycho-linguistic construct became an ideological dagger for the European war of destruction and domination as simple words like boys and dogs proved to be invincible social concepts, conveying a message of their superiority and conversely of natives' inferiority. Moreover, it allowed the colonizers to mask their own most predatory and barbaric actions against the native peoples of their colonies across the globe.

For example, a parallel can be drawn between the treatment of nature and animals and the treatment of the colonized peoples. As Sheldrake (1991:3-4) points out in his fascinating book, *The Rebirth of Nature*, in the industrial world nature was viewed mechanistically, "conceived of as the inanimate source of natural resources, exploitable for economic development." As such, "Nothing natural has a life, purpose, or value of its own;...their only value is the one placed on them by market forces" or the "economic man." Destruction of nature was justified. Europeans viewed the indigenous peoples in a similar fashion, as a source of physical labor with no purpose of life or value of their own. Their only value was the one determined by their colonizers. They were good enough to serve Europeans, but barely anything more than that. Not surprisingly, the desecration of nature went hand in hand with human subjugation as a mechanism to exact labor. That is, the drive to exploit natural resources of the colonized world in order to fuel Europe's progress and prosperity led to the subjugation of humans which, in turn, set the stage for the destruction of nature. As vividly captured in the PBS series on *The Africans: A Triple Heritage* (part 4) and on *Vietnam* (part 2), Europeans carried out their so-called civilizing mission in a most gruesome form: outright murder and mutilation of those natives who refused to submit themselves to the colonizers! How ironic that most barbaric methods were deployed to achieve the mission of civilization!

In his analysis of poverty in Asia, Myrdal (1970) argued that the colonial theory was a shrewd instrument of European domination, for it offered a rationalizing defense of the colonial structure of power. He (1970:494) stated:

> The `white man's burden' was, in the final analysis, his duty to govern those who could not govern themselves. The racial inferiority doctrine, in particular, helps us understand why colonial rulers often felt that nothing much could be done to raise the standards of the indigenous peoples, because their plight was the consequence of immutable biological facts. Explanations in terms of social conditions led to the same defeatist conclusions; the social environment was held to be outside the jurisdiction of the colonial governments. In turn, the more basic racial inferiority doctrine supported the established *laissez-faire* attitude in social matters.

To summarize, while the geography of European imperialism was driven by the mission of economic plunder through territorial conquest, it was the conquest of native bodies and minds, however, that served as its primary instrument. That is, the colonizers firmly planted the culture of imperialism in the colonies not only to systematically denigrate the colonized's national culture and mode of life as barbaric, but also to present themselves and their value system as being superior in every respect. Once the native minds were colonized, subjugation of their bodies as a source of cheap labor followed. While the native elites led the way in terms of accepting the presumed superiority of the colonizers' mode of life, the poor paid the price with their blood and bodies. As a result, the culture of imperialism gained permanency in the colonized world, faithfully serving the conquerors. That is why despite the fact that imperialism in its classical form (i.e., direct colonialism) saw its demise about half a century ago when the colonies started dismantling the saddle of colonialism, it has not ceased exerting enormous influence in their cultural and economic spheres, but in a far more polished manner than in the heyday of colonialism.

The cultural sphere of imperialism extended well beyond its immediate colonial boundaries, reaching even a remote and mountainous country like Nepal. Although Nepal was never formally incorporated into British India, it was tightly kept within the overarching domain of the British raj, particularly during the period of hereditary Rana autocracy (1846-1951).[1] The Ranas fondly absorbed British culture (Regmi, 1978). This small acorn of Western cultural emulation, planted by the Ranas more than a century ago, has today grown into a huge oak tree, molding the mindset of Nepal's ruling elites as well as sheltering their vested interests. It is this process of continuous molding and colonization of the elite mind and subsequent distortion of national development that this chapter attempts to expose through a personal story in the following pages.

THE BARBIE DOLL: A METAPHOR OF REALITY

The spring of 1983. I was back in Nepal to do research. One day, I went to visit a relatively affluent family who had gained its wealth from participating in "development," i.e., from being close to the Western expatriates in Nepal. The family was quite Westernized and acculturated to the prevailing culture of development. When I entered their living room, there was a Barbie doll, prominently displayed by the window. What was even more astonishing to me was that the Barbie doll was situated close to the pictures of *Laxmi* (the goddess of wealth) and *Ganesh* (the elephant-headed god of success). I was not sure whether the display of Barbie was equated with wealth or whether she represented an expression of the Western standards of beauty that white girls are more beautiful than Nepali (non-white) girls, but it was quite a fitting exhibition of how Western values had cast a spell on the Nepali elites' values and development thinking. A year later, Ken, Barbie's boyfriend, had joined her. Barbie and Ken! How interesting!

Unable to blot that image from my mind, it has prompted me to examine my own values and rethink the whole culture of development, rooted in the Western trajectory of growth (with the underlying assumption that it can be replicated in Nepal). In fact, whenever I reflect on the scene, conflicts and contradictions hound me. It takes me back to my boyhood days when my development odyssey began. Then I begin to realize how my colonized mindset was formed along that odyssey, the kind of mindset that the European colonizers systematically grafted and nurtured among the colonized to convert them into native agents of colonialism in order to rationalize and perpetuate their rule. Memories can be so cruel, sometimes! The past continues to haunt the present.

Ever since that encounter with the Barbie doll, I often find myself recalling the many faces of suffering I have seen over the years—all victims of development, some struggling to survive, some going hungry, and others rejoicing at their financial success and ostentatious material acquisitions. Despite immense suffering caused by development, its magnetic charm does not fade. Nepalis are seduced by development and by its voracious materialistic culture. I have been seduced. We have all been seduced. And in this process of seduction, there has been a structural violence of our psyche. But who caused it?

Materialistic development is *seduction*, which Webster's dictionary defines as "the act of seducing to wrong acts or beliefs." Seduction is an interesting experience, however. It makes people euphoric, but only until they realize that they have been duped into doing something shameful or even harmful. Yet seduction involves no physical conquest, but only an irresistible bait. Sometimes, the seduced do not even feel violated. Many simply choose to suppress any feelings of violation. Are we ever going to realize the deep wounds that the seductive culture of development leaves on us? If we ever do, what can we do to heal such wounds?

With these questions in mind, this essay begins with an account of the process of my own seduction by development. In a way, this is a wrenching dialogue with myself, based on my encounter with development as a young student aspiring to join the ranks of educated and affluent elites. However, my objective here is not to present my own personal biography; rather it is a postmortem, an analysis of the impact the ideology of development has on the colonized mind. Such a personal narrative is designed to reveal how and why the seductive power of development, with foreign aid acting as its irresistible bait, becomes deeply entrenched among the country's ruling elites, molding their cultural values, thinking, behavior, and actions. It also shows how the whole notion (and culture) of development is distorted.

BECOMING UNDERDEVELOPED

As a *garib* (poor) boy growing up in a rustic town of Pokhara in Central Nepal more than 45 years ago, I had few possessions of material value. My material aspirations were limited to my occasional desire to have enough food and some nice clothes. I grew up in a tiny house with a leaky roof. My family had about 1 acre of non-irrigated land. Along with some vegetables, we usually grew maize and millet. My mother sometimes brewed and sold millet liquor, locally known as *raksi.* This is how my family eked out a meager existence. Life was always hand-to-mouth, a constant struggle for survival. It was not unusual at all for me to go to school hungry, sometimes three or four days in a row.

I specifically recall one *Dashain,* the biggest Hindu festival. It is celebrated for 10 days every year with great fanfare. The festival signifies a celebration of victory of good over evil, namely the victory of Goddess Durga. During this festival, most temples are littered with blood from sacrificed animals (uncastrated goats, roosters, ducks, and buffalos). The smell of blood and raw meat is everywhere. Tremendous amounts of meat are consumed during this festival. Even the poorest are expected to consume some meat. (In fact, this is one of the very few times during the year most poor families get to eat meat). It is not just a religious celebration; it is also equated with status. There is tremendous pressure on every family, rich and poor, to celebrate it with as much pomp and show as possible. Parents are expected to buy brand new clothes and other material items for their children. As a result, each year countless families plunge deep into debt. Many mortgage, if not sell outright, whatever little land or other assets (e.g., gold) they have to raise money to celebrate this so-called auspicious occasion. Because the festival is very expensive, many households fail to recover from debt. My father used to call *Dashain dasha* (misery) or the "Festival of Sorrow."

That particular *Dashain*, I was eight or nine years old. My family had no money to acquire any of the necessities for the *Dashain*. It was the 8th day of the *Dashain*, two days before its culmination. On the 8th or 9th day, families are supposed to sacrifice animals to please and honor Goddess Durga, but we had not even a rooster. We all sat in the house the whole day, huddled around and feeling sad, not knowing what to do. My parents could not get me even one new shirt, let alone a complete outfit. Even today, the memory of that *Dashain* brings tears to my eyes. Anyway, finally, in the morning of the 9th day, I received a small sum of money from my brother-in-law, for whom I had done some work, actually for one of his clients who had just reimbursed him. That money saved that *Dashain*, and my family was barely able to ward off a social embarrassment.

To my innocent mind, poverty looked so natural, something that nobody could do anything about. We accepted poverty as a matter of fate, caused by one's bad karma. That is what we were routinely told. Little did I know that poverty was largely a social creation, not a by-product of karmic configuration. Despite all this, poverty rarely seemed dehumanizing.

So, poor and hungry I certainly was. But underdeveloped? It never occurred to me that being poor meant being "underdeveloped." True, there is no comfort and glamour in poverty, but such a Darwinian concept was alien to me. The whole concept of development (or under-development) was totally alien to me and perhaps to most other Nepalis. It is not that the word for development did not exist in the Nepali language. It did. It is called *bikas*.

Following the overthrow of Rana autarchy in 1951, the word *bikas* began to gain currency as one of the most commonly used terms in the Nepali vocabulary. A status divide was erected along the *bikas* line between the *bikasi* and the *abikasi*. Those who had acquired some knowledge of so-called modern science and technology identified themselves as *bikasis* (developed), supposedly with a "modern" outlook, and the rest as *abikasis* or *pakhe*[2] (uncivilized or backward). Soon, some of the localites, especially those associated with the *bikasis*, came to appreciate the value of being identified with them because there was money in *bikas*, lots of money, made available through foreign aid.

Development was no longer just a concept. It became a social ideology, an ideology which fortified the already existing class divide. The majority of the wealthy class who also happened to be relatively more educated and enjoyed access to power aligned themselves with *bikas*, thus becoming *bikasis*. The international division of the world into "developed" and "underdeveloped" countries solidified Nepal's internal division of classes. Such division left the *garib* (the poor) as *abikasis* and the *dhani* (the rich) as *bikasis*. The ideological foundation of Malthusian poverty was thus being played out in Nepal as the poor were regarded to be poor because they were *abikasi*. They were accused of impeding *bikas.* Such economic Darwinism had suddenly developed a life of its own, a myth giving an appearance of reality.

Bikas was generally associated with objects such as roads, airplanes, dams, hospitals, fancy buildings, etc. Also viewed as a key component of *bikas* was education, for it was proclaimed to be essential to building human capital. By implication, education could salvage the *abikasi* mind. But education had to be modern emphasizing science, technology, and English, the language of *bikas*. Sanskrit, previously the language of the learned as well as the language of Hinduism, was generally regarded as a deterrent to *bikas*. For example, modern science taught us that the earth was round, contrary to what our parents had told us. Suddenly, we began to reject everything they had taught us as being defective, including their deep-rooted experiences. Such devaluation of indigenous knowledge created a big knowledge void.

There was tension in the family. Educated children were viewed as future agents of *bikas* whereas our parents were usually seen as barriers to *bikas*. To wit, there were things our parents did that had little scientific basis or made any sense. But there were also many things they did that had more practical values than the theoretical science we were learning at school. There was wisdom in their experiential knowledge (Chapter 1). Yet, in the eyes of *bikasis*, whatever human capital and productive forces our parents had accumulated over the years did not count for much, for it was considered archaic and primitive. We ignored the basic distinction between book-based education and experience-based wisdom. We got the education, but rejected the wisdom. It was sad that many students even felt ashamed to be seen in public with their parents.

The new education gave us the impression that even our parents' labor—manual labor—was antithetical to *bikas*. So the educated children started sneering at manual labor, treating it as something that only an *abikasi*, intellectually underdeveloped mind would do. The colonial conception of manual labor as something to be done by inferior natives was thus revived. The new educational system was producing a whole new thinking on the value of labor. There was a clear demarcation between non-manual labor and manual labor. In this sense, *bikas* meant, to apply Ivan Illich's (1992) logic, denying as well as uprooting the existing labor use system, traditional bonds, and knowledge base, rather than building on them. A totally different development mindset was being shaped.

This new attitude toward labor created a backlash against education in general as some parents resented it. My father opposed my education although I always did my manual labor. Many children were actually pulled out of their schools by their parents even before completing their elementary education. In an agrarian society like Nepal, children formed a vital source of labor or economic assets, but they had developed an aversion to manual work as a result of education. So what good was their education if it meant depriving the family of much needed family labor and potential supplementary incomes their children would generate when hired by others to do manual labor? Such a calculation was particularly important among the poor parents who did not see much prospect for their educated children's employment in the non-manual civil service sector, the principal source of salaried employment for the educated. Since the poor, in general, had historically been excluded from civil service jobs, to most poor parents, their children's education did not mean an investment in future prosperity. Instead it entailed, at least in the short run, an opportunity cost in terms of lost labor and potential incomes.

Before the spread of development ideology, hard manual labor was a fairly common way of life. The vast majority of people did it from their very early childhood, by the time they were seven or eight years old. Now the delusionary vision of *bikas* had made it anathema as if *bikas* could be achieved without hard physical labor. The devaluation of manual labor by the educated was being hardened by their observation of resident Westerners who rarely did any manual work. They all had at least one local maid. Some had two or three. They were living like a maharajah, a life of opulent luxury. They saw themselves as advisors and exhibited an aura of superiority. Even meagerly paid Peace Corps Volunteers (PCVs) had personal cooks. We thought that their life-style represented that of a modern, educated *bikasi*. Consequently, the local educated people began to emulate them and aspire to the "good life" the Westerners enjoyed. That was the kind of image of development that was purveyed to us.

Today, this emulation process has become so pervasive that it has actually undercut *bikas*, however defined. The high rate of unemployment among the educated is not only a function of the lack of employment opportunities. It can be directly traced to their increasing refusal to take manual jobs which they consider to be beneath them. Certainly, the Brahmanical Hindu conception of education conferred status and prestige upon the educated and civil service jobs. It is also true that high caste households, mainly brahmans, did not do certain types of menial work such as plowing the field, removing carcasses, and things considered unclean. Teachers and high-level government officials also generally disliked hard physical work. Yet, there was no precedence to degrade manual labor *carte blanche*, as was happening under the *bikas* rubric. Before *bikas* came, even the educated would usually perform manual labor. Today, the whole concept of such work is almost totally alien to them.

There is, however, another side to the saga of new education. Not all parents resented Western education. For the elites, who drove the engine of the national culture, modern education was the umbilical chord that linked them to the West. In other words, vestiges of British colonial influence were alive, and the elite parents behaved just like the loyal cadre of civil servants the British had carefully created in India. The ruling elites thus acted in their own vested interests, and did so at the expense of national interests. Since they greatly cherished such Western linkage and wanted to be associated with *bikas*, educating their children in modern schools and in the West was their high goal.

For instance, Nepali elites preferred to send their children to St. Mary's School (girls) and St. Xavier's School (boys), the only English schools in the country back then, both run by Christian missionaries (also see Gyawali, 1994b). One notable feature of missionary education is that while Nepal's official policy prohibited Christian preaching and proselytization, the country's ruling elites had no qualm about allowing these two schools to offer Bible classes as part of the overall curriculum. Established in the late 1940s and early 1950s by a Jesuit priest named Fr. Marshall Moran (Shah, 1993:38), they were heralded as the standard bearer of modern education in Nepal. Why all this? Simply because they served the interest and aspirations of the ruling elites.

Several wealthy families in Pokhara sent their children to these schools, both located in Kathmandu. When their children, some of whom lived in my neighborhood, came back home during breaks, we could hear them converse in English. Those children would have little contact with us, and sometimes view us as *pakhes* (uncivilized). Educationally, we felt very deficient in front of those elite children. Just like in the past, it was primarily the wealthy who could afford to educate their children and turn their education into an investment (human capital), thus further advancing their individual as well as class interests. In essence, the new educational system was preparing a new generation of elites who not only controlled the rapidly expanding bureaucracy, but also dominated the development enterprise. As the elites became the lopsided beneficiaries of *bikas*, education and *bikas* both displayed their distinct class roles and characters from the very outset.

By the mid-1950s, the ideology of *bikas* (development) had been firmly grounded in the Nepali psyche. It mattered little whether actual development was being achieved or not. But it had permeated almost every Nepali mind, from peons to the prime minister and the king. The higher the bureaucratic authority, the louder the voices of development advocates. *Bikas* was definitely regarded as a secret passage to material paradise. To evoke Ullrich's (1992:275) commentary on modernity and materialism, the myth of *bikas* was projecting materialism as human salvation, the sole source of happiness, emancipation, and redemption from all social evils such as hunger and poverty. Materialism appeared to have replaced a traditional Hindu conception of *bhakti* (devotion) and *dharma* (duty, good deeds) as a channel of *moksha* (salvation). This does not imply that Hinduism was (is) completely void of material values. It does have a tendency to play cat-and-mouse with materialism. That Laxmi (the goddess of wealth) exists in the Hindu mythology, and is actually highly revered, certainly means material values have been woven into the fabric of Hinduism, at least in terms of its practice. But even Laxmi was subordinated to this new form of materialism as it had emerged as a modern deity.

Development had become the hottest and fastest growing enterprise in the nation. Development projects were beginning to mushroom. Ironically, while anti-colonial sentiments were still riding high in the colonized world, we were enchanted by their industrial growth. Growing emphasis on development only lent credence to the Eurocentric paradigm of economic Darwinism which placed colonizers' capitalist system at the zenith and those of the colonized at the nadir. By adopting Western development models, we had affirmed the presumed superiority of their industrial economic system as well as their cultural values. We had helped them justify their branding of us as underdeveloped.

Similar to what Esteva (1992) notes, we had converted history into a social and economic project, a project to replicate the European form of social life without ever taking into account our own geographical resource base, indigenous pool of knowledge, local needs, and cultural roots. As Esteva (1992:9) remarks:

The industrial mode of production, which was no more than one, among many forms of social life, became the definition of the terminal stage of a unilinear way of social evolution. This stage came to be seen as the natural culmination of the potentials already existing in neolithic man, as his logical evolution. Thus history was reformulated in Western terms....The metaphor of development gave global hegemony to a purely Western genealogy of history, robbing peoples of different cultures of the opportunity to define the forms of their social life.

We had thus condemned the utility and strength of our own indigenous economic system and development path—in fact all non-North Atlantic modes of existence. We had fully accepted the Western standards and categories of development and underdevelopment. Ironically, while colonial rule was being rejected in the name of nationalism (national pride), colonial mentality and colonial economics were being profoundly internalized. Political liberation had simply turned into a vehicle of transferring ruling power from the colonizers to the national elites as it failed to bring about economic liberation or to liberate the colonized mind—which anti-colonial champions like Gandhi and Mao identified as critically necessary for navigating safely the murky waters of economic progress in a manner that was both sustainable and consistent with both national needs and capacity. Put another way, the culture of imperialism remained intact, affecting our every action.

Bikas had become our modern-day intoxicant. The more we drank from the spring of this intoxicant, the less control we had over our senses, eventually becoming oblivious to the reality that the so-called ladder of modernity, imported and imposed from the West, was actually a trap. To apply the logic embedded in Memmi's (1965) and Nandy's (1992) analysis, the dark colonial shadow that the British raj cast over Nepal for more than a century had left indelible marks. The thinking of the colonizers had been transposed onto the minds of the colonized. We had learned to welcome such thinking as a ladder of progress and modernization.

Although Christianity had already penetrated some other parts of Nepal (Shah, 1993), it was around 1951, I believe, when the first group of British Christian missionaries arrived in Pokhara. This does not mean that was the first time the people of the Pokhara valley were exposed to white people. Because of the deliberate British policy of Gorkha (Gurkha) recruitment, many recruits from the surrounding hills had already offered their unrivaled service to the British. While the citizens of other colonies were exploited as slaves, indentured plantation workers, and coolies, Britain's exploitation of Nepali youths was some-what unique in that they were used as raw materials, as cannon fodder for the war machine of the British imperial army (Des Chene, 1996; Onta, 1994; Pahari, 1991). The youths of Nepal had, like other colonized people, lost control of their labor. While Nepal was responsible for raising and nurturing their bodies, their labor—and too often their life blood—belonged to the British. In this sense, the dance of British imperialism was already in full swing across the country. To the valley of Pokhara, the missionary activity was new, however.

Along with Christianity, the missionaries brought modern medical facilities to Pokhara as they set up a small hospital called the Shining Hospital. While some would declare that the missionary hospital spawned a new, modern era of Western medicines and medical miracles, it undermined the local medical knowledge and practices. Medical services and medicines were provided either free or at nominal prices. It is noteworthy that "...in the world's only `Hindu kingdom' for much of the post-Rana period...the best schools and hospitals were run (and set up) by Christian missionaries" (Gyawali, 1994b:13; words within parentheses added).

As Christian missionaries arrogantly claimed that they were there to save both our bodies and souls, they made few attempts to cooperate and coexist with local medical and religious practices. In fact, the missionaries often mocked our practices, degrading the time-honored local Ayurvedic medical tradition as quackery. With the rising popularity of Western medicines came the rapid decline of Ayurvedic medicine. Furthermore, the presence of Christian missionaries and their hospital in Pokhara led to a dramatic psychological change in the native people's perception of whites.

Almost everybody started addressing those white people as *gora sahib* or *sab* for males and *mimsab* for females (white master, boss, teacher, or sir/madam depending on the context), a practice that was largely carried over by the Nepali mercenaries serving in the British army. Although the word *sahib* is a fairly common honorific term, it clearly has a dominant-subordinate class connotation. The fact that whites were called *sahib* meant that they were bestowed with a dominant position. The *sahib* culture became engraved in the Nepali mind and soil, a culture in which whites were placed at the highest pedestal, and the Nepalis looked up to them the way devotees look up to the statues of their gods, begging for blessings. This, I have no doubt, accentuated whites' pre-existing feeling of superiority over us, thereby rationalizing their treatment of us as uncivilized inferiors who needed to be saved—almost in every respect.

What is so ironic about the emerging relations is that when I was growing up, white people used to be commonly referred to as monkeys (meaning ugly). Additionally, the Hindu caste codes regarded them as *mlakshas*, the polluted or untouchable, relegating them to the bottom of the caste hierarchy. If any Nepali (except those belonging to the low caste group) touched a white person, that individual would be considered unclean, and thus required to undergo a cleansing ritual. In fact, as late as the 1940s, all Nepali recruits serving in the British imperial army and those who had crossed any of the oceans were, upon their return home, subjected to a cleansing ritual, for they were presumed to have come in physical contact with whites. Now they were no longer viewed as monkeys (ugly) and *mlakshas*. They were instead seen as beautiful and addressed as *sahibs*. They were treated as though they belonged to a master caste (race), even higher than the highest ranking caste group: the brahmans. So even the most sacred of the Hindu social codes were no longer sacrosanct when it came to applying them to white folks. It was a fundamental metamorphosis of the Nepali national culture, attitude, and behavior toward whites.

While it was certainly a positive development that whites were no longer viewed as *mlakshas*, it was hard to fathom why they had been elevated to the top of the social hierarchy. In other words, the oppressive and archaic caste system—itself a social Darwinism type of concept which actually predated Darwin by many millennia—had not broken down. Its caste hierarchy had only been rearranged in accordance with the emerging *sahib* culture and nascent *bikas* enterprise; caste relations had been transformed into power relations in our dealings with whites, the latter occupying the position of power and prestige. The ideology of *bikas* had supplanted everything as we had willingly chosen to travel down a Westernized path that downgraded our humanity to a lower status.

The Shining Hospital served as a sign of development, the first such sign in Pokhara. And this development was brought by white people, the harbingers of *bikas*. It was obvious that they were regarded as economically superior. They spoke the language of *bikas*; they knew the modern science and technology of *bikas*. They were the *bikas*. Since everything associated with whites was viewed as good and desirable, developing close contact with them, learning their language, and imitating them became valuable attributes of development.

Shortly after the British missionaries, came an airplane, an old DC 3. When some citizens of Pokhara heard the roaring sound of an approaching airplane, it caused an incredible commotion. I vividly recall racing down with my friends to the pasture where the plane had landed. Frightened by the plane's roaring sound and unusual shape, the cows and buffalos grazing in the pasture were running in all directions. The bucolic serenity of Pokhara was suddenly disrupted by that noisy machine. When the airplane landed, pandemonium broke. We were clamoring to touch it as if it were a divine creation sent to us by God. Some wondered how something so big could fly while others searched in their Hindu religious tradition to see if they could identify some divine figure resembling that airplane. They sure did find one: the *Garuda*, the eagle-like Hindu mythical bird, the heavenly vehicle of Vishnu, who in the Hindu trinity of Brahma, Vishnu, and Shiva is the universal god of protection, the Savior. We had noticed another facet of development. Not only could *bikas* cure the sick, but it could also fly like the *Garuda*, carrying *bikasis* around the country. We found a good adaptation of this development symbol to our own Hindu tradition. *Bikas* looked justified!

Then came a used jeep, flown in by the mechanical *Garuda*. The jeep was brought in pieces, along with a foreign mechanic, who assembled it in Pokhara. The jeep was later followed by bicycles and oxen-driven carts. Such was the order of transportation development in Pokhara and in many parts of Nepal: a retrogressive order. This was quite symptomatic and symbolic of the whole process of development occurring in Nepal—everything backward. What we were observing was imported *bikas*, not true progress from within. We had achieved very little on our own.

Following the advice of Western experts, Nepali *bikasis* or elites advocated industrial growth. Some actually built factories, even before embarking on the path of agricultural improvement and setting up infrastructural networks. For instance, a merchant family in Pokhara established a match factory, but the venture collapsed within a couple of years because of the absence of marketing networks and transport facilities. Yet this regressive trend has not ceased to mar the national development horizon. That is, we have ignored the message embedded in an old Nepali saying: *"ghati heri had nilnu"* (Size your gullet before you swallow a bone). We consume what we don't produce, and sometimes produce what we hardly need. While the national production structure remains practically pre-industrial and hence incapable of meeting local demands, our consumption patterns have prematurely leaped to the postindustrial phase. As noted in Chapter 2, the North-Atlantic culture of consumerism has invaded every nook and corner of Nepal, generating previously non-existent wants and therefore undue scarcity, a situation which ultimately thickens the sediments of poverty.

Anyway, imported development had arrived in Pokhara with various objects acting as its various manifestations. Though of little use for the general public, in our minds these objects signified *bikas*. Excitement seemed to fill the air even though few outside the development circle were climbing the ladder of progress in terms of being able to reduce the levels of hunger and poverty. This early wave of development was captured in the first five-year development plan launched in 1956 and almost entirely financed by foreign aid. As this plan institutionalized the development enterprise, the march of *bikas* was officially on. Although few of us knew where this march was leading us, development had become our new religion, with various material objects representing the pantheon of *bikas* gods and goddesses. The resemblance between *bikas* and Hinduism in terms of symbolism was uncanny.

As the first five-year plan came to an end in 1961, *bikas* emerged from its infancy, ready to take off on the wings of foreign aid. It was around this time that my development odyssey got underway, an odyssey that has yet to end. To be precise, it all happened with the arrival of the first group of Peace Corps volunteers (PCVs) in Pokhara in 1962 when I was in the 6th grade.

With the financial aid and guidance from the United States, a plan for vocational education was launched, and our high school was chosen as one of the first multi-purpose schools in the country. Part of the American PCV operation in Nepal was directly tied to this new educational agenda as many of the volunteers taught vocational courses. Prior to their arrival, however, a new building was built to house our high school. Along with the regular courses, the school offered four vocational tracts: *Trade and Industry* (carpentry and rudimentary drafting and electric wiring), *Home Economics* (cooking, sewing, and knitting), *Commerce* (typing and some shorthand writing and bookkeeping), and *Agriculture*. This new educational system was designed to produce a pool of skilled workers who would build the foundation of human capital, needed for development. So vocational students were expected to fill the knowledge and skill void, as well as play a big role in national development, at least on paper. We were being subsumed in this tide of *bikas*, both as its recipients and groomed as its future agents (and as valiant neo-agents of the American agenda of global domination, I believe). I was not only a member of the very first batch of vocational students, but also belonged to one of the earliest crops of Nepali *bikas*.

In order to carry out the vocational training plan, fancy chairs, desks, and tables were flown in from overseas. All sorts of tools and equipment came from the United States as parts of its aid package.[3] The headmaster and three vocational teachers were sent to America for training. Not even once were we told that what was going on at our school, in Pokhara and throughout Nepal, was all part of the grand plan that President Truman had formulated in the late 1940s for the poor, underdeveloped people like us.[4] The Truman plan was largely a post-colonial version of the colonial plan. One basic difference was that it reflected the changing geopolitical configuration.

Later, by implementing the Peace Corps plan, President Kennedy took the Truman plan to a new height and placed his own stamp on it. The Peace Corps plan was the least expensive yet most effective mechanism of intensifying American influence and countering communism across the underdeveloped world. Perhaps, most PC volunteers were not aware of the grand plan either. There was a good mix of volunteers. Some had joined the PC for an idealistic purpose: the do-gooders. Some had joined it, we found out later, to avoid being drafted for the Vietnam war, and others did it for adventure and curiosity, perhaps in search of invigorating cultural relief from the material opulence of stale suburban life in the United States. A few did it to indulge in the hippie movement or alternative lifestyle (see Chapter 6). Whatever the reason, Nepal fit the image as it was described as a Shangrila country, a view later popularized by Cat Stevens in his 1971 song entitled "Katmandu" ("I want to go to Katmandu"). How funny that many volunteers, who were sent to promote American values and materialistic development, were actually yearning for reprieve from that very same material life, in a culture that was depicted as most backward and poverty-stricken!

Whatever the hidden agenda of the American plan, we cared little. After all, the degrading specter of direct colonialism had vanished like a shadow in the dark. The vituperative language of colonial hegemony and racial superiority had been replaced by such euphemistic lexicon as American partnership and collaboration for development through foreign aid, a potent, seductive force in the modern diplomacy of domination. So we were sold on *bikas*. We found ourselves in a brand new school with a corrugated tin roof that had nice windows and blackboards, fine furniture and tools, objects beyond our imagination, and of course a horde of Westerners. For us, who grew up going to school in an open field or in open sheds made of bamboos and thatch, who used to play football (soccer) with green grapefruits, our school looked like a castle in a fairy tale, complete with glitters and grandeur. We never dreamed of such things, but they had suddenly become integral to the daily reality of our education.

Our school even had a generator to produce electricity so we could operate our fancy equipment. When electricity made its debut in Pokhara in the late 1960s, we already knew how it worked and how to do wiring to use it. So, evidently, *bikas* looked glistening and sumptuous, at least on the outside and at school. A little bit of US aid had done wonders, or so we thought back then. We were all bewitched, and our lives were changing very fast. It was almost like taking a giant leap from the bottom of a stairway to its top without climbing any of the steps. We did not even have to work, let alone work hard, to obtain these items. As we increasingly indulged in the Western concept of development, foreign aid began to pour in; it soon became the medium of material nirvana. However, because we were not producing *bikas* from within, the pride that came with self-achievement and self-reliance was conspicuously absent. We were only getting a piggyback ride on the back of the ideology of imported development.

Hindsight reveals a great deal of sadness to all of this emerging national culture of *bikas* and all the glitter surrounding it. First, although plenty of imported *bikas* seemed to surround the school, little change was forthcoming on the home front. As previously mentioned, development had not done much to reduce our hunger. For most poor children like me, our life at home was one whole ocean apart from our world at school. Every morning we went to school excited, ready to enjoy our new chairs and work with fancy tools, but after school the hard reality of life would set in as many of us returned home to face the same prospect of haunting hunger. Our expectations had, nevertheless, been raised, and disappointments were becoming more frequent as the distance between what material goods could be available and what was actually available to us was widening. Furthermore, since wants were rising, poverty had grown a new face, one with a much deeper materialistic undertone than ever before. Poverty had rarely been so frightening, and so degrading, in the past.

Second, we all got the impression that development could bring material benefits instantly, and we did not have to work hard to acquire what we wanted. Consequently, most educated people, as already discussed, shunned physical labor; they looked for work in the civil service sector where they could order their juniors to humiliating submission. Nepal, to be sure, has a long history of what is locally referred to as the *chakari* (servitude) mentality. Those who are possessed by the *chakari* mentality invariably wear two disparate faces: one looking meek and saying *hajur, hajur* (yes sir, yes sir) to those above them and another acting obnoxious and disparaging to those below them as subhumans. *Bikas* had further cemented this bifocal mentality.

This anti-labor, technocratic tendency has become epidemic as exemplified by the booming enterprise of development consultancy in which consultants get the most amount of money for the least amount of work. The majority of consultants are state civil servants and professors, who are routinely engaged in several projects at one time, collecting full fees from all. Especially those educated in America—or the so-called "America-returned"—command a high market value. About four years ago, I talked to a Nepali professor from Tribhuvan University in Kathmandu, who was finishing his Ph.D. in the States. During the course of our conversation, he informed me that he had already made arrangements to do consultancy work on the side after his return. This did not surprise me at all because, on several occasions, I had myself seriously considered working as a development consultant, and actually did some consultancy in the early 1980s. Since it pays handsomely and produces instant wealth, this line of profession has a magnetic appeal. It has become the opium of the educated.

It is interesting to note that most of the consultants—both domestic and international—rarely spend any time in the field, observing the reality and listening to the voices of those for whom development is supposedly meant. They consider themselves too important to be engaged in fieldwork. To most of them, therefore, consultancy means sitting at their desks and churning out baseline studies and project feasibility and evaluation reports that few bother to read. They are like the American bull discussed in Chapter 2. Since actual fieldwork is seen as messy work, they send assistants to field sites to collect data. They are also well aware that their data is worth very little because much of it is self-constructed and self-invented by their assistants, many of whom fill out the prepackaged questionnaire forms themselves, sitting in a tea stall or under a tree. Even when field assistants take their tasks seriously, many of them have few clues about the nature of the project in which they are involved. As a result, they have little idea as to how to record and report the data, the obvious casualty being the accuracy of such data. But, to consultants, it makes little difference, for their reports are predetermined and preconfigured in that they already know what they want to write or how they want to prepare their reports. In other words, their output is only a job, a matter of professional obligation, not a commitment to professional integrity or national progress. Yet, incredulously, these are the very self-serving consultants who project themselves as high-minded development experts and feel gratified by their claim that they are contributing to national development. The irony is that while the development enterprise itself continues to expand by leaps and bounds, the levels of inequality, unemployment, and poverty have witnessed little decrease.[5]

Third, the ongoing mode of development was merely reenforcing the colonial myth that whites were superior to the peoples of color (of the colonized world); that development could be brought only by whites and through their aid; and that we were indeed underdeveloped because we did not have the wherewithal of development. It was solidifying the notion that we were incapable of doing things for ourselves and by ourselves. While such colonial psycho-linguistic words as "boys" and "dogs" had been replaced with less loaded words like "poor" and "underdeveloped" in the postcolonial era, the underlying message was the same. The colonial civilizing mission was resurrected all over as the mission of development. These new Western "civilizers" first made us dependent by eroding the foundation of our relatively self-reliant mode of life, and then categorized us as inferior, helpless, and poverty-stricken. That's not all.

The new civilizers are the embodiment of Prospero (colonizer), a character in Shakespeare's play, *The Tempest*, who first occupied Caliban's island and learned from him all the qualities of the island, and then turned him into a vassal subject. Prospero tormented Caliban by conjuring up vicious attack-dogs to chase him down (Recall the civil rights episode of recent American history in which similar tactics were deployed by white policemen against black marchers and demonstrators?). When Caliban claimed that the island was his and complained of Prospero's predatory behavior and action, the latter demanded gratitude for having brought him the blessings of civilization. Later, Prospero explained to his daughter why they could not get rid of Caliban altogether now that they had the island:

> We cannot miss him: he does make our fire
> Fetch in our wood, and serve in offices
> That profit us.

Poor Caliban! And poor Prospero! What a way to buy into and express "the white man's burden!"[6]

Closely interwoven with nature and its cyclical rhythm, our way of life was certainly different, but by no means inferior. To wit, we were not equipped nor prepared to subjugate nature. Our relatively harmonious coexistence with nature was, therefore, interpreted as a sign of our primitiveness and technological weakness. Development was measured in terms of the distance between humans and nature, i.e., ruthless human domination of nature. As the logic went, the greater the distance between the two, the higher the level of development. Well, the distance between the two has definitely increased, in some cases literally as poor Nepali village women are having to walk farther and farther every year in search of fire wood and animal fodder. But true, progressive, and indigenous development has yet to occur.

We did not help ourselves either. The common practice of self-reliance and cooperation had given way to dependency and despondency. In the past, for example, if a trail was damaged, the villagers from the surrounding villages would organize a work force and repair it. But the new attitude among the villagers is to wait for somebody, perhaps a donor agency, to come and fix it. This mentality has become pervasive at all levels.

One evening in the fall of 1988 a reporter for Nepal Television was interviewing a high-ranking transportation department official about a bridge in Kathmandu which had just collapsed. When asked how he planned to rebuild the bridge, he replied without any hesitation that some foreign donor agency would provide aid to rebuild it. As shamefully lamentable as his answer was, it truly reflected the degree of dependency on foreign aid. Chained to the shackles of development, Nepal is immobilized, especially at the central level. In short, there has been a remarkable breakdown of the spirit of cooperation and self-reliance, as well as a severe corrosion of local knowledge base. Nowadays, at the national level few things function or move without foreign aid. The system is in a state of paralysis and total disarray.

The national ruling elites had internalized the new civilizing mission of development as the national agenda. And, in the name of carrying out this agenda, they had formed a cozy partnership with the various capitalist agents of the West. Nepali elites were doing what Nandy (1992:269) has observed in different national contexts: "When, after decolonization, the indigenous elites acquired control over the state apparatus, they quickly learnt to seek legitimacy in a native version of the civilizing mission and sought to establish a similar colonial relationship between state and society." Expressed in simple terms, development had legitimized the ruling elites' authority and control over national policies. Already well-accustomed to the Western way of life or material cultural values, the national elites had not only blindly subscribed, irrespective of their political ideology, to the mistaken belief that Western-style development was the solution to pervasive poverty, but they had also managed to project themselves as champion of the poor. Our prevailing mode of life was thus vilified by development fetishism. While development itself was touted to be a frontal attack on poverty, the poor were being blamed for their poverty. The only ones doing *bikas* and reaping its benefits were the elites. As Gyawali (1994b:12) reveals, the Nepali "intelligentsia has no clothes," yet, like the naked emperor, the elites can't see their own bare flesh. In fact, they are the impostors who are swindling the country.

Finally, before the onslaught of *bikas*, the poor and poverty were rarely stigmatized and reviled. Despite the prevalence of selfishness and the oppressive nature of the feudalistic social structure that existed in Nepal, the rich seemed to have borne at least some sense of shared moral responsibility toward the poor. For instance, the patron-client relations, though onerous in many ways, offered some economic cushion for the poor (see Brass, 1990). Poverty in the past was padded with some security, but now it was surrounded with almost total economic insecurity. The principles of *bikas* informed that such traditional behaviors and relations of production undermined individual profit motives and capital accumulation, both much needed for Western-style material development. Everything was defined in stark capitalist economic terms. Those who disregarded such principles of development were labeled irrational. Categories and labels were being constantly invented and reinvented, used and reused to denigrate us and our mode of life.

In making these points, I am not suggesting that whatever was old was good and desirable and that every aspect of our lost heritage should be reclaimed. Nor am I implying that the old social structure should be revived in its entirety and that we should adopt an exclusionary position and advocate nativism. Such a fundamentalist position is neither desirable nor acceptable. Nobody should be callous about the many tyrannical characteristics of our feudal-religious heritage. My contention, however, is that the indigenous economic system and values were generally self-reliant, self-sufficient, sustainable, and far less destructive to both humanity and nature. It served as a hedge against total deprivation. But now under the banner of development, the dignity and humanity of the poor were being questioned whereas poverty itself appeared to be deepening.

The modern medical technology was helping the poor live longer. While the looming glare of death was being rapidly cast away leading to a population explosion, the means of sustaining the growing number of survivors remained a mere mirage. While early death (short life expectancy) was characterized as a sign of underdevelopment, there appeared to be little solace for the poor in being able to live longer. Embroiled in prolonged misery and embittered by endless dehumanization, for the poor in general, increased life span was no miracle of life. Under so-called *bikas* and modernization, beating death did not necessarily mean celebrating life. For the poor, life has become one huge drudgery, a burden that can be neither tolerated nor overcome.

Yet these issues seemed to matter little. We had already developed a blind faith in *bikas* and its objects. We accepted development as a *fait d'accompli*. We seemed to have convinced ourselves that more *bikas* meant less poverty. What a historical fallacy! Although I had read several British literary pieces which graphically portrayed the poverty-filled social conditions stemming from the industrial revolution, it never occurred to me back then that England, the cradle of industrialism and hence the capitalist civilization, had experienced a parallel growth of poverty and prosperity. Sorry, Charles Dickens! How could I have so easily forgotten imperial England's social filth that you showed me through your rich and passionate description? Let's not forget that its imperial drive to colonize foreign lands was as much a direct response to its rapidly growing industrial needs (or greed) as it was to its deepening domestic poverty, unemployment, and attendant social ills. Cecil Rhodes, an ardent advocate of British imperialism, stated that "...The Empire, as I have always said, is a bread and butter question. If you want to avoid civil wars, you must become imperialists" (quoted in Lenin, 1969:93-94; also see Harrison, 1984).

We failed to see that *bikas* objects were not necessarily the same as actual *bikas*, achieved with local resources and rooted in the cumulative expansion of the indigenous knowledge and technology base. We sought ways to be close to Westerners for we viewed them as the messiah of development. Since the Peace Corps (PC) policy presented the best opportunity to be close to whites, we hailed it. Peace Corps volunteers (PCVs) were usually friendly and accessible unlike most high-flying diplomatic types and so-called development advisors. Moreover, they lived and socialized with the local people of the communities where they worked. We constantly hung around the PCVs and fantasized about going to America with them.

When I reflect on my own personal experience, there is little doubt that I had developed a colonized mind. As already pointed out, it all started in the 6th grade when I first came in close contact with American PCVs (teachers). I was proud of my contact with them. Being able to speak a little bit of broken English was a big thing. I viewed my association with American teachers and English-speaking ability as my *bikas* ladder, a ladder to carry me to the summit of modernity. Acquiring American values and copying their habits made my colonized mind feel more gratified. My mind was molded in the American cultural thought process albeit I had no idea what that really meant or how it actually worked.[7] Enamored by the notion of Western-style development, I absorbed its emerging culture, a belief system, that if a person spoke English, s/he was very bright, *bikas*-minded, and, of course, sophisticated.

Guided by such a mindset, I chose a vocational tract, namely *Trade and Industry*. I was excited about it because we were told that if we passed the national high school matriculation examination in first class, we would receive a full scholarship to go overseas to study. Such a prospect was irresistible to my colonized mind. Since foreign education was deeply cherished, students aspired to go to America and Europe to study. Of course, we had erected in our minds a geographical hierarchy of countries for foreign education, America being the most preferred destination, followed by England and other countries.

I passed the examination in first class. But no scholarship came my way. A sense of betrayal surrounded me as *bikas*, the mighty goddess of modernization, had failed to deliver on its promise. With my *bikas* hopes and dreams dashed, my life felt like a punctured tire, hollow and useless. Having nothing left to look forward to, I became a primary school teacher, attended college in the morning, did some tutoring, and stayed active in student politics. Then one day in 1971, my life suddenly took a new turn. I received a letter from a Peace Corps friend who had returned to the US in 1968. Thanks to his efforts, I obtained a full scholarship from Gustavus Adolphus College in Minnesota. It seemed like the Santa Claus of *bikas* had at last arrived to deliver my development goodies. In early 1972, I came to America, perceived across the globe as the magnificent Mecca of materialism, a country where many thought the roads were paved with gold. I was on my way to *bikas*. At least, so I thought back then.

Such was the development odyssey of my colonized mind.

In recent years, I have come full circle, from being a passionate subscriber to Western development ideology to being its vocal critic. The more I observe what this ideology is doing to a country like Nepal, or how it is leading Nepal down a self-destructive path, specifically with respect to its social, economic, and cultural consequences, the more I question its utility, objective, and, of course, *modus operandi*. With this comment, let me now shift to a more general discourse on development. The focus is particularly on planning as a vehicle of development and how Nepal's ruling elites have actually deployed planning as an indispensable source of wealth and instrument of their power base, both political and economic.

PLANNING, FOREIGN AID, AND NEPALI ELITES

From the dark clouds of World War II emerged the dawn of independence across Asia. India's freedom from Britain in 1947 dealt a death blow to Rana autocracy in Nepal. Rana rulers had flourished under the tutelage of the British raj. When the British left India, the Rana regime lost its imperial patrons and consequently became defanged. Four years later in 1951, Nepal was able officially to shed the yoke of Rana rule. The euphoric trumpet of liberation was, however, tempered by the formidable task of rebuilding the national economy left in shambles by the Ranas who had bled the country white.

Like other newly emerging nations, including its immediate neighbors in South Asia, Nepal faced, to use Baran's (1973) phrase, two stark post-liberation realities: "the revolution of rising expectations" and "the steep ascent" of development. While the question of whether or not the masses felt the so-called revolution of rising expectations and the need for Western-style development remains debatable, there is no dispute that the new rulers of Nepal certainly did. To them, development was not only a national goal, but also a class imperative.

Apart from their political claims and character, the overall class interests of the new Nepali rulers were not much different from those of the Rana rulers. In this sense, the battle between the two was not a clash of two polarized classes. Rather it was largely a power struggle between two different factions of the same class lineage—one bent on openly autocratic (repressive) rule and another pursuing a relatively democratic path. The social history of Nepal is essentially a history of feuds between different factions of the ruling class (see Joshi and Rose, 1966; Shrestha, 1990). However, unlike the previous ruling factions brought down by palace intrigues and coups, the Ranas' factional rule was dethroned by a faction with a relatively large popular base.

Anyway, the new rulers, along with a new breed of national elites, ascended to power at a critical historical juncture. While the tide of "modernization" was beginning to sweep across Asia, Nepal's new rulers faced a grim prospect of producing enough internal surplus to lay its foundation in the country as well as to enhance their power base and economic position. Since 104 years of Rana rule had, as indicated above, bled the country white, the country had a barren look. In the absence of other natural resources (with the exception of subtropical forests in the Tarai), most of the national economy was directly tied to its narrow and underdeveloped agrarian base. Consequently, the new rulers' ability to extract necessary or enough surplus from it was quite limited, especially given the fact that they already controlled much of the country's land (Shrestha, 1990). In light of the fact that peasants had too little land and hence were too poor, they could not resort to the time-honored tradition of squeezing peasants to generate a surplus. Any attempt to apply the saying that "Peasants are like sesame seeds; the harder you press them, the more oil you get from them" could have led to peasant reprisals and rebellions which, in turn, would have severely crippled the new rulers' authority and power base or even deposed them from power. The agrarian base was thus out of the picture as a means to meet the new elites' modern demands.

Given such a scenario, the new rulers found themselves in a difficult position, one in which they could neither elevate their socioeconomic position to a higher plateau, nor climb "the steep ascent" of development (modernization) in order to quench the thirst of "rising expectations." The two objectives went hand in hand in that the new rulers' economic fate was directly predicated on their faith in national development. So development was both a national and class imperative, for, without it, they would not, to repeat, be able to fulfill their class interests; nor could they expect to generate employment for their educated members whose number was already on the rise.

Thus guided, Nepal's new ruling elites, despite their strong feudal roots and ties, regarded the country's agrarian base as anti-*bikas* and hence in need of rapid transformation. That is, the country's agrarian base was the last place where the educated with a modern outlook and urban bias would seek, nor could find, employment. In their eyes, therefore, modern development patterned after Westernization became the inevitable national goal and demand, for it was the only viable avenue to produce and extract enough surplus. Yet the basic questions remained: what is the most expedient approach to development and how to generate enough resources, namely capital and technical expertise, to embark on this national project?

While foreign aid cogently filled the development resource gap, "planning" was embraced as a logical institutional instrument of national economic development. In view of the new ruling elites' socialistic national slogan and capitalistic goals, there was little doubt about its efficacy. Because planning involved state control of development by a centralized authority, it allowed the new ruling elites to monopolize all the resources, mostly from foreign countries. It had a natural appeal as it acted as an effective medium of collusion between their vested class interests and national development.

As previously mentioned, Nepal implemented its first national plan in 1956. Planning was naturally flaunted as a grand chariot of both social justice and economic development. It was a form of social engineering of development that had its parallels with genetic science, e.g., agronomy. As Escobar (1992:132) notes, "Generally speaking, the concept of planning embodies the belief that social change can be engineered and directed, produced at will. Thus the idea that poor countries could move more or less smoothly along the path of progress through planning has always been held as an indubitable truth, an axiomatic belief in need of no demonstration, by development experts of most persuasions."

For instance, in the late 19th century, Engels (1978:11) had envisaged "...the planned utilization and extension of the already existing enormous productive forces of all members of society, and with uniform obligation to work" as a vehicle of establishing "a new social order...for enjoying life." About a century later, Myrdal (1970) was no less sanguine about it than Engels. Even those economists who were often hostile to socialism jumped on the bandwagon. Such a messianic vision of planning was, to apply Wallerstein's (1992:5) perspective, based on the basic belief that reason and consciousness would prevail; humanity could act as a rational and harmonious social unit, building a good society in the common interest of all and that the state was the fundamental apparatus of such rational, conscious, and collective construction of the good society which the human race presumably savored.

Paul Baran (1973) articulated in the mid-1950s why planning was the most logical and efficient path to progress. Two main goals of comprehensive planning can be discerned from Baran's analysis: (1) to maximize the realization of potential economic surplus[8] as a source of capital accumulation to propel economic development and (2) to establish a socialist order by eliminating privatized control of the means of production.[9] Although Baran derided capitalism, he remained true to his Marxist persuasion in that he was unwavering about his belief in the presumed superiority of the industrial mode of production (or technology) as a means of Western-style material achievements. In essence, Western Europe and America were seen as a technological model of economic growth. In the same vein as the Western model of economic rationality discussed in Chapter 2, planning implied that the indigenous economic system was wasteful of economic surpluses and therefore anti-*bikas*. So, to achieve development, a country like Nepal was required to steer away from, or even dismantle, its indigenous knowledge base and production system rather than to build on them. In this sense, both the capitalist and Marxist conceptions of development had plenty in common although their approaches and objectives varied.

The empirical validation for planned development came from the former Soviet Union which had posted dramatic industrial growth in a far shorter period than capitalist countries (Myrdal, 1970). Although

Soviet planning provided the general guidance, Nepal followed the Indian model which was implemented within the framework of democratic socialism, a political system that was heralded by most leaders of the non-aligned movement (e.g., Nehru, Tito, Nasser, and Sukarno) as a genuine and appropriate alternative to both capitalism and communism. Planning, as practiced in Nepal, was (is), however, neither democratic nor socialist. After my return to Nepal in 1979, it became clear to me that the Nepali elites had completely derailed planning's core mission, turning it upside down. They had used planning not as the vehicle of creating a new social order, but as a mighty populist tool, maintaining a firm grip on development funds (foreign aid) for their personal advancement. The vision of building the good society for all had been completely thwarted.

As a large-scale national undertaking, modeled after Western-style development, planning, as pointed out above, required the very things underdeveloped countries like Nepal sorely lacked: development resources such as capital and technical expertise. This is where the development planning needs of new countries like Nepal and the Truman plan for global control converged (see note #4). Under the Truman plan, America was actively offering foreign aid—capital and technical expertise—purportedly to help poor nations execute their economic plans. Foreign aid was made available, initially as free grants. For the US, the sum of foreign aid was too small to inconvenience its treasury. From the capitalist world's viewpoint, a few million dollars of aid scattered in the newly emerging nation-states did wonders as it sowed the seeds of their dependency on the US and on former colonial rulers. Foreign aid was an inexpensive but very effective instrument of control. As a result, although colonialism as a vehicle of territorial domination has been defunct, its imperial culture thrives vibrantly in the minds of native elites. Foreign aid is not merely an economic issue; it is a device to manipulate the recipient state's national culture, casting and recasting it into a North-Atlantic mold. During the formation of my colonized mind, I was too seduced to understand such issues; nor did I ever care about them.

In 1951, America gave Nepal 22,000 rupees in aid. Though tiny in amount, that was the first foreign aid to reach Nepal, and it was directly connected to the Truman policy of communist containment.

During the anti-colonial movement that swept Monsoon Asia, Marxism was received warmly both by its urban intellectuals and rural peasants. Marxism's appeal in Asia did not, however, stem from the breakdown of the capitalist system. Ironically, it was rooted in the fact that many of the colonial intellectual class that the imperial order educated to serve as its domestic agents had actually turned against it. As Feuer (1959:xx) succinctly states:

> The symbols of the Marxist philosophy became the vehicle of the resentment of Asian intellectuals. The Marxist terms were filled with a new content. The `capitalist' was identified with the Western rulers, the `proletariat' was taken as the Asian people generally, and the `class struggle' became the equivalent of racial and national liberation. The Asians were particularly receptive to Marx's apotheosis of technology in historical causation. For through building up industry they could guarantee their independence, eradicate their own inferiority feelings, and assert themselves as equal to the white men. And lastly, Marxism as a science of political leadership offered to Asian intellectuals a new ideology for their role as society's administrators.

Even after several Asian countries gained independence, there was no sign that the appeal of Marxism was waning. In view of the sweeping wind of Marxist influence and the rising "Red Tide" in China in the aftermath of its communist victory in 1949, even a tiny and isolated country like Nepal was figured into the US geopolitical plan. It was viewed as a key chip in the Domino Theory of communist march into South Asia—a view that received more credence especially after the Chinese takeover of Tibet in the 1950s. Although Nepal's towering Himalayas were generally seen as an imposing physical barrier to communist expansion into South Asia, it was by no means impregnable. Hence this physical barrier had to be reenforced by a cultural moat, constructed in the image of Western material values, i.e., induce Nepalis to act as local agents of America's interest. This meant seducing Nepal's ruling elites into thinking that they too could, through foreign aid, bask in the dazzling glow of West materialism.

Thus came foreign aid—an integral component of Truman's foreign policy—to the rescue of both the American agenda in Asia and the ruling elites of Nepal. To the latter, as an invaluable source of surplus, foreign aid not only helped them control the leverage of political power, but also the treasury vaults to fulfil their economic interests and aspirations. And, in the meantime, it was convenient because they could obtain it free and without any hard work. So the lofty vision of socialist construction (that is, development and justice for all) turned into an empty slogan as it was tactically used as a populist tool to fool the general masses starved for justice and basic economic security. Nepal's ruling elites had no intention of implementing such a vision, for it would have meant sacrificing their own vested interests.

As King Mahendra, following his 1960 coup against the elected government, usurped all the political power, foreign aid became even more critical for the survival of his rule (Mihaly, 1965; Shrestha and Conway, 1996).

> ...[Foreign] aid has assisted the monarchy both directly and indirectly to create a better-equipped and better-trained army and to put a large number of potentially restive young men on the bureaucratic payrolls. It is true that aid-giving agencies of several nations have pressed the king for reforms, but aid programs have been maintained despite the confirmed absence of significant reforms because for these nations change had a lower priority than maintenance of status quo, which they all found to their advantage for different reasons. Thus, in the short run at any rate, foreign assistance has enhanced the monarchy's chances of survival and has inhibited the growth of pressures for fundamental change.

This is what Gaige (1975:200) tersely wrote about the role of foreign aid in the 1960s and early 1970s. While the Nepali king no longer holds absolute power, at least not according to the constitution, every ruling class (including the king) since then has been increasingly enslaved to foreign aid both to keep the dimming flame of development burning and its coffers expanding continuously. So, as one can see, foreign aid—a favorite child of American diplomacy born in the chilly chamber of the "Cold War"—is a perfect match between the Nepali elites' vested interests and the Western agenda of global influence.

Development was thus bestowed upon us by the Western gurus in concert with our national elites as the mantra of material nirvana, and we chanted this mantra like a daily prayer. Under the pretext of development and democracy, we absorbed the American values. Hindsight tells me that the American agenda of sprouting local agents to defend its interest worked. As a leader of student politics in Pokhara, I recall fervently defending America against leftist activities in Nepal, at times engaging in fist fights with communist students. When the Apollo 11 Lunar Module landed on the moon in July 1969, we were exuberant.

America's celestial triumph became our political bragging rights on the earthly ground against communist students. The ideology of development was, without a doubt, tightly intertwined with American presence and aid and with the capitalist belief in the supremacy of individual material gains as the ultimate measure of progress and good life.

Nepal went along with the Truman plan. The initial lure of 22,000 rupees provided as pure foreign aid (grants) has turned into a mountain of foreign debt (see Tiwari, 1992). Today, the debt figure stands at nearly two billion dollars (not counting grants). While this sum is like a drop in the debt bucket when compared to the amounts of foreign debt Brazil and Mexico owe (more than $120 billion each), for Nepal it represents 50 percent of the country's total gross national product (GNP): approximately $100 per person (i.e., 50% of its per capita income). Nepal is suffering the fate of a fly trapped in a spider web, awaiting death at the spider's convenience. What is noteworthy about the contemporary debt situation is that, unlike in the past, Nepal has hardly any leverage to reject or negotiate the terms of foreign loans, benignly camouflaged as foreign aid (see Panday, 1992; Shrestha, 1992; Tiwari, 1992).

Despite such gravity, the total amount of foreign debt keeps mounting rapidly because, for the ruling elites, it is free money. They express hardly any shame about their constant begging for foreign aid and then bragging about their ability to secure it. During an interview in 1993, Mr. Mahesh Acharya, who at that time was the Minister of State for Finance under the Nepali Congress Government, was giving an update on the state of the Nepali economy. Mr. Acharya boasted about his Nepali Congress government's success in securing additional foreign aid: "...there has been a noteworthy increase in the volume of foreign assistance after the formation of the elected government. During the fiscal year 1990-91, foreign assistance amounting to Rs. 5,665.4 million (Rs. 48=US$ 1) had been approved. The amount reached Rs. 21,084 million in 1992-93" (*Nepal Press Digest,* 1993:376-77). The minister, however, avoided to point out that 62 percent of this so-called foreign assistance was actually loans, which translate into more debt for the country.

Since the elites do not have to pay back this debt personally and stand to gain the most from it, they have little interest in killing the goose that lays the proverbial golden eggs for them. It is entirely in their personal as well as class interests to obtain more and more foreign assistance. To them, it makes no difference whether the money comes in the form of outright grants or loans and where it comes from as long as it does. Foreign borrowing has been "depersonalized," and foreign aid has now turned into a national preoccupation. As the massive build-up of foreign debt saps its energy, ability, and resources, Nepal finds itself caught in a downward spiral, sinking deeper and deeper in the sea of dependency, thus becoming too debilitated to chart a relatively self-reliant and sustainable course of development.[10] Yet the ruling elites are little worried about it. It is clear that the deeper the overall socio-economic condition of Nepal sinks, the better-off the ruling elites are because the sinking ship gives them more reasons to beg for more foreign aid. There is little doubt that the elites of Nepal truly are the modern day merchants of poverty and degradation.

Today, in Nepal, foreign aid and development projects are syno-nymous, and so are the elites and development. One cannot exist and function without the other. Planning has long been subverted to serve the political and economic interests of a small class of Nepali elites. Instead of creating a new, progressive social order and the good society where everybody could enjoy life, planning has legitimized the authority of the ruling elites, thereby propagating the old order as well as socioeconomic disparities and poverty inherent in it. Simply put, *bikas* is a class ideology, with planning acting as its populist decoy.

CONCLUSIONS

In this self-reflective narrative, I have attempted to recount the development journey of my own colonized mind and how it evolved and operated. I have also discussed how the common national goals of planning were subverted by the ruling elites to serve their own vested interests. In essence, my attempt in this chapter has been to demonstrate how the culture of imperialism is transfused into Nepal, how the colonial mindset is created and recreated among its ruling elites, how both external and internal forces have worked in tandem to devalue its indigenous economic system and deform its national culture, and how the Western notion of development was imposed. In all of this, foreign aid has played a critical role, captivating most elites' hearts and minds as well as framing their attitudes and behaviors. The age-old adage that money corrupts seems to be painfully true. Seduced by the dazzling temptation of foreign aid, the ruling elites of Nepal have opted to completely ignore what King Prithvi Narayan Shah, the founder of Nepal, most emphatically instructed some 200 years ago: to vigorously pursue a self-reliant economic policy, keeping British interests (today it can be translated as Western interests) at bay.

NOTES

1   Although Nepal was never formally incorporated into the British raj, its overall status was little different from that of a colony. The British maintained firm control over it after the conclusion of the Anglo-Nepal war of 1816. In that sense, it was virtually a colony without formal colonization (for a detailed discussion see Des Chene, 1993; Shrestha, 1985).

2   The term *pakhe* technically means somebody from a hilly area, frequently referred to as *pakho* in Nepali. But in its colloquial usage, the word has somewhat of a derogatory connotation meaning somebody who is uncivilized, uneducated. It is equivalent to the American term, "hillbilly."

3   By the time I graduated from the high school, some of the tools had disappeared, and most tools and equipment had become almost useless because of the lack of proper maintenance facilities and budget. Fancy chairs had been damaged. The school building itself was deteriorating. I was recently informed by a Pokhara friend that all the tools and chairs have completely disappeared, and vocational courses are no longer offered (except for *Commerce*).

4   The Truman Plan was a direct response to the post-World War II realities: the sweeping tide of anti-colonialism fueled by the forces of nationalism; the rise of the United States as the leader of the capitalist world; and the spread of communism. The plan contained three interrelated goals: (1) to contain communism, (2) to ensure the capitalist world's continued access to the former colonies' raw materials, cheap labor, and markets, and (3) to consolidate the United States' new super power position in the world, extending its dominance beyond the Western hemisphere.

   The Truman Plan was a two-pronged, stick-and-carrot approach to international diplomacy, carefully designed to preserve and promote capitalist interests. The military component acted as the tool of gunboat diplomacy, ready to strike any time, as it has in many countries—most recently in Iraq. It was the foreign aid component, however, that was deployed worldwide as a more practical and seductive lure. In 1950, President Truman's Secretary of State, Dean Acheson (1950:553), flatly stated the value of foreign aid: "...as a security measure, it is an essential arm of our foreign policy... It will open up sources of materials and goods we need, and new markets for the products of our farms and factories."

In 1949, President Truman declared: "We must embark on a bold new program for making the benefits of our scientific advances and industrial progress available for the improvement and growth of *underdeveloped areas*..." (emphasis mine). Regardless of its soothing tone, the plan essentially retained the colonial order without the colonial garb, under the pretext of American cooperation and partnership for the development of underdeveloped nations.

Furthermore, the speech unveiled a brand new era of development. The chant of the mantra of development was heard in every new country. Moreover, the Truman speech, as Gustavo Esteva (1992:6-7) succinctly notes, formalized the term, underdeveloped, to be emblazed permanently in our minds as a category (and backward state) of development on the Darwinian totem pole.

5   The culture of development is undergoing another trend, one that is often touted as participatory, bottom-up, or empowering development. Foreign non-governmental organizations (NGOs) are invading Nepal in growing numbers, dwarfing Peace Corps volunteers and Christian missionaries. Although most Western NGO advisors/workers, who can be called the missionaries of development or neo-civilizers, possess only superficial knowledge of Nepal, they audaciously claim to be bringing *bikas* to Nepali villages and villagers. Recently, several local NGOs have been established, which, I have been informed, are syphoning foreign NGO funds for the personal benefit of their creators. Quite an example of local entrepreneurial spirit that the World Bank, USAID, and NGOs are aiming to engender among the local people!

6   I had read an abridged version of *The Tempest* during my first year in college back in Pokhara, but had completely forgotten about the story. Furthermore, I had failed to make any contextual connection to the colonial relations expressed in the play until I read Annette Rubinstein's brief 1992 correspondence in *Monthly Review*.

7   I thought Americans were better than the British whom I associated with Christian missionaries. I must confess that despite my *bikas* mindedness, I resented Christian missionaries. To me, they were the high priests of colonialism.

8   Baran (1973) argued that planning was indispensable for maximizing
     national economic surplus, which he divided into actual surplus and poten-
     tial surplus. Actual surplus is roughly the difference between what a society
     actually produces and what it actually consumes, and potential surplus is the
     difference between what it could produce and what it needs to consume. To
     Baran, it is the potential surplus that is most critical.

     In Baran's view, both feudal-mercantile and capitalist systems are inherently
     irrational. In both, there is not only a wastage of accumulated (actual)
     surplus, but also less than full realization of potential surplus for several
     reasons. As a result, the amount of potential surplus is substantially less
     than what could actually be "available for capital accumulation and
     economic development with a different organization of society from the one
     which exists" (Sutcliffe, 1973:91).

9   Despite seemingly successful implementation of planning in the Soviet
     Union since 1928, Baran (1973:43) did not overlook the power of the
     dominant class to co-opt it. Since the prevailing pattern of resource allo-
     cation corresponded to the vested interests of the dominant class, Baran
     believed it inevitable that any serious planning endeavor would come into
     sharp conflict with the dominant class and its allies at home and abroad. As
     a result, the Planning Board, could be taken over—like the government
     itself—by the ruling class, its activities sabotaged, and its existence used to
     serve the dominant interests while at the same time nurturing the illusion in
     the general masses that "something constructive is being done" about
     development to benefit them.

10   The total volume of foreign debts of underdeveloped countries climbed from
     $22 billion in 1962 to $60 billion in 1970. Today, according to the data
     published by the World Bank, their total debt has ballooned to nearly $1.3
     trillion. Susan George (1992:xv) reveals that "...between 1982 and 1990,
     total resource flows to developing countries amounted to $927 billion....
     During the same 1982-90 period, developing countries remitted *in debt
     service alone* $1,345 billion to the creditor countries...(a difference of) $418
     billion in the rich countries' favour" (emphasis in original). In the name of
     development, underdeveloped countries are trapped in what can be
     described as a situation of international debt bondage.

4

I AM A
DEVELOPMENT VICTIM, SIR!

If the soil is gone, our whole *jiban* (life) will be ruined. How are we going to survive?

— A peasant

Why apply all those *bikasi* (modern) farming inputs? *Bikasi mal* (chemical fertilizer) and *bikasi biu* (hybrid seeds)—they all cost money. In order to purchase those inputs, farmers like me have to take a *wreen* (debt) from a *sahu* (money lender, merchant). Any debt is bad for peasants. When they fall in debt, they are ruined. How many peasants do you know who fall in debt and not lose their lands to their *sahu*? When the land is gone, there is nothing left for a peasant like me. What am I going to do? See, land is my life. So what good does it do to buy all those *bikasi* inputs if you have to end up losing your land?

— A peasant

Agriculture is the backbone of Nepal's agrarian economy. It is the primary source of livelihood in the rural sector which supports about 90 percent of the country's 20 million people. Virtually every phase of life revolves around agriculture, from birth to death. So farming is the barometer of life chances in Nepal. Every harvest serves as a solid indication of whether people will have a relatively good year or suffer hardships. When agriculture fails, life suffers, often immeasurably. From an ecological angle, the economic fate of almost every Nepali is inseparably linked to the fate of farming and hence to the sanctity of the soil.

My attempt here is not only to portray this entwined relationship between Nepali life and agriculture, but also to uncover how it has changed in the past few decades as a result of so-called development. While this chapter is heavily based on both personal observations and informal discussions with numerous peasants over the years, it also draws from my own background as a peasant boy. Even though my family had only about 1 acre of land, my father was a skilled peasant, well-known in Pokhara for his farming knowledge; he taught me quite a bit about farming.

Although limited in number, the stories highlighted in this chapter reflect a broad spectrum of peasant life in Nepal. To be sure, these individual stories and experiences vary from peasant to peasant and from region to region. Yet the running theme and outcome of Nepal's agricultural development attempts are almost identical, one common denominator being an increasing disintegration of the ecological relationship between Nepali life and agriculture over the past few decades. Since Nepal still remains predominantly rural, one may argue that the impact of agricultural modernization is quite confined to urban areas and those areas situated along transportation routes and nodes. While such an argument may seem plausible on the surface, it ignores the changing reality. Evidence suggests that it has reached many rural areas, especially those in the Tarai, a region which accounts for over 60 percent of national agricultural production.

While the cost of modern agricultural inputs such as fertilizer keeps rising, modernization has failed to generate any mass benefits in terms of peasants' improved life chances. Government statistics reveal that despite an increasing infusion of modern inputs, crop yields remain low at the national level (Shrestha, 1990). For instance, the average yield for paddy, the most dominant crop in Nepal, has hovered around 2,000 kilograms per hectare, the figure which is almost one-third of the average paddy yield in Japan. It is important to note that, although the Tarai has received over 80 percent of the agricultural development resources earmarked by the central government, its average paddy yield is much lower than that in the hills. The Tarai's yield is barely 1,800 kilograms compared to over 2,400 kilograms per hectare in the hills. The picture for four other major basic crops (maize, wheat, millet, and barley) is similar. Overall, there has been little improvement in peasants' life chances. With this background information, I would now like to proceed to the main story of this chapter.

THE WAY IT USED TO BE

Imagine, for a moment, that there is a small village where the material dimension of people's daily life is very simple. Life seems all natural as it is intrinsically intertwined with nature and its rhythmic cycle. Villagers find meanings in every natural phenomenon as it is interpreted in the context of their own life experiences, often as an omen of things to come or as inevitable outcomes of their past deeds. Such is the perception of their karmic cosmos. They are keenly watchful of every cycle of nature. Whenever nature fails to deliver what is expected of it such as a timely rainfall and its timely recession, villagers suffer a common fate although it is a lot harder for some than for others. They all retreat into their belief system by proclaiming that the god is angry. Occasionally, they even organize to perform a common ritual to appease the wrath of a particular god. They all treat such events as natural parts of life.

They wake up at the pre-dawn crow of a rooster that serves as a natural alarm clock. This is true particularly during the major planting and harvesting seasons. They get ready for a long day of hard work that planting and harvesting demand. Once awake, their daily routine begins as they move from one chore to another. While women prepare breakfast (often popcorn) to be taken to the field, take care of children, and fetch water from a stream, men often gather tools and take care of animals. And then there are farms to tend. During planting and harvesting, many peasants spend the whole day in the field, literally from dawn to dusk, returning home only after the evening falls. When household animals are herded into their sheds and chickens seek shelter in their little nests, and when the nightly darkness covers the mountains and valleys obscuring their contours and terrains, they ready themselves for a night of rest. Little kerosene lamps are turned off. And in the quiet of the night villagers fall asleep. Everything is peaceful. But peasants' work is not finished yet; it only takes a short break. Such is the rhythm of life in that village.

The next morning the routine resumes. There is little variation in life from day to day. Villagers' expectations are generally minimal. Invariably everything in life is viewed as a karmic *chakra* (wheel). Just like the rhythmic cycle of nature, events in their daily life are taken as a given, as if predetermined by some cosmic force, something beyond their control. Such is the human (peasant) ecology of Nepali agrarian life. Separation between humanity and nature is minimal if any. In this ecological configuration, the survival of humanity is not based on its ability to distance itself from nature by subduing it. Rather it's predicated on being able to live in harmony with nature, on its ability to endure the vagaries of nature as well as enjoy its blessings. If peasants fail to take care of this delicate ecological balance, nature often suffers, consequently inflicting pains on them.

Peasants constitute an integral component of the environment. They are the stewards of nature. They look after the land, fixing the broken bunds and gullies, fences and terraces to prevent soil erosion. They protect the forests, a vital source of their peasant ecological existence. They work the soil and nurture it. They raise livestock to supplement their livelihood as well as for manure which replenishes soil nutrients. Nothing goes to waste. Everything is used and reused. What they do not or cannot consume, their animals do. And, if animals don't, then it is thrown into the compost pit. Not even water used for dish washing is wasted as they usually wash their dishes near vegetable plants being grown in the front yard. They cannot analyze the chemical components of the soil from a theoretical angle, but the depth of their practical or experiential knowledge is rarely in doubt. They can feel the texture of the soil and tell how good it is. They judge the quality of the soil based on the number of earthworms found in it. The greater the number of earthworms, the better the quality of the soil. Their knowledge base is simple but very practical to their reality.

They may not have scientific explanations for their experiential knowledge, but they certainly know what works and what does not. For instance, they see earthworms as vital allies in the ecological mystic of nature, a barometer of soil quality. They can even tell what grows best in what type of soil. For them, the soil is the source of life. They call the soil their *Dharti Mata* (Mother Earth). Without it, there is no life. Peasants are fully cognizant of the fundamental tenet of peasant ecology that if they fail to nurture the soil, *Dharti Mata* will cease to nurture them. Every object is interrelated and mutually dependent. In such existence of mutual cooperation and dependence, land as an ecological entity plays a central role. Land is a life-giving and life-sustaining force, not a commodity to be exchanged in the market for a profit.

Such a portrayal of agrarian life does not imply that peasants were always angelic guardians of nature. History reveals their abusive behaviors. As much as they were aware of the need to nurture nature, they exhibited a periodic tendency to damage it in their attempt to avert any threat to their immediate survival, a tendency that seems to be occurring much more frequently than ever before (Shrestha and Conway, 1996). Such an abusive behavior surfaced, especially when population growth rapidly exceeded nature's existing ability to sustain its human children or when the oppressive agrarian relations of production denied them their basic survival rights.

In essence, however, what is portrayed above used to be a close approximation of normal village life in Nepal. The above depiction still holds true in remote areas of the country that remain relatively untouched by the onslaught of development. No, I am not suggesting that a typical Nepali village was a replica of *Balmiki ashram*[1] where life was peaceful as well as plentiful. It was essentially a subsistence-based economy where the prevailing mode of life was simple and relatively natural. Except for a few daily necessities such as salt, kerosene, and cloth, villagers generally produced their own basic means of subsistence. The village was a self-contained economic system. Even the population was composed of all occupational groups necessary to sustain the community as a relatively self-sufficient unit in terms of its production structure. Although deeply tainted with the degrading caste system, villages included a wide array of low caste functional groups such as the Damai (tailors) to sew clothes, the Kami (iron or metal-workers) to make utensils and farm implements, and the Sarki (leather-workers). Also generally included among the village population were local merchants to make available certain necessities such as kerosene, salt, spices and clothing materials, all imported from outside. And, of course, they rarely lacked a local elite class that was directly correlated with the high caste groups, namely bahuns and chettris. This is how they formed a complete, interdependent community, sometimes made of a single village and other times several small villages.

In spite of a relatively high level of self-sufficiency, most villages were strapped for cash because they had few reliable mechanisms for internal cash generation. Cash was needed mainly for purchasing certain daily necessities that could not be produced locally. So during the agriculturally slack months of November to February, hill villagers normally left (as they still do) their villages in search of wage employment opportunities in cities and in construction and plantation sites, both within Nepal and in India. Many of them even journeyed to the Kashmir and Nainital areas in northwest India to work as porters, transporting

apples to market centers (Bishop, 1993). Besides such seasonal migration, many hill dwellers left the country seeking long-term household and
army employment in various parts of India, thus linking Nepal's agrarian
hill labor with India's semi-capitalist economy (for a detailed discussion
of migration, see Shrestha, 1990).

Despite the linking of the hill economy with India's semi-capitalist
economy through labor and mercenary migration, the hills remained
relatively free from capitalist or Western influences until the 1950s. The
village as a socioeconomic unit generally defied the notion of so-called
"economic rationality" which asserts that people are driven by their
inherent desire for incessant material accumulation and advancement.
Instead the village and its constituents were invariably guided by the
principle of what Karl Polyani (1957) called "reciprocity," a practice
which can be defined as mutual dependence among the villagers for basic
goods and services. In fact, until recently *parma* (mutual labor sharing)
used to be almost universal in Nepal; it is now becoming a fading
memory of the past.

This does not, however, imply that the village represented a utopia,
filled with social harmony and justice, economic equality and security
for all. Disharmony existed. There was much disparity and oppression
in the social relations among the villagers. Some had more land than
others, and commanded a greater power base. Others were totally
landless and hence powerless. The landless depended on the landed for
their subsistence, often working as tenants, sharecroppers, or domestic
workers. As such, landless villagers' interaction with nature (or land)
was mostly mediated through their land tenancy and sharecropping. In
light of such tenuous class relations centered around land access and
control, there was tension among the villagers. In addition, family feuds
and clan discords were part and parcel of life.

Such feudalistic tension was, however, tempered by their need for
coexistence as a community bonded together by their common fate that
intrinsically tied both classes to nature. It is this very common bond that
engendered mutual dependence, serving as a centripetal force and
countering many centrifugal tendencies inherent in the oppressive nature
of existing class relations. Under such circumstances of mutual dependence, the survival of one class was directly contingent on the survival
of another. Therefore, poverty which back then was almost exclusively
equated with sheer hunger was often shared although admittedly some
bore its burden a lot harder and definitely much more frequently than

others. The rich gave food to the poor in times of crises. Even religious festivities and rituals served their social purpose as, during these occasions often organized as acts of good deeds or to insure good karma, the rich shared their resources with the poor or other villagers. While such sharing lasted only a day or two, it was an important mechanism of resource distribution because religious festivities occurred fairly frequently. Various other forms of redistribution also existed. In fact, it would be no exaggeration to assert that sharing and mutual dependence formed the foundation of the patron-client relations of production although they were, no doubt, tilted in favor of those who controlled resources. Social relations were certainly unequal, but definitely interdependent. Given these realities, the distinction in life style between the rich and poor in a village was generally manifested in terms of land ownership and food security rather than modern material possessions. The stark differences between the two were few and far between. As such, villagers' lifestyle was normally monotonous and uniform, and poverty was invariably a matter of local concerns rather than a national and international development issue.

THE WIND OF CHANGE

Now imagine further. The wind of development blows across the nation, reaching even remote and rustic villages where life was once very simple and natural. Development, by conventional definition, is an economic Darwinian concept. As such, it implies moving up the economic ladder—from a lower level of material life to a higher level, from a reciprocal production structure to a more market-based system. And, by its very nature, it tends to be disruptive of the existing mode of life and the traditional way of doing things. It even affects the way of thinking and cultural patterns and processes as it often brings about unforeseen changes. As the rustling whisper of development blows across the rural landscape, it grows in strength. The question is: what happens when the rustling whisper turns into a howling wind?

The official purpose of development was to cast the country's economic climate and culture into a modern mold. It was, in essence, a project in socioeconomic engineering. The argument was that as modernization diffused across the underdeveloped world, it would cause the downfall of their precapitalist modes of production, subsequently paving the way for the industrial mode of production (Corbridge, 1986). The vision of development was, therefore, scripted in the grand theory of modernization. Given such a vision—or propaganda as some might call it—how could anybody resist the temptation of materialism that development represented? That is how the notion of development was sold, as a mighty engine of material nirvana (Chapter 3).

But, in order to induce economic rationality, the sociocultural as well as physical infrastructure of development had to be established. Western gurus of *bikas* initiated various development projects, ranging from education to transportation to industry and many others. Also included among them were various projects designed to develop the farming sector. Although the agrarian sector was commonly viewed as backward and tradition-bound, its development was deemed necessary because of Nepal's overwhelming dependence on farming. Producing economic persons thus required implanting the notion of economic rationality among peasants (Hayami and Ruttan, 1971; Mellor, 1968; Schultz, 1953). There had to be a fundamental metamorphosis of their subsistence-based practice. So development arrived in rural areas as well, intent on changing the way farming was done and transforming the peasant mode of life and peasant ecology. The process gained speed after the Green Revolution got under way in the mid-1960s. It was designed to improve farm productivity, inducing peasants to engage in commercial farming which was heralded as the culmination of agricultural development (Griffin, 1974; Yapa, 1977).

As intended, arrival of *bikas* began to disrupt the traditional (peasant) way of life and its social fabric. As the howling wind of *bikas* managed to supersede the existing patron-client relations of production, it removed the built-in system of social obligations on the part of the landed and rich to shoulder some of the burden of poverty on the poor. Furthermore, prior to the *bikas* wave, poverty was normally viewed as a communal and collective problem rather than as an individual family problem although individual families were the ones who endured it. But now development, as defined and measured in materialistic (capitalistic) terms using such indicators as per capita income, energy consumption, resource use, and literacy, individualized poverty, meaning that the poor were generally viewed as *abikasis*, as cases of personal deficiency or self-inflicted failures. Poverty was thus projected as an unfortunate creation of the poor, not as an inevitable outcome of growth-driven development and social inequality (Chapter 3; Yapa, 1993). This new, Malthusian outlook offered a very convenient outlet for the dominant class to believe that their wealth was a fruit of their own mental dexterity and forward-looking economic mentality (rationality) rather than a benefit of their social position and that they had no role to play in causing poverty (Myrdal, 1970). So they were absolved from any obligations and responsibility toward the poor and their poverty.

Needless to say, poverty emerged as a welfare issue as it was appropriated by the national government and international development agencies. In other words, while the problem of poverty remained localized because of its deep roots in the local social relations of production, its purported remedies were shifted to the state and international development establishment, often totally removed from the local reality. In the meantime, there was no provision for the poor to play any role within the development establishment, nor offer any voice to determine its course. To tell the truth, the ruling elites in charge of the ongoing development enterprise had no vested interest in tackling poverty, for it was their golden goose. It was important for them to perpetuate poverty because the grimmer the picture of poverty, the more foreign money it attracted. And whatever foreign money was poured into Nepal in the name of poverty alleviation, most of it was siphoned away by the ruling elites. For the ruling elites, it paid to play up the marauding ghost of poverty.

Development had not only arrived in rural areas, but it was there to stay as a national enterprise. Pursuing the path of agricultural development meant applying new inputs such as chemical fertilizer and hybrid seeds as well as growing cash crops for the market, for they are presumed to be more lucrative because of their higher values. For some, it also meant embarking on commercial farming ventures such as fish, goat, or poultry farming. In short, these ventures required capital investment, but not too many had the means to pursue them. The opportunity to practice economic rationality and become an economic person was, therefore, available only to a limited number of farmers, those with sufficient land and/or other assets.

THE WAY IT IS NOW

October 1979. I was in Rampur, Chitwan, with my field survey team to investigate rural migration from the hills to the Tarai. Chitwan was selected as a fieldwork site because of its status as the first Tarai district to be opened for planned resettlement by hill migrants. With the help of American aid, the scheme was officially implemented in 1956 as an integral component of the first five-year plan (Shrestha, 1990).

One early morning in late October, my field team and I were on our way to a village to interview some hill migrants about their migration histories and experiences. We were riding our bikes, chatting and laughing. It was a little chilly, but very refreshing as the early morning breeze gently caressed our noses and cheeks. The sun was breaking out of its deep sleep. Red and rosy like a fresh flower just plucked from a garden with the morning dew still sparkling on its petals, the morning was stunningly beautiful. Suddenly our laughter was broken by a deep voice coming from far afield. And the morning breeze and the beauty of that sunrise yielded to the melancholic tone of that deep voice. We all stopped, almost motionless. A man, perhaps in his mid-40s, was running toward us. "Help! Help!" he shouted. He approached me and held onto my bike. And then he said in a sobbing voice, "I am a development victim, sir! I am a development victim!"

Somewhat surprised and confused, I asked, "What is wrong?"

"I am a development victim, sir! Please help me. I have lost all of my land." He sounded desperate. "I had 3 *bighas* of land (1 *bigha*=0.68 hectare). It was more than adequate to support my family. I even sold some excess rice and corn in the market. But the Agricultural Development Bank was pushing the idea of opening commercial fish and goat farming. It was offering loans to those who could afford to launch such a venture. Using my land as collateral, I obtained a loan from the Bank's local branch to develop a fish farm. The Bank gave me no technical support."

"Did you seek it?"

"No, I did not. The Bank does not provide technical support. Anyway, it seemed simple, and I was excited about the idea of fish farming. I thought it was an easy way to make money," replied the man. "I dug a pond and launched a fish farm. But it did not last long. One day there was heavy flooding and the whole fish farm was washed away. The fish were gone, almost all of them. I lost everything. I had to sell my land to pay the loan."

"Then, what did you do?" I asked him.

"Later, using my remaining land as collateral, I got another loan to do goat farming. I purchased four hybrid goats, one male and three females. In less than a year, two of the female goats had produced four little baby goats. The venture seemed to be going well until a deadly disease struck them (and other goats in the area). Since there was no timely veterinary help available to save the goats, they eventually died. Only one survived the disease. So the goat farming venture also failed. I lost my land. Misery is my company now, and I cannot support my family. What can I do?"

Once again he asked me to help him. Unable to do anything about his situation, I informed him in a faint voice that there was little I could do. After a while he left, looking somewhat disappointed by my answer. His was a moving story, one that was quite disheartening to those who see development as the modern incarnation of Laxmi, the goddess of wealth. I later did some probing into his life story, and discovered that he had arrived in Chitwan from the adjoining hills in the mid-1960s in search of land. He was not a poor migrant when he relocated to Chitwan. He had already been swayed by the wind of development in his desire to join the *bikasis'* club. Since the opening of Chitwan in the mid-1950s represented a first step along the path of Nepal's development march, he saw his migration to the district as a window of opportunity to accumulate more land at the frontier and make money.

He sold his land in the hills and with the money he managed to buy land in Chitwan. He had indeed lost most of his land because of failed commercial farming ventures. This was independently verified by some of his village neighbors with whom I spoke. They said he had no more than one-half *bigha* of land left. After we returned from our fieldwork, I reflected on how that peasant had described his situation. How cruel and sardonic that the very development, as embodied in commercial farming, that was supposed to have ordained him to merchanthood had made him a victim. A development victim, indeed!

Here is another story, one that illustrates a different sort of victimization although no less painful than the above case. One day I saw a peasant plowing his field, using two oxen and a hand-made plow. There was nobody around except for a few birds trying to catch worms in the freshly plowed field. In the world of natural configuration, everything has a purpose. Worms are not only good for the soil, but they also serve as a source of food for birds. The peasant seemed oblivious to his surroundings as if he was completely immersed in his own world of thoughts. Or perhaps, with his feet moving along the empty furrows, he was simply flowing with the slow, rhythmic pace of his oxen, pulling the plow and turning the earth over. While I could occasionally see him swatting the oxen and hear him commanding them to move a little faster, he did not even hear me approaching him until I got very close to him and said hello.

He was not startled or anything. He greeted me with a Nepali hello. Wiping his sweat off, he stopped his oxen and we both sat down. He pulled out of his pocket some tobacco, filled the *chilam* (a tobacco pipe made out of clay) with the tobacco, lit it up, and smoked it. He offered me the *chilam*. That was his way of asking me if I wanted to take a puff, too. I politely declined. He then asked me what I was doing in the village and where I had come from. I told him about my research work.

"How much land do you have, *ba* (father or somebody who represents a father figure, often used to show due respect for his seniority)?"

"I don't have any land, *babu* (a common term used by seniors to address juniors in a loving way, like a son)." He replied in a sad tone.

"How come? You never had any land or you lost it?"

"No, I never had any land except for a little *chhapro* (lean-to). I used to work for a *jamindar* (landlord) as a *hali* (plowman). Every year I used to plow a certain amount of his land, and in return he used to give me grain. During my free time, I used to plow other farmers' lands to earn a few rupees. My *jamindar* also gave me about one *bigha* of land to cultivate on a sharecrop basis. At the end of each harvest I would give him half of the crop. He was not a bad *jamindar*. Sometimes, he even loaned me money, especially when I needed it for some emergency purpose."

"So you mean you don't work for that *jamindar* any more?"

"No, unfortunately, I don't work for him, *babu*. But I wish I did though because life would not be this difficult. It was better back then when I worked for him. Life is very difficult these days for this *dukhi* (poor, unfortunate, or somebody in despair). Today I will earn some money because I am plowing this land for somebody in the village. He will pay me 15 rupees, and with that money I will be able to feed my family. But tomorrow... I don't know what I am going to do tomorrow. I don't know if anybody will ask me to plow his field. No job, no money, and no food. Such is my karma, *babu*. What to do? Life is always very hard for this *dukhi*."

When asked why he didn't work for that *jamindar* any more, he replied: "This is a sad story, *babu*. A couple of years ago, his son purchased a tractor and began cultivating his land by himself, using hired labor. His tractor could till all of his land, and faster than we could. He is a very educated man. He was studying in India. When he came back from India, he took charge of the family. His father does not do much these days. He is getting old, and stays home most of the time. From what I know he is very ill. We rarely see him. The young man said he did not need any *hali* (plowman) like me anymore. He did not want any sharecroppers (tenants), cultivating his land either. So no land for share-cropping. He does not keep any *halis* like his father did. The old man could not say anything. Oh, yes, he hires people whenever he needs them, mostly during the rice planting and harvesting seasons. He also hires *madhesis* (in common vernacular, this term is used to denote Indians) to work for him. But it is all temporary work. He pays about 7 or 8 rupees a day (about 50 cents at that time). *Babu*, money does not last very long like land and grain. We have to spend it to buy food. The one *bigha* of their land I used to sharecrop, he took it away. There was nothing I could do. Such is *dukhi's* life, *babu*. Very hard."

"I am very sorry to hear that the young *jamindar* let you go, *ba*. But didn't the land reform law protect your tenancy rights over the land you used to sharecrop for the *jamindar*?" I queried.

"Yes, they say it does. But I don't know. Who listens to a poor, uneducated man like me? We don't have any rights. The rich *jamindars* bribe government officials and always win. We never win, so why bother? I can't afford to go to the court. No money. And if I go to the court, who is going to work and earn money to support the family? See, *babu*, if you are poor, you are poor. Nothing works for you. Nobody cares about people like me. We have no power because we have no money, no land. We can't afford to pay bribes to *hakimsab* (a government official with authority)."

The old man also added that when the landlords learned that the land reform act of 1964 was being passed, they started evicting their tenants so that they could not have any claim to the land they were previously cultivating. In fact, during the course of my fieldwork, many people I spoke with held the opinion that politicians, planners, and policy-makers—most of whom are directly or indirectly connected to landed families—leaked the contents of the land reform act well in advance to give landlords a chance to take protective measures before its passage. As a result, even the very law that was passed to protect tenants from oppressive property relations played hooky with them, thus generally denying them the opportunity to have partial claim to the land that they had been cultivating for years (Zaman, 1973). For countless peasants, the land reform act had a boomerang effect as they lost their access to sharecropping land, but failed to gain any tenancy right to the land they once used to cultivate. As landlords generally viewed their previous tenants with suspicion, some of them even avoided, whenever possible, hiring them for casual work. Mutual trust was replaced by mistrust.

I could hear in his voice an entrenched sense of frustration and dejection. He seemed to have silently accepted the injustice of the existing social reality. Apparently, the young *jamindar* had mastered both the art and science of modern economics, actually to the point of fully applying it. In the vernacular of capitalist economics, the tractor that he purchased embodied technology, an unmistakable symbol of agricultural modernization. His decision to consolidate all of his land was the height of economic rationality. That is, he was fully applying the logic embedded in the concept called the economy of scale, which essentially asserts that the larger the scale of operation, the lower the cost of production (and the higher the margin of profits). Such is the basis of development economics. As long as he stood to gain from his new production arrangements, it mattered little to him how many tenants he evicted and made superfluous and hapless, eventually pushing them toward the margin of misery and destitution. Nor did he care about personal relationships and loyalty of the evicted tenants to his father. There was no concern for his social obligation to his father's loyal tenants. In the true spirit of his economic training, the only thing the landlord's son was concerned about was his profit.

Yet, cursed with the burden of survival under the condition of extreme hardship, life had to go on for those tenants evicted from sharecropping. That is the curse of poverty—one can neither live like a full human being nor die with dignity. Hardened by both the instinct and daily struggle for survival, life in rural Nepal, however, seems amazingly resilient and seasoned. Given this reality, the plowman, I am certain, will survive despite all the hardship of life he faces every day. And so will the tradition of *hali* work. It won't be defunct—at least I don't believe so—in the near future despite the growing use of tractors, especially not in the hills where the terrain alone demands the use of *halis* to till the land. Even then, there is no doubt that uncertainties loom heavy as life has, within a relatively short span of time, witnessed tremendous changes in the demand and use of traditional professions. In many areas of Nepal, *halis'* is not the only traditional profession that has come under growing assault from tractors. Traditional tailors have increasingly succumbed to ready-made and imported clothes, shoe-

makers to shoe factories, and ironsmiths and metalworkers to mecha-
nized manufacturing. Tossed around and banged up by the howling wind
of development, all these professions are facing a slow death not only
due to technological competition, but also because the new generation
has little interest in pursuing them. The cord that once insured the gene-
rational continuity of caste-based as well as family professions is wearing
thin fast and furiously.

The plowman's story is not unique, however, as it is all too common, and has been repeated many times over, especially in the Tarai.
Ever since the arrival of tractors, a growing number of sharecropping
peasants have been displaced, thus severely affecting their life chances.
Sharecropping and/or traditional production arrangements based on
patron-client relations used to be, as pointed out earlier, a critical source of subsistence. While such arrangements rarely paved any path to
prosperity, they did form, for many, a vital bridge to the basic means of
survival—land. They gave almost every tenant a sense of purpose in life.
They sustained the ties that bound patrons and clients together, thus
reinforcing their coexistence as well as mutual dependence. They demonstrated the overall commonality of life and purpose whether one was a
tenant or a *jamindar*. It was this commonality of life, mutual dependence, and communal bond that usually blurred the sharp lines of social
class distinctions. But that is no longer the case. Sharecroppers had no
choice, but to become wage laborers, which meant being dependent on
the vagaries of the labor market in a country with extremely limited
wage-laboring opportunities. These days, there is very little commonality
of life and purpose between the social classes. Nor is there any real
sense of an organic community as a mutually dependent and intrinsically
interlinked socioeconomic unit. They are all rapidly becoming relics of
the past as they are increasingly fragmented (more in Chapter 7).

Direct human tragedies are not the only trademarks of agricultural
modernization. There seems to be another type of tragedy looming over
the horizon, one that is neither readily visible and discernible nor easily
curable.

During my fieldwork in the Tarai, many farmers brought to my
attention the deteriorating quality of soil, its changing texture. They all
attributed it to the growing use of chemical fertilizer. They also revealed that they had started seeing in the past few years insects that they
had never seen before. Those insects, they swore, were damaging their
crops. Two farmers actually brought a couple of new insects to show

me. Since peasants' knowledge is experiential, based on years of repeated observations and practices, they could not explain the recent changes
in the soil texture and increasing insect populations. They had not had
enough time to form a knowledge base about those new insects. Yet they
could tell the adverse changes that were occurring in their fields. Their
eyes were not deceiving them.

There was also some indication that the number of earthworms
inhabiting their fields had decreased over time. This phenomenon too,
they felt, was attributed to the growing use of chemical fertilizer and, in
some cases, insecticides and pesticides. The decreasing population of
earthworms was an indication of soil degradation, they surmised. The
farmers, with whom I spoke, acknowledged that their crop production
had certainly increased as a result of chemical fertilizer. They were torn,
however. While they were generally tempted by fertilizer's role in increased crop production, they were very concerned about the deteriorating soil quality and new insect populations, something that they did not
recall experiencing until the use of chemical fertilizer. There also seemed to be a broad consensus that they were having to increase the amount
of fertilizer applied in order to maintain the level of their crop yields.
Perhaps, the diminishing return of fertilizer use had already set in.

Clearly, I did not possess the necessary expertise to address many
of their questions and concerns. I am neither an entomologist nor a plant
biologist to have a good grasp of what those farmers were beginning to
experience. Yet I could not help but ponder what the future might hold
for them. What those farmers informed me of during field-work about
their changing agro-ecology could spell a bad omen for the soil quality.
True, the application of fertilizer is quite limited in Nepal, primarily to
the Tarai belt and fertile valleys situated close to urban centers such as
Kathmandu. Nepali farmers in general use much less fertilizer per unit
of land than those in advanced countries. Furthermore, the percentage
of farmers using fertilizer is still low, perhaps no more than 15-20
percent. Since more than 50 percent of the households own less than half
a hectare of land, it is rarely considered wise to apply chemical fertilizer. It simply is not cost-effective. At the current rate of use, the extent
of soil degradation due to chemical fertilizer will most likely remain
confined. However, if the application of fertilizer were to increase—a
scenario that is more than likely to occur given the current trend—it
could intensify the soil's chemical imbalances and degradation and
consequently damage local peasant ecologies, especially in the Tarai

where the degree of chemical fertilizer use is much higher than elsewhere in the country, both in terms of total volume and rate. Since the Tarai is considered to be the granary of Nepal, any long-term damage to its peasant ecology will upset the nation's food supply. It could also eventually affect the quality of water.

This is not a comforting scenario. First, for a predominantly agrarian country, Nepal's current supply of cultivable land is already extremely low—barely 0.15 hectare per person (Shrestha, 1990). What is more, the prospect of further expansion of cultivable land is even less. This means the peasant ecology of Nepal hangs in delicate balance. Soil degradation would further exacerbate growing ecological pressure. Second, peasants' current knowledge and technical ability to reclaim chemically degraded soil is almost nil except to stop using fertilizer well before it is severely damaged. In a world rooted in experiential knowledge, sudden changes, particularly those outside the domain of their knowledge base, have a tendency to play havoc with their peasant life. Since they are equipped with little experiential knowledge to deal with such chemically-rooted ecological problems, their response may actually end up magnifying the problems.

In a situation like this, blessed are those who refrain from using chemical fertilizer or use it only in small quantities, well mixed with organic manure and compost. Two farmers actually told me that they were planning to stop using chemical fertilizer. They did not like what it was doing to the soil. To be sure, they would have to forgo the gains that chemical fertilizer could provide in the form of increased crop yields. In that sense, there was an opportunity cost involved in their decision to stop using chemical fertilizer. Yet they were so concerned about the soil quality that they did not want to take any more chances with their most important environmental resource: the soil. They said, "What good does it do to increase crop production in the short run if it is going to kill the soil in the long run? We don't need agricultural development at the cost of our land, the bedrock of our existence. Our forefathers did just fine without chemical fertilizer; why do we need it, anyway? If the soil is gone, our whole *jiban* (life) will be ruined. How are we going to survive?" In response to my query about the possible decline in crop productivity and about the need to balance between the increasing family size and food production, they replied that they could manage it. They had reverted to using organic manure which their animals produced. To peasants, the soil was sacred, and protecting its sanctity was, therefore, more than a modern environmental imperative. It was their duty, a matter of life or death as it was directly linked to their existence.

During the course of my fieldwork, I also happened to meet a farmer who had stood his ground in refusing to fall prey to the whims of agricultural modernization. He was not being defiant; he was simply operating under a different logic. The preachers of modernism would label him a laggard, an ignorant traditionalist who does not understand the prize of progress. But I could not call him that, for he was, in my assessment, quite rational and calculating, in fact no less so than any hard core adherents of the economic rationality doctrine. His economic reasoning for his refusal to tap-dance to the tune of modern agricultural development was actually fascinating.

I doubt this peasant was even aware that what he was talking about was pure economics, but he was certainly lecturing me on Economics 101. Perhaps, to him, it was peasant Economics 101. It was still all economics, logically sound. I just sat there in front of him in a tea stall, almost motionless, intently listening to his logic and at the same time marveling at the explanation of his decision. "Why apply all those *bikasi* (modern) farm inputs?" he asked sarcastically. "*Bikasi mal* (chemical fertilizer) and *bikasi biu* (hybrid seeds)—they all cost money. We have to purchase them. In order to purchase those inputs, farmers like me have to take a *wreen* (loan) from a *sahu* (money lender, merchant, or trouble). Of course, you know what *sahu* means, right *bhai* (younger brother)? It means they harass you, they trouble you all the time. A *sahu* is a sure source of your *dukha* (akin to misery and trouble). Taking a *wreen* from a *sahu*—that is debt, that is tantamount to inviting misery and trouble into your own kitchen, *bhai*. Any debt is bad for peasants. I don't want any debt. When they fall in debt, they are ruined. How many peasants do you know who fall in debt and not lose their lands to their *sahu*? See, what I mean. When the land is gone, there is nothing left for a peasant like me. What am I going to do? See, land is my life. I have seen many peasants lose their lands to their *sahu* and become landless."

"See, *bhai*, *jamindars* can purchase all those inputs. They don't have to take any *wreen*. They are the *sahus* and they can afford it," he continued. "Even if they lose their harvest, nothing is going to happen to them. They have lots of land, lots of grains in storage. But for me it is an entirely different matter. I don't have much land. Listen, *bhai*. I take a *wreen* and buy all those inputs. By the way, do you know how expensive *bikasi mal* (chemical fertilizer) is? In the past few years its price has doubled and tripled. Then what happens if the harvest fails? See when you apply those inputs, you have to be able to sell your crops so you can make money and pay back the loan. But if the harvest is bad, how can you sell your crop and make money? See, you can't do that. I will be in deep trouble. The *sahu* will come knocking on the door, and they always come knocking on the door when your fortune is down, when you are hurting most. They are like vultures circling over a dying cow; they know when to go after you. They hit you hardest when you can least absorb the pain. They are very good at that. Then I will have to sell my land to pay the loan back; otherwise he will not leave my house. As you know, when you have to sell your land under duress, the buyer will dictate the price. As a debtor, you don't have much leverage. See, you can't win! So what good does it do to buy all those *bikasi* inputs if you have to end up losing your land?"

I was not surprised at all by the underlying logic of his lecture. Recall the earlier story about the man who identified himself as a development victim—the man who tried to launch a fish and goat farm, but ended up losing much of his land because both ventures failed? But this peasant wasn't about to be swayed by the current. His was a risk aversion strategy, quite reflective of peasants' general proclivity to play it safe. Such a strategy is quite important for peasants whose agricultural fortunes rely heavily on the weather conditions. They have very little control over whether they are going to have a good or bad harvest. Given his small amount of landholding, combined with the high cost of chemical fertilizer and limited market, modern farming practices are not simply practical. It was, therefore, clearly a strategy based on the security of survival rather than the profitability of modern farming. Still it was pure economic calculation, and nobody could contest its rationality, at least not on a logical ground. I certainly could not, and would not, quibble with his argument, especially when he informed me that he used as much organic matter as possible to increase his crop production. He also mentioned that he was fully aware of the importance of seed quality in farming. He carefully picked out, after every harvest, best quality seeds for the following season. He produced his own seeds which are much hardier and more resistant to varied climatic conditions than commercially-marketed hybrid seeds.

What we have seen are different forms of development victimization within Nepal's agrarian sector, some because of the lack of complete knowledge and necessary auxiliary services and others because of *jamindars'* profit maximization drive. While one form of victimization is hardly any less painful than the other, there is little doubt that the latter is much more sinister than the former. Moreover, it not only affects a greater number of households, but its victims are often those whose socioeconomic position is already weak because of their landless and/or tenant status. It clearly demonstrates how one *jamindar's* decision to execute the principle of economic rationality, so loudly heralded by development advocates, denies many resourceless peasants access to land—their lifeline—and consequently undermines their survival chances. When many *jamindars* apply the same logic, the number of victims swells as is already happening throughout the Tarai. It is logical to assume that when *jamindars* apply the economy-of-scale (i.e., large-scale production) model to farming, total yields may go up, signaling that both land and labor productivity has increased. In modern economic lexicon, that is "growth," a true index that economic persons have emerged. Funny, modern economics sometimes works in a very queer fashion: when labor productivity goes up, unemployment rises. What a way to achieve growth! Yet, we cannot fault *jamindars*. The most fundamental logic of modern economics bars us from faulting them, for they are doing exactly what they are supposed to: maximize their profits. But that is not how moral or humanistic economics works. There is something fundamentally incompatible between Westernized economic growth and the socioeconomic viability of the masses.

MODERN DEVELOPMENT: A FOOL'S GOLD?

As already stated, development is supposed to be a stairway to a better life. But for the Nepali masses in general, development is anything but the path to prosperity and to the good life which the development establishment promised them. In reality, it is bankrupt as it has turned into a series of economic ruins and social disintegration.

To repeat, social history serves a bitter lesson for the poor and deprived as development has demonstrated a historical proclivity to leave them behind during its march, forcing them to not only fend off vile attacks from the rich, but also fight against each other for a few leftover crumbs. In this dichotomous configuration of development, the poor happen to be generally less educated and almost solely dependent on manual labor for their survival. As the poor become increasingly separated from their rural peasant ecology, they are subjected to the vagaries of the labor market. Also equally distressing is the fact that while the poor become dependent on selling their manual labor, development makes manual labor progressively redundant as it moves from the labor-intensive, subsistence-oriented, primary economic activities to the capital and technology-intensive commercialized production structure (e.g., the *jamindar's* case). What is so doubly treacherous is that when the peasants dispossessed from rural areas move to cities, they find little gainful employment opportunities awaiting them. As a result, regardless of which geographic space they occupy—rural or urban—their lot rarely improves (also see Harrison, 1984).

With respect to societal development, underdeveloped countries like Nepal have generally failed to climb up the Marxian economic trajectory (or the Rostowian scale), i.e., step-by-step development, moving from the communal mode of production to the feudal mode and then to the capitalist mode. They have bypassed the industrial-capitalist phase and have been thrust upon Rostow's postindustrial landscape that is highly commercialized, capital-intensive, and consumerist in its orientation, an economic system in which low-skilled manual labor is either in low demand or trapped in jobs that barely pay even subsistence wages (Broad, 1995; Sweezy, 1994). The whole process of development as gradual progression has been short-circuited. Even a casual visitor to Nepal can notice that the country has leapfrogged from the agrarian mode to the world of consumerism and high-tech. Yet it has barely waded its feet in the waters of industrialism. Nepal reveals a typical juxtaposition between the old and the new, with one foot grounded in agrarianism and another floating in modernism. While a select few have already achieved mastery over the computer technology and begun to navigate the global information superhighways, the vast majority remain illiterate and in the bipedal mode. And accompanying this antipodal trend is the "Wall Street" mentality that "greed is good" or "make money any way you can." This is the mantra that pervades the Nepali elites.

Yet development has engendered *hopes* and *aspirations* among the people. The poor see hopes in development—hopes of survival, hopes that one day they too will be able to reap the benefit of development and lift themselves up from the swamp of poverty. Their hopes are based on the fact that development has fulfilled the material aspirations of the rich and powerful, making them even more prosperous and prominent. A great deal of faith has thus been vested in development as the only solution to poverty. Development has an almost spellbinding appeal.

In the midst of these hopes, however, lie many poor peasants' unsettling doubts about the messianic faith in development as the salvation of their poverty. What they have experienced is the gradual disappearance of their traditional bases of subsistence such as kinship networks, patron-client relations, and peasant ecological resources—all in the name of development. Frustration is mounting.

Some may vehemently dispute such contentions, but is it by design or default that the World Bank, the most powerful agent and arbiter of the development enterprise, has been forced to parade and promote one development model after another in the underdeveloped world (Payer, 1982)? The latest model in this procession is "sustainable development" (see Chapter 2). Such a parade of one after another development model clearly testifies that development has failed to fulfill its self-proclaimed mission which, according to Seers (1973), is to reduce poverty, inequality, and unemployment. It is no remedy for mass poverty, for its moral infrastructure is built on "economic rationality" (alias profit) rather than genuine concerns for the general masses (Amin, 1993).

Nepal exemplifies the development enterprise's utter failure to tackle the shackles of poverty. "Nepal is poor and is daily becoming poorer," said one report published in 1974 (ARTEP, 1974:1). In the late 1970s, 40 percent of the Nepali households were estimated to be living below the poverty line (Jain, 1981). Today, it is estimated that over 60 percent of the households fall into this category (Shrestha, 1992:13). Such grim statistics of poverty have provided a cogent rationale for foreign aid begging. A shameless beggar, that is what the modern Nepali state and its ruling elites have become (Pandey, 1992). There is plenty of foreign aid poured into Nepal so there is no lack of development money. As the level of poverty increases, so does the amount of foreign aid. So the only thing falling short in the fast moving drama of Nepali development is the alleviation of poverty.

Development funds have proved to be not only a fantastic boon for the elites, but also a powerful tool of control in their class (power) relations with the poor, an instrument that helps to keep the poor in check while issuing themselves fat checks (Gaige, 1975). To wit, some of the development money has certainly trickled down to a few poor, mainly in the urban-commercial contexts. Consequently, one can find a few poor who have become rich, thus providing good anecdotes of development (capitalist) success. And development advocates are quick to hail such anecdotal rags-to-riches stories to stress their message that development works. For instance, a poor butcher in Kathmandu has become the owner of a relatively large supermarket-like grocery store which is quite popular among Kathmandu's elites and Westerners. But what they fail to announce openly is that, for the poor, development is a lottery game and that buried under every success story are scores of tragic stories of development victims. Simply put, poverty remains the stepchild of development, with foreign aid now acting as its sponsor.

This is the reality of contemporary development, and there is a dilemma facing the poor. They are caught in a tug-of-war between their own hopes and despair, their aspirations and frustration, their anger and anxiety, and their dreams and nightmares. And increasingly entangled in this cobweb are both Nepali peasants and their subsistence. The deeper the roots of contemporary development penetrate, the more land alienation peasants experience. The more disenfranchised the peasants become from the land, the more difficult it is for them to protect their peasant ecology. Since peasant ecology holds the lifeline of subsistence for millions of Nepali peasants, any damage to it, especially in the absence of meaningful alternative sources of livelihood, is bound to aggravate poverty and hence their life chances.

Such an ominous outcome will ultimately lead to more destruction of the peasant ecological system which, in turn, will degrade the overall physical environment. In fact, such a destructive course is already being played out in the Tarai, the land frontier of Nepal, which produces approximately two-thirds of the country's total agricultural output (Shrestha et. al., 1993). Over the past four decades, there has been a massive shift of population from the hills to the Tarai in search of land, the anchor of peasant ecology and subsistence. Failing to procure land in the Tarai through official channels or to find other reliable sources of subsistence, frontier migrants from the adjoining hills have resorted to the encroachment of common lands (for a detailed discussion, see Ghimire, 1992; Shrestha, 1989). An overwhelming majority of these land encroaching families were either landless, totally alienated from land both in the hills and Tarai, or near-landless with a family holding of less than 0.5 hectare. In my recent field survey of Bardiya district in the western Tarai, it was reported that there were more than 20,000 families who had encroached on common lands.

This raging land encroachment movement is not only an undeniable symptom of Nepal's development failures in general and agricultural development failures in particular, but also a clear peasant protest against these failures. Although this form of protest may vary from other peasant protests being waged in other parts of the underdeveloped world, it is still a struggle for their basic survival rights and justice (see Guha, 1989; Hecht and Cockburn, 1990; Peluso, 1992; Shiva, 1988; Chapter 7). Interestingly, the official version presents land encroachment as the cause of the Tarai's environmental degradation, namely its forests. The argument is linear in nature in that land encroachment is an act perpetrated by encroachers who are, in turn, assumed to be the descendants of "overpopulation"—the historical bogeyman that Malthus invented almost 200 years ago to provide a cogent rationale and socially-protective umbrella for the landed gentry and its oppressive production relations vis-a-vis peasants. So logically then, the ultimate blame rests on overpopulation, accused of being the root of all social and economic ills in society.

This is the foolish stance of developmentalists. It would, however, be no less foolish to counter such an extreme argument by pretending that Nepal's rapid population growth (growing at the rate of nearly 2.5%) has played no part in its current problem of poverty and environmental deterioration. While I fully reject the mainstream position that overpopulation is the sole cause of all ills, there is little doubt in my mind that the country's rapid population growth has contributed to the problem (see Patterson and Shrestha, 1988; Shrestha and Conway, 1985). Furthermore, landless and near-landless encroachers are not the cause of forest destruction in the Tarai as has been widely circulated within the development establishment (Department of Resettlement, 1973). Commercially valuable forests (trees) are destroyed by contractors and loggers, both legal and illegal, not by land encroachers whose prime environmental crime—which is the label the state prefers to use—is occupying common lands such as some community pastures, forest fringes, and river banks. During occupation, they do tend to remove any secondary growth that encumbers their efforts to grow crops on the occupied lands.

Land encroachment in the Tarai shows no sign of abating. As more and more poor and landless hill peasants migrate to the Tarai in search of land, it is destined to increase. Since land encroachment is tantamount to a determined ecopolitical movement by those peasants who have been alienated from land, it brings encroachers dangerously into direct conflict with the Nepali state and its dominant interests, including its environmental protection policy funded by foreign donors. Over the past 25 years, several violent confrontations have occurred between the state's eviction forces and land encroachers. In those conflicts, several encroachers have been reported killed by the state's armed eviction forces (Ghimire, 1992; Kaplan and Shrestha, 1982). One recent confrontation between the state's armed forces and encroachers occurred in Bardiya in the fall of 1993. More than 10,000 encroachers (including their family members) had, in a well-organized fashion, occupied forest fringes. During the course of eviction, one encroacher was killed and several severely beaten and driven into the jungle. A mother who had delivered a baby the night before was forced out of her hut with the baby in her bare arms. Both were left in the open field despite the fact that the temperature outside was quite chilly. According to one account offered by the principal leader of the movement and later corroborated by the then assistant forest officer who was in charge of the state's armed eviction forces but had quit the job since, the number of casualties would have been much higher had the majority of adult males (encroachers) been present at the site when the actual eviction took place. The leader of the movement was quite emphatic about this point (for a detailed discussion, see Shrestha and Conway, 1996).

The point is that despite the history of periodic evictions and some fatal battles, it is unlikely that encroachment will subside in the absence of other viable subsistence options for landless and near-landless peasants. Theirs is a battle for survival. In this ecopolitical battle for survival, there is no tomorrow for the landless peasants of the Tarai. To use a crude metaphor, a hungry peasant is an angry peasant. When poor and landless peasants are forced to traverse the space of vulnerability, one in which their immediate survival is under siege, they are uprooted from their ecological roots (Foster, 1995). They are no longer an integral part of the soil and the overall environment. They are no longer connected to the mutually supportive (and dependent), triangular relationships of the peasant ecology: people, land (soil), and domestic animals (see Chapter 2). With their subsistence base thus cut off, hungry peasants, who choose to remain in their rural niche, are essentially forced to abrogate their reverence for *prakriti*, their long tradition of environmental responsibility to take care of her so she can, in turn, continue to provide them with subsistence. The environment as a source of common resources becomes, ironically, the innocent target of hungry peasants' wrath in their desperate struggle for survival. As the hungry peasants attack the common land to access it as well as to make a political statement about the rapid deterioration of their life chances, their attack unfortunately poses a further threat to the security of the Tarai environment, particularly to its common lands which constitute the primary bone of contention between the state and encroachers.

The security of peasant subsistence is directly interlinked with the security of both peasant ecology and the larger environmental system of Nepal. As such, the security of peasant subsistence is at the core of Nepali agricultural development. Any attempt at agricultural development that is solely driven by growth motives without any regard for its human and environmental costs and that fails to first ensure peasant subsistence will have profoundly adverse ramifications for both the environment and peasants. The logic of this argument dictates that in order to ensure peasants' subsistence they must be allowed to have secure access to land, a situation that has unfortunately been eroding over the past few decades as a result of distorted agricultural development.

REVIVAL OF PEASANT ECOLOGY

The ray of hope within this generally gloomy picture is that when peasants are given secure access to land, they breathe vibrant life into peasant ecology and protect it. It is true that there are cases, in which land recipients have sold their lands off and become professional land encroachers, moving from one area to another (Shrestha, 1990). Notwithstanding these cases, there is enough evidence to show that peasant ecology undergoes a dramatic revival when peasants are given secure access to land. Returning to the case of land encroachers in Bardiya, a number of peasants evicted by the government forces were later resettled and given 2 to 15 *katthas* of land (30 *katthas*=1 hectare), depending on their family sizes. There is little doubt that the Nepali Congress Government's distribution of land to encroachers was a calculated political decision, mainly designed to: (1) win land encroachers' votes and (2) squelch their revolutionary fury before its spark turned into a raging fire. Such decisions have a historical precedence in the agrarian politics of Nepal as they have been carried out by successive governments, including the communist government during its short reign in 1994-1995 (for a detailed historical discourse of this issue, see Shrestha, 1990).

Regardless of the political implications, my personal observation of several of these settled families in Bardiya revealed a remarkable scene. Their small plots of land were full of vegetable plants. Virtually every yard was green and lush. The villagers had even dug a pond to collect rain water to be used as a reservoir for plants and animals. They had also planted a few trees at the edges of their properties, a practice that used to be one of the hallmarks of peasant ecology. Almost every family had at least one or two domestic animals, in some cases goats and in other cases cows and/or water buffalos. They all seemed to have chickens and some had a few ducks. These animals and fowls not only supplemented family food and income sources, but also produced manure for the field. Peasant ecology was live and vibrant and the sanctity of the soil had been restored. I observed many such cases in the Tarai.

One particularly memorable example comes from a village near Rampur in Chitwan district where I first did my fieldwork in 1979—a year that can be regarded as a defining moment in the history of landless movement in Nepal. It was relatively organized and quite large in terms of participation. Despite its short life span, that was the first landless movement that Nepal had ever witnessed. That village near Rampur was established by landless encroachers in the course of the 1979 landless movement (for a detailed discussion, see Kaplan and Shrestha, 1982). It used to be a pasture field that was essentially barren with no trees, not even secondary growth. After the invasion, the encroachers carefully divided the land among themselves in equal amounts. When I first went there, it had just been occupied by encroachers who had erected a few make-shift huts with no walls. Roofs were made of leaves. They were erected simply to stake their claim to the land which was considered to be a very poor area in terms of its soil quality. Because of this reason the area, I was told, was left unoccupied during the early stages of land settlement in the district. When I returned to the same village nine years later in October 1988, I could not even recognize it at first. Only after I saw a few familiar faces with whom I had spoken in 1979, did I realize that it was the same village. Most of the peasants who had gathered for a cup of morning tea in the village tea shop recognized me immediately.

Besides the joy I derived from being able to spend some time with the same people nine years later, the ecological scene of the village was simply sublime. The pasture field, once barren, had now been turned into a self-contained village where peasants had vividly demonstrated their uncanny ability to revive their ecology, almost anywhere. Those peasants had turned the soil upside down, renewing its life. With its bright golden color shining against the backdrop of the morning dew, the paddy crop looked as good as anywhere in the district and was ready to be harvested. There were vegetables growing in every backyard, with the pumpkin vines and ripe pumpkins covering the roofs of many huts (so the vines don't cover the precious little land that can be used to grow other vegetables). There were domestic animals in sheds and chickens running around almost in every yard. Every conceivable component of the peasant ecological landscape was in place. They had even collectively dug small irrigation channels to irrigate their fields. It was a sight to behold. That was pure agricultural development, in every sense of the word. True, it did not quite fit the mold of agricultural modernization, but that was the beauty of their achievement. It was both indigenous and ingenious, self-motivated and self-reliant—all achieved with their own sweat without any outside advisors and aid. True agricultural development and truly sustainable. There was pride. It had not only protected the sanctity of the soil and hence peasant ecology, but also uplifted peasant subsistence in that village, peasants who were once alienated from land and whose survival was at stake.

So to conclude, the argument in favor of peasants' secure access to land, especially in an agrarian society like Nepal with a limited natural resource base, is more than a matter of peasants' subsistence and basic survival rights. It is also a matter of overall ecological security as well as sound and truly sustainable agricultural development. It is a matter of protecting and reviving the indigenous economy in a manner that ensures its long-range sustainability while at the same time guaranteeing the security of subsistence for the masses, not just for the elites.

NOTES

1. Balmiki is a famous Hindu sage who had established a small *ashram* or hermitage in the middle of a lush green jungle, surrounded by fruit trees, where wild animals roamed freely right around the *ashram*. In the ecological imaginary, the *Balmiki ashram* is the Hindu equivalent of the Garden of Eden (for a historical and theoretical discussion on *ashram*, see Olivelle, 1993).

5

PROSTITUTION:
AN UNFINISHED STORY

Goodbye
Don't cry, I'll be back
Crossing white hills, black hills, powder-dry hills
With heavy steps over the road to Seoul
To sell myself
I'm going now
Don't cry, I'm going now
Even the sky hangs heavy with sorrow
Over powder-dry hills
Heavy, heavy I go towards Seoul
To sell myself

— Kim Chi Ha quoted in Matsui, 1983:64

Kumari is a beautiful young girl, chosen at a very early age to serve as the living goddess. And worshiping the *kumari* is a very popular and time-honored religious tradition in Nepal. Presumed to be the incarnation of the "virgin goddess," the *kumari* is the ultimate symbol of the "virtues" of virginity. This tradition which is believed to have been established by the Newar ethnic group of Kathmandu elevates female virginity to the highest level possible: a goddess status.

In Nepali, the word *kumari* literally means a virgin girl. From a biological viewpoint, the concept of female virginity has no sexual value, nor any virtues. The value of virginity is a male creation, a sociocultural construct, intended to satisfy men's fantasy of having sex with virgin girls. In some societies, it is also rooted in the mythical belief that sex with a virgin not only cures venereal diseases, but also increases male virility and life expectancy (Truong, 1990). So, if one sifts through the tradition of *kumari* worship, it is quite apparent as to what its hidden motives are. This tradition translates into a social myth couched in religious terms, a myth designed to inculcate in the minds of young girls that remaining virgin until marriage has its rewards as they will be seen as pure and clean and hence most desirable. Virginity is thus tantamount to attaining a goddess status like the *kumari*.

For ages the symbiotic nexus between the notion of feudalistic religious piety and female sexual "purity" has engendered a gender-biased sociocultural structure, thus locating female sexuality in a subservient position as an object of male sexual satisfaction, with little concern for women's pleasure. In fact, girls were (are) raised to sacrifice personal interests and pleasure for the sake of men. Accordingly, if women happened to satisfy their eros and derive any sexual pleasure from such a subservient sexual position, that was fine. But they were accorded little right to demand personal sexual pleasure from their male partners, for such a demand would be considered immoral. In classic Thai love poetry, orgasm was consistently treated as a kind of miracle, a gift of divine grace, not the result of physiological stimulation (Robinson, 1993:497). Very few men placed any value on their female partners' (wives') sexual pleasure and satisfaction. Crudely expressed, as soon as they achieved their orgasm, they were done and showed little interest in women's orgasmic pleasure. This is true even today since not too many wives in Nepal—or in any society where female sexuality is subjected to social repression—are believed to be the beneficiaries of deep sexual pleasure. In essence, sex is a male play, with women serving as its warm-bodied vibrators.

Although unique to the Newars, worshiping the *kumari* has long been incorporated into Nepal's Hindu and Buddhist religious practices. There are several *kumaris* in the Kathmandu Valley, but the principal *kumari* is known as the Raj (Royal) *kumari* because she is worshiped by the King. She lives in the Kumari Bahal, a mid-18th century stucco temple, featuring intricately carved wooden windows. Situated right at the core of Kathmandu, the Kumari Bahal is a popular tourist point.

As the incarnation of the "virgin goddess," the *kumari* is always carefully selected from a group of girls four or five years of age. She must have a flawless body, free of any scars and defects or deformities; she must be fearless and satisfy 32 specified, distinctive signs. In addition, astrologers must confirm that her horoscope is in complete harmony with that of the ruling king in order to insure his safety and security. Myth has it that any misalignment in their horoscopes spells a bad omen for the ruling king. If she passes all these tests, the girl is then crowned as the *kumari,* inheriting the clothing and ornaments of her predecessor. Once chosen, she can no longer act and play like a free-spirited normal, innocent girl. Maids are assigned to take care of her 24 hours a day, to nurture and safeguard her with utmost care, making sure that she never falls sick or injures herself. She is often carried around in order to minimize the chances of her falling and hurting herself. In reality, she is a goddess in bondage, with little freedom to be herself.

The *kumari* remains the living goddess until she reaches puberty or sheds blood in any form, for example, from a cut. What is so tragic is that menstruation, one of the most natural functions of a woman's body, perhaps designed by nature to remove certain toxic impurities from her physiological system, becomes in this sense a sign of sin or lost innocence, thereby instantly disqualifying the *kumari* from continuing to perform her goddess role. In fact, if her attendants detect any indication that she is on the verge of experiencing her first menstruation, she is removed immediately. Menstruation is seen both as a mark of female pollution and sexual maturity. Therefore, the *kumari* is suddenly stripped of her goddess status. She becomes an ordinary girl, but one who has lost her entire childhood, perhaps the most joyous phase in one's life cycle.

Not only is she no longer worshiped, but the ex-living goddess is rarely welcomed with open arms into any household. Her life is damaged, like a temple in ruin. She is a wounded spirit with few places to go. The blessing of being chosen as the *kumari* instantly turns into a curse upon her departure from the throne as she is forced to live bounded and hounded by the myths about the ex-living goddess.

As the primary basis of societal codes and belief systems, myths are often far more powerful than facts and realities. They guide and govern people's lives. It is believed that the ex-*kumari* brings an early death to the man who marries her. She is a cursed woman. As a result, many ex-living goddesses have ended up living lonely and rejected as marriage partners, some turning to prostitution. By inventing such a myth, this cruel religious tradition has not only taken away their precious childhood, but also destroyed their adulthood. While one may surmise that their pursuit of prostitution makes a mockery of the institution of *kumari* worship, exposing its naked contradictions and fallacy as well as its distortion of female sexuality, it often leads them to destitution. It is hard to fathom that the *kumari's* fall from grace can be not only so sudden, but also so sad. Yet the tradition continues and the myth lives on.

This portrayal of the *kumari's* rise and fall reveals a gross tragedy, the numbing reality of women's lives, sexuality, and status in Nepal: even the ex-goddess status cannot prevent them from being subjected to social cruelty and humiliation. Although this chapter is not about the *kumari's* rise and fall, her sad saga does set the stage for exploring some of the basic questions about female sexuality, focusing on how women are forced into prostitution and how prostitution deforms their lives, often beyond repair. Specifically, this chapter is divided into three major segments. In order to illustrate the nature of prostitution, the chapter first reflects on the life of one prostitute named Gita, a real-life parable that remains unfinished.

Although some of the Nepali colloquial contexts of Gita's narration of her own story are minimized in the process of translation, it still provides a chilling glimpse into how Nepali women's social status and life can be turned into a heap of rubbles. This segment is followed by a discussion of the feudal-religious nexus (roots) of prostitution, that is, how men have drawn lines through myths to control women's virginity, repress their sexuality, and ultimately degrade their status and humanity. Finally, the discussion deals with the broader issue of how the development-tourism nexus has given a global dimension to prostitution, a profession that used to be largely localized and practiced by a limited number. It will also show how the feudal-religious nexus and the development-tourism nexus have converged together in the past few decades to spread the global net of the skin-trade market in a manner that not only devalues women, but also undermines society in general. The main objective is to draw a broader portrait of prostitution, stressing both its religious-feudal roots and contemporary manifestations.

GITA: AN UNFINISHED STORY OF A DAMAGED LIFE

One early morning during the winter of 1988, I went to visit Gita at her home located on a gravel street on the north side of Kathmandu, an area that could be considered a suburb. When I arrived at Gita's place around 9:30 in the morning, the sun was just beginning to break out of the thick blanket of mist that shrouds the Kathmandu Valley until about 10 o'clock, virtually every morning in the winter. Under the veil of the dense fog, the city of Kathmandu looks like a shy Nepali girl trying to take a sneaky peek at passers-by. Sometimes the mist is so heavy that one can actually feel the dew dropping like a sprinkling rain. The air is very cold and damp, and remains so until the sun burns the mist off and warms the streets.

Gita lived in a one-story house which was attractively landscaped. There were many flower pots with a variety of plants lined up around its open front porch. As I walked toward the front door past the gate, a small dog looked out the window and started barking at me. Even before I had a chance to knock on the door, the door opened. There she was, Gita, with an irresistible smile, quite befitting of her beautiful face. She was fully built and relatively tall for a Nepali woman. In her very early 30s, she looked almost 10 years younger. That was remarkable for a Nepali woman, for they usually age early because of the physical strain of life as well as the burden of bearing many children. By the time women are 30, most of them have already given birth to three or four children because they marry young, before reaching the age of 20. In the past, the majority of girls would be given in marriage by the time they were 15, some even before reaching puberty. My own sister, the oldest of the seven children, was married away at the age of 13, and had her first child within 2 years.

In a sweet voice that perfectly complimented her face, Gita welcomed me. The house inside was no warmer than the temperature outside. This was not surprising at all because the houses in the Valley are damp and cold in the winter; they are neither insulated nor centrally heated. But her personality exuded enough warmth to easily overcome any discomfort caused by the chilly temperature inside.

Tastefully decorated, her living room was free of clutter and the gaudy decor, generally found in the living rooms of most rich families. She did have a TV and VCR set. Since these two items have recently emerged as important status symbols in Nepal, most Westernized families tend to display them prominently in their living rooms. Contrary to my *a priori* thinking that Gita lived a very glitzy life, simplicity marked her decor. I felt very ashamed of my distorted preconception about her life style. But after having met her in person I could not see her as a prostitute. Instead I saw a sister, an innocent woman, in Gita, victimized by circumstances and by the societal milieu in which she matured to be a beautiful woman.

When I arrived at her house, Gita had just returned from the Temple of Pashupati, situated at the bank of the Bagmati, a river considered to be holy by Hindus. It runs right through the heart of Kathmandu. Her hair was still damp. Obviously, she had gone to Pashupati to worship Shiva (also called Pashupati) and bathe in the Bagmati. Many sins have been washed in the water that has flowed down the Bagmati. In the Hindu tradition, taking a bath in the morning, before consuming anything, is regarded as an important religious, devotional ritual as it signifies an act of purification. The common belief is that, like fire, water is a purifier, a cleanser of sins. Anyway, after the bath in the Bagmati, Hindus worship Shiva and return home, presumably blessed and cleansed of their sins, at least for that day.

In a typical customary fashion, Gita brought me a cup of tea and one boiled egg. She sat on the floor, across from me. Keeping up with the Nepali tradition, we were acting like a perfect host and guest, very polite and respectful. Despite this normal host-guest distance and some degree of awkwardness, I felt at home, as if we had known each other for a long time. She was aware that I was a professor and visiting her to learn about her life. Mindful of my teacher status, Gita was very respectful (in spite of the fact that teachers' social status has greatly eroded in Nepal, they still command significant respect, particularly among the older generation). Similarly, I had already gathered some background information about her life through a mutual friend who had helped arrange our meeting. While I was concerned that somebody might see me visiting her and view me as one of her customers, she might have felt ashamed to openly talk to a stranger like me about her life as a prostitute.

Once our sense of shame and fear melted away under the warmth of mutual respect, our conversation flowed freely. The conversation lasted the whole day. Gita did not seem to be in any hurry; nor did she display any signs of discomfort and hesitation to answer my questions even though a few of them were quite intimate and personal in nature. At times, I was the one who felt somewhat uneasy about asking her such questions because in Nepal such conversations rarely occur between opposite sexes. Sexual taboos run deep. I must admit that I was very surprised about her unusually candid response.

Gita was born into a poor bahun (Nepali variation of Brahman) family in a small village, near Dhulikhel in Kabhre, a district situated to the east of Kathmandu. She was the oldest of the five children in the family. Two of her younger siblings, one brother and one sister, fell victim to the claws of death long ago when they were only about two or three years old. Her father passed away just a few years ago, at the age of 46. She has two brothers, one 26 years old who is married and already has two children, and another 18 years old who is finishing high school. Both live with her mother back in her village. They have about 2 acres of land which is barely enough to support the family for 6 months of the year. Gita sends money home, to her mother, on a regular basis to support the family. The money is also used for her younger brother's education. She wants to make sure that he is not, due to financial constraints, deprived of the opportunity to receive a good education, something she so much desired but could not get. She has 8 years of schooling, but can speak some English which she learned through her contacts with Americans. Despite her minimum education, she acted and spoke in a relatively sophisticated manner.

Gita is not alone in this respect. Many poor children are deprived of educational opportunities, especially girls, because their education is viewed as a waste of time and money. As a result, girls' future welfare is sacrificed. Almost in every respect, boys are the center of attention. According to Hinduism, having a son is very critical to clear the passage to heaven for the parents upon their death. In case the parents are barred from climbing the stairway to heaven because of their sins, sons are supposed to perform necessary rites to atone for their sins so their souls can enter heaven or rest in peace.

Unlike sons who are bestowed with the honor of being the bearers of the family name and heritage and regarded as a vital link of the family lineage from the past to the future, daughters are treated as somebody else's property because they are given in marriage to others. This is a common precept of family life both in Nepal and across Asia. To some, the birth of a girl is not an occasion for celebration; it is a sorrowful event or as an economic liability, for her marriage may require a large dowry. As Mazumdar (1992) has revealed, in the past female infanticide was quite common in India. It is believed to be still practiced in China, especially since the country implemented its strict one-child-per-couple family planning policy in the late 1970s. If the first born happens to be a girl, the probability of infanticide is high. As a method of population control, it was widespread in pre-war Japan, too. Given Japanese women's historically low status, it is safe to claim that infanticide took a heavier toll on female infants.

What is ironic is that while the girls are required to work much harder than boys, they are generally relegated to a second class status within the family. They are normally given less food, less care, less education, and less of almost everything than boys, and this pattern intensifies if there is more than one daughter in the family. The situation is worse among poorer families because of intense competition for food. Girls fare better, however, in wealthier families because of less sibling competition for food and other resources. Daughters are denied property rights in Nepal unless they remain unmarried until the age of 35. The burden of being born female is thus a constant reminder of the vicious cruelty of life in a socially oppressive society like Nepal.

Back to Gita. Though never married, she has a 7-year old daughter who lives with her mother back in her home village in Kabhre. Gita made a conscious decision to leave her daughter with her mother as long as possible so she would not have to "be stigmatized as a prostitute's daughter and pay for my sin." Gita visits her village whenever she can in order to see her family and daughter. Her mother also periodically brings her daughter to Kathmandu to see her, but Gita rarely asks her mother to come to stay with her in Kathmandu for any length of time. "My mother knows what I do, but I don't want to put her in a situation where she has to actually observe the daily grind of my life and my shame."

Gita went on to point out that whenever her mother came to visit her, the trip would last only a few hours. The visits were infrequent. The decision to leave her daughter with her mother was very painful, she said, but one she had to make for the sake of her daughter. While talking about her daughter, her emotional pain burst into crystal streams of tears, rushing down her cheeks in search of some consolation. I was mum as if words had deserted me. As Gita stopped talking, suddenly an eerie silence enveloped the room, occasionally punctuated by her sobs and nose-blowing. I couldn't do much to comfort her, so I let her cry, hoping that tears would somehow heal her pain and anguish.

I looked out the window. The sun had completely broken free from the veil of dense morning fog. It was getting warmer outside. The sun rays were piercing through the windows, as if trying to piece together Gita's torn life. The flowers were glowing in the garden. The dew drops on those flowers were sparkling like diamonds against the sun light. Everything appeared to have suddenly come alive as do dormant plants in a desert after the first rain. But that was outside, in the front yard.

Inside, it was totally different. There was much grief and pain, Gita's grief and pain, spread out across the living room. Only her shadow could hear her crying pain, that she could not even keep her own daughter, a natural extension of her own body and soul, at home with her. She had lost hopes about turning her own life around. She emphasized that she was hollow like an empty tin can that produced only noise, but no music. But she was driven by her desire to stuff her daughter's life and dreams with hopes, build her daughter's future on her own body, metaphorically, that is.

Gita got up, politely excused herself, and went into the kitchen. Yet the eerie silence remained undisturbed. My thoughts were deeply plunged into Gita's grief whereas my eyes kept roving aimlessly from object to object. The whole room was filled with one vast emptiness like a huge blank canvas. On the one hand, I felt like leaving so she would not have to talk about her life, her daughter, and her family, so she could keep her pain buried. On the other hand, I did not think it right to leave her alone under that circumstance. Leaving her would have been an easy solution for me, but not an appropriate one. It would have been insulting, like sprinkling salt and pepper on her already burning wounds. Gita was not just a part of my inquiry or somebody's sexual object; she was a human being in pain, who needed moral support. After several minutes, she came out with two cups of tea in her hands. Her eyes a bit swollen, she wore that embarrassed smile on her face and apologized profusely although there was no reason to do so. Gita then asked ever politely why I was so interested in learning about what she called her "lowly life."

I informed her that my interest in the issue of prostitution arose from an incident in Bangkok. The moment I mentioned Bangkok, she smiled. Obviously, she was aware of Bangkok's reputation as a hub of prostitution. During the summer of 1979, I was returning to Nepal after 7 years of sojourn in America. On the way back, I stopped in Bangkok to see a few Thai friends I had met at Indiana University. Being new to the city, I did not know much about the place and its local custom. In fact, I had very little prior knowledge of prostitution in Bangkok. My friends were supposed to pick me up at the airport, but for some reason they were not there. I decided to take a taxi to the hotel where I had already made a reservation and paid for the room. But a mind-boggling incident happened on the way to the hotel. The taxi driver asked me if I would like to stay in a different hotel which was much closer than my hotel. Not knowing his plan and intention, I innocently said that was fine with me as long as the hotel manager accepted my reservation so I would not have to pay twice. He took me to a brothel-cum-hotel. When I saw the scene inside, I was angry with the taxi driver, but concealed my anger because I did not want to be left alone in that place. I asked the driver to take me to my hotel, which he did. It was hard to believe that immediately after checking into the room, the bellhop who carried my luggage asked if I wanted a girl friend, bed partner. I was shocked as well as bemused, and could not resist wondering why prostitution was so rampant in Bangkok, whether it was common in Kathmandu too, and how much these women were exploited or abused. Ever since then, I have always been interested in exploring the issues of prostitution.

When I was talking about my Bangkok experience, Gita kept quiet. Looking somewhat sad, she just stared out the window right past me. The comment about my encounter in Bangkok appeared to have reverberated through her veins.

The time was passing by. It was already 1 o'clock in the afternoon. Gita asked me to stay for lunch, which I did. Even though it was my first visit to her house, I felt comfortable enough to walk into her kitchen and offer to help her fix lunch. We both sat and began eating lunch, like two close friends. I felt welcomed and accepted by her. We finished our lunch and moved back into the living room. Breaking the flow of our casual, lunch conversation, I asked Gita: "So tell me, *bahini* (younger sister), how you ended up in Kathmandu and got involved in this profession."

"It's a long story," said she hesitatingly.

"That is fine, *bahini*. I would like to hear it if you don't mind telling it to me."

"I don't know where to begin. You know it is very difficult for me to talk about my life. My life is like a cabbage, filled with almost endless layers of bitter memories. It hurts me greatly to peal those layers because the more I peal, the more painful it feels. Life weighs very heavy on me," said Gita in a very sad voice, and taking a deep breath.

"I understand. If you don't feel like talking now, I can come back tomorrow," I interjected.

"No, no, no, that is not what I meant. Please stay. I don't mind talking to you at all. Just that it is very difficult for me to express my pain. You know I don't even know how to tell it. My words are all clogged up in my throat, and all of my pain right here," said Gita, placing her palms on her chest.

"Well, anyway, where was I? Oh, yes! my family was very poor. We didn't have much land. My parents worked very hard to support us. From the very childhood, I had to do chores in the house to help out my parents. As you already know, girls don't get to go to school as much as boys do. I didn't start going to school until I was about 10 or 11 years old. I wasn't a very good student; there was never much time to do my homework. I never finished high school." Gita seemed somewhat sad and ashamed when she was talking about her education.

She then went on to talk about marriage inquiries and proposals that her parents received when she was about 17. She said, "There was no lack of suitors willing to marry me. For some reasons, I was in big demand, and several times, my mother hinted, not too subtly, that I should get married. My parents particularly liked this young bahun man who was working in Kathmandu. He was from a relatively well-off family. My mother said this young man's family liked me very much. He had everything that a bride's parents would want in a son-in-law. A perfect match for me, they thought. You know they were quite impressed by the fact that he had earned a B.A. degree and was working for the government. Government jobs are popular. You already know that. I vaguely knew him, but I simply was not interested in getting married. When I responded negatively, my mother was not happy."

"So what happened then?"

"You know how the Nepali marriage custom works. If my parents had forced me to marry that young man, there was nothing I could have done. I could have run away, possibly. Fortunately, my parents did not force me to marry him. I sometimes wish they had made me marry him as most parents would have done with their daughters. If I had married him, I won't be living this lowly and disgraceful life," said Gita with her head buried in her palms. "I can't even raise my head in front of my neighbors and relatives? That is why I avoid any social contacts with them. They say I make dirty money. They are right. Some of my relatives treat me like a leper, but what can I do? Who wants to associate with a prostitute like me unless they want to crawl up under my sari for a fleeting moment of thrills. A typical life of a prostitute: men enjoy rubbing their bellies against mine, but don't want to be even seen with me."

Gita seemed very disturbed about her outcast status, and regretful that she had shunned the marriage proposition from that young bahun man's family. In addition, she was blaming herself for the kind of turn her life had taken.

"So you turned down the marriage proposal. Then after that?"

"After that...!! Marriage inquiries still kept coming. The same bahun man's family sent another person with the same proposal a few months later. I turned it down again, and several more. After a while my parents gave up pressing me to marry. I continued to help around the house as well as on the farm. I would also work as a farm hand, whenever possible, to earn some cash to ease the load on my parents."

Gita became quiet and somber as if some memories were haunting her. "About ten years ago," she continued, "my life took a bad turn. I met an American man, I think, at my friend's wedding ceremony. He used to visit my village frequently. I gradually realized that he was showering me with a great deal of attention. He began visiting my house quite regularly. Every time he went away to Kathmandu or other places, he would bring me gifts. At first, I felt very strange about his behavior. But slowly my fascination about his attention turned into my attraction toward him. I was mesmerized by his charm, his attention and gifts. Pretty soon, we became very close."

"How intimate?"

"I lost my virginity to that American man; yes, I did," said Gita without any hesitation.

"What did your neighbors have to say about a bahun girl like you seeing an American man?"

"You can probably tell what they said about me. As a bahun girl, I was supposed to be shy and reserved, not appear sexually inviting or get close to men. They say it is okay for hill girls (she meant women from such hill ethnic groups as the Gurung, Magar, Tamang, Thakali, Rai, and Limbu) to go out with Americans.[1] But a bahun girl like me is not supposed to do that. Such a behavior is not approved as it is equated with a prostitute. So gossip about me started to swirl all over the village. They called me a loose girl, a shameless girl. It hurt me a lot, but what could I do? I thought once I married him and moved to America, I won't have to hear those nasty remarks. At least that's what I thought because there was no doubt in my mind that he would marry me and take me to America. What a fool I was!"

"What happened between you two?"

Visibly agitated while talking about the American fellow, Gita said, "I was stupid to trust that man. Our relations lasted almost one whole year. One day, he asked me to come along with him to Kathmandu. I thought that was a prelude to his marriage proposal. My excitement was boundless. But I was afraid that my parents would find out about my visit to Kathmandu. Going away with him alone prior to marriage was not acceptable because that would have brought to my parents dishonor, shame, and lots of pain. People think that if a girl goes away with an American, she would not return a virgin. Americans are seen as sex-mongers."

"So what did you do?"

"So I devised a sneaky plan. I told my parents that I was going to Narayanghat (a small city in Chitwan) to visit my close girl friend who had moved down there. But I went to Kathmandu to meet him. He had made arrangements for us stay in a fancy hotel. He bought me many presents: new clothes, cosmetics, and jewelry. After that romantic trip, I became even more convinced that he would marry me very soon. I was ready to tie the nuptial knot with him regardless of what my parents said. But I am sure they would not have objected."

"So it never happened?"

Once again, Gita became quiet. Her eyes were somewhat red and filled with water. I could not tell whether she was angry or remorseful. But, after some silence, she told me that her visit to Kathmandu was her last fling with the American fellow, a final rendezvous. About a week later, he said to Gita that he had to return to America and would be back in Nepal soon, in about a month. She even took that as a sure signal of him gearing up to ask her to marry him. Her thoughts were that he was returning to America to discuss the matter with his parents, buy certain things for the wedding, and finally get everything ready for the occasion she had been eagerly waiting for. He left for America and Gita returned home. Day after day she waited for his return. Weeks passed by and months passed by, but there was no news from him, no nothing. Suddenly, four or five months later, Gita said she received a short letter from him. He said he was getting married back in America. It hit her like a lightening bolt. "I was totally stunned; my whole body felt numb as if I had just fallen from a tall tree," said Gita. "It was the worst moment for me. I was used and betrayed by him. More than my virginity, he took away my dignity and ruined my life. I lost face. I could no longer face my relatives and village neighbors without feeling humiliated. I walked with my head down for months, and I still do. Even now there is a profound sense of rage simmering inside me."

Gita abruptly got up as if she were going somewhere. She was angry as well as in great pain as if her old wounds were gnawing at her heart. Then she sat down and started staring at the ceiling, almost totally blank.

"What did you do after that?"

"I was distraught and confused; I didn't know what to do. My life turned upside down. I became a woman with a past, but without any future. My value as a marriage partner vanished once people found out that I was involved with that American man. In society's eyes, I was an outcast, a damaged property that nobody would want to touch. No more marriage inquiries! My parents were too poor to buy me a groom by flaunting large sums of money, land, or some other forms of dowry. I was doomed. Nowhere to go. I was almost entirely drowned in my own self-pity and self-contempt. It was a vulnerable time in my life."

"What did you do then?"

"Along came a chhetri fellow (*chhetri* is a Nepali derivative of Kshatriya, the second highest caste)," she said. She knew him from her school days. He began to come to see her on a regular basis. She did not care whether he intended to marry her or not. She just wanted somebody to talk to, to lean on, anybody—it didn't matter. So she was happy that the chhetri fellow came along. He was a source of her consolation. Of course, they soon became physically involved. "After all, I had no fear of being a first timer, and socially there was nothing left for me to protect. No more inhibition," said Gita.

"Well, I became pregnant. Believe it or not I was ready to have an abortion, but my mother talked me out of it although she knew full well that having a baby out of wedlock was absolutely disgraceful to the family. My father said nothing to me, but I could tell he was ashamed and hurting badly. I believe he was in a state of shock when he learned what I had done to myself and to the family name. He quit mingling with his fellow villagers. He became completely withdrawn and introverted. Even though my chhetri lover was willing to marry me, his family did not allow him to do so. They thought I was a cursed whore and, therefore, socially untouchable. So once again I was burned. I was deeply embittered. It was my bad karma."

Finally, Gita said, a baby was born, a girl, the same daughter who lives with her mother. She did not know what to do. For men, even when they become outcasts for whatever reasons, there are several routes to escape neighbors' scornful gossip and remarks. Even those men involved in incestuous relations can weather social condemnations. They can simply move to a different community in a faraway place. Simply because they are men, nobody will question if they are outcasts or why they moved to a different place. It is normal for them to move from place to place. Since there is no social suspicion and hindrance to their geographical mobility, they can easily put a lid on their past, leave behind their outcast status, and carry on with their lives in a new place without suffering any societal indignation. But for women, it is totally different. They are supposed to be geographically confined. We can't just pack up and move because if they migrate to a different community alone, without being accompanied by at least one family member, many will raise all kinds of questions. They will essentially equate such women with prostitutes. They have to be; otherwise women would not dare to move alone. So goes the tattered logic. Unfortunately, if a woman moves to a different area alone, that's what she frequently ends up becoming, a prostitute. It is a self-fulfilling prophecy.

After the baby was born, Gita's life went downhill even faster, like a massive landslide during the monsoon season. Any shred of hope she might have had about getting married perished completely. Her life was buried in the debris of a social landslide, almost beyond rescue. Yet she could not afford to let her sins foreclose her daughter's future. The very daughter who smothered her any marriage hope ironically gave her life a new purpose. Bent on building a nice future for her daughter, she decided to do whatever she could to regain some control over her life, put together whatever pieces she could gather, and try to make the most out of her life. "That meant," Gita said, "leaving my daughter with my mother so she could be raised at least halfway decently; it was a very agonizing decision. For her own sake, I couldn't allow her to obstruct my path. Determined to earn some money to support my daughter and family, I moved to Kathmandu, hoping to find a way to rearrange my life. I had nothing more to lose any way."

Ironically, of all the people Gita searched for, in Kathmandu, to seek some help were two American men she had met through her American lover. She tracked down one of them. He already knew that his friend had left her like a dead fish, rotting on a river bank. They met several times. Not surprisingly, pretty soon he began making sexual advances toward her, and she went along with that. The only thing that was constant in her quirky life was sex; it turned into a cheap reprieve from her self-contemptuous life. Deficient of educational skills or other talents, her youthful physique was her biggest asset. Desperately in need of money to support her daughter and family, she decided to milk that asset as much as she could. She had no illusion about developing a permanent relationship with the man. Nor was there any desire left in her to do so. No more! Once hit by a burning stick, a dog never gets near a fire again. "There was no way I was going to let him get away without paying his dues for the pleasure he derived from my flesh and skin. Although I never fell short of giving him full attention, he was merely a customer, my first true customer."

Gita went on to point out that "Pretty soon, other Americans began to approach me. This new American fellow must have spread the word about me. That was good for my business. There was a steady flow of customers seeking sex from me, this fresh flower from Kabhre. I always gave all of my customers full attention." Gita claimed that some of her customers complimented her for the quality of her service. They were particularly pleased with her innocent mannerism, naturalness, and the sincere attention she showed them. They liked those qualities, and she had a way of making them feel desired and did not come off heavy, like some educated Kathmandu women who radiate an aura of overbearing sophistication. "Whatever it was they liked about me, they kept coming back over and over. I did regard them as guests, not just as my customers, in-and-out in 30 minutes. Rather than rushing them right into my room, I always offered them tea and some Nepali snack and struck conversations, slowly lifting them up the scale of their sexual thirst. They really liked that. Many came on a routine basis. That was good for me because I did not have to worry about who, or whether somebody, would be coming next."

"Sounds like you have a good operation!"

"Yes, financially, I am doing alright. Until a couple of years ago, I satisfied four or five customers a day. Those days, I badly needed the money, not only to support my family but also to buy a few nice things. I wanted to buy a piece of land and build a nice house. If I had to live a prostitute's life, I might as well have some of the nice things people enjoy, not look shabby. At least, maintain a certain level of economic security even though my social life is a total wreck. Two years ago I built this house. These days, I entertain only two-to-three a day, rarely more than three, and usually work five days a week. That is enough. No set price for regular customers; I accept whatever they give me. They pay a fair price, but it is a very small sum for them. I gross on average about 1,000 to 2,000 rupees a day, depending on the customers, enough to support my family."

Gita was quite content with her economic security. But socially...? That's a totally different story. "A few years ago, my father passed away. He was ill for almost a year. I blame myself for his illness and death. He became a recluse after I became pregnant. I am absolutely certain that my reckless acts exacted a big toll from his life. I returned to my village for my father's funeral and mourning, and stayed there for two weeks. I really miss my father," said Gita. She started crying while talking about her father.

"I feel very lonesome. All empty inside. I rarely go out except to buy necessities. Hardly ever socialize with anybody. I have few friends to confide to. If my neighbors ever see their children talking to me, they order them back into their houses in a stern voice. It is their way of sending me a message to stay away from their children. Once inside the house, they scold their children for talking to me, I am sure. That makes me feel very bad. My life is one huge social desert, in fact, drier than a desert. Yet in my business there is little room for any personal emotions. It is all physical, living in pretenses. Faking has become a routine part of my life—both emotionally and physically. What can I do? I have to support my daughter and family back in the village. They are dependent on me." As she correctly remarked, she is the link to their economic survival and, hopefully, to her daughter's bright future. She wanted her daughter to get a good education which would help her dodge the shadow of her demon that trailed her. Gita stated that if her daughter succeeded, that would bring smiles to her face and some relief to her heart, thus helping to reduce the load of her sin that hung like a heavy chain around her neck.

"One day," Gita wished, "hopefully after my daughter is all grown up and married—I pray hard every day that she does not suffer my fate or relive my sin—I'll be able to renounce this life and become a *jogini* (hermitress) so I can spend the rest of my life in peace. I want to wash away as much sin as possible during this life. I do not want to be born a prostitute again in my next life. I can't bear it."

I found myself completely engulfed by her life story, immersing deeper and deeper into its depth. My head was getting heavy. I wanted to take a short recess so I asked Gita if she could make me a cup of tea. While she went into the kitchen, I walked out into the front yard to stretch my legs and catch some fresh air. It was very pleasant outside. The sun was approaching the western horizon. While I was checking out her pretty flower plants, Gita came out with a cup of tea and some snack. We both sat on the front porch, enjoying a mild late-afternoon breeze. We then resumed our conversations about her life.

"Please tell me who your customers are. Are they mostly Western expatriates living in Kathmandu, tourists or others? Can you shed some light on them?"

"Mostly Americans who reside in Kathmandu, not many tourists. I try to avoid tourists as much as possible because of the fear of contracting sexual diseases from them. Not that resident foreigners don't carry such diseases. I know many of them often go to Bangkok for sex. I hear lots of prostitutes in Bangkok have contracted various diseases. Still I feel a lot safer with resident foreigners. I have been lucky. So far no infection with any form of sexual diseases. I do go to see my doctor for regular checkups to insure that I am safe."

"Anybody else?"

"A few Japanese come sometimes. Also four or five high-ranking Nepali government officials, all married men. I don't care for them because what they offer is pittance, but they demand a lot. It is not the money so much, it is their attitude. While they enjoy getting under my sari, they often treat me rudely. Yet I can't refuse to have sex with them because of their authority. If I did that, they could cause me trouble, and that is the last thing I need. What can I do? Fortunately, they don't come too frequently."

She informed me that many of her foreign customers are married men with children. Their families live in Kathmandu. "Moneywise," Gita said, "the Japanese men are quite generous, generally more so than most Americans. With them, however, it doesn't seem to make much difference whether I gave them extra attention or not. That's my impression. But Americans, they really appreciate that extra attention. They love that polite, slow, and gentle touch. For some reason, they are hungry for attentiveness. Do you know why that is the case?"

I did not answer the question. I politely sloughed it off.

"I could also tell you a little bit about some of their sexual habits or peculiarities," volunteered Gita.

"Please do," I replied. Prostitution, after all, is not merely a social mirror of various conditions that force women to become prostitutes; it is also reflective of sexual fantasies and peculiarities, or sexual acts that lead men to prostitutes—acts which the sex customers think they can demand from prostitutes without any fear of sounding weird, but not necessarily from their wives or fiances. They see prostitutes as vicarious objects hired to perform the kind of sexual act that gives them a sense of personal gratification and power.

She described one situation. "Once a Japanese man came to visit me. He worked at the Japanese Embassy in Kathmandu. He was polite enough to ask me hesitatingly if I would be willing to do what he wanted me to do. When I nodded, he said he didn't want to have any inter-course; he simply wanted me to play with his *linga* (phallus). He took off his clothes and then took mine off very slowly. He did not want to lie down on the bed; he preferred the carpeted floor, and asked me to sit next to him. He had even brought with him some kind of ointment which he wanted me to apply to his *linga*. It was basically a *linga* massage. It felt awkward, but it was a learning experience, and a very fascinating one. While my palms kept rubbing his *linga* gently and slowly, his fingers were running through my hair in a caressing motion as if they were ready to play a melodic tune."

"Or perhaps those fingers were indulged in a search for romantic solitude," I interrupted.

Gita said, "I must confess that was the first time in many, many years I experienced true sexual pleasure. For some reason, it was very erotic as well as romantic. My sexual life is so routine and predictable that my personal sexual sensation seems to be all gone. I don't feel it any more," lamented Gita about her lost sexuality.

"Did that man ever come back again?"

"Yes, he did, a few other times. Another time, an American man, a high-ranking official with the USAID office in Kathmandu had drawn up his own sexual fantasy plan. He wanted to have sex in a particular position. He had even brought a photograph to show me that position. He was very quiet, and didn't talk much." Gita let me know that, as a seller of her body, she could not refuse his request. Her job was to fulfill their fantasies. She saw herself simply as an object of their play, one with a warm body and certain sexual organs, one who could help them navigate their sexual flights and "see the flashes of twinkling stars in their heads (this is Gita's figurative expression for a man's orgasmic experience)." Over the years Gita had seen quite a lot, different men's different sexual idiosyncrasies and fantasies.

I asked Gita whether she had any hope of getting married one day. She did express a yearning to do so if she was presented with a genuine opportunity. "I doubt any decent Nepali man would ever want to marry me. I have heard about some Nepali prostitutes married to Americans. They are the lucky ones. But right now my marriage prospect is virtually nil. As much as I hate such a life, I can't quite quit it. Not yet. I still have to raise my daughter and support my family. Her future has to be built even though mine is already ruined. But it is hard to tell how much longer my attractiveness will last, perhaps five more years. As a prostitute, my best years are actually behind me. Who wants to have sex with a prostitute with shaggy breasts, flappy thighs, and a wrinkled face that looks like hill terraces? At least not the ones who can afford fresh girls, especially when there are plenty of them to pick. Many young girls are coming to Kathmandu from Darjeeling and from the surrounding areas to become prostitutes. I hear they mostly work in different fancy hotels. Prostitution is very common and widespread nowadays. So far, many still want me, but the day will come, I know, when they will discard me like a banana peal. The sun will set one day. Even a thought of that day gives me chills." Gita seemed depressed and resigned to her current fate as if all the avenues were closed.

It was getting late. The sun had already faded into its nest. The darkness was falling fast, and once again Kathmandu was being embraced by cool evening breeze. As I was getting ready to leave, Gita was melancholic. Although she had detailed the story of her life, I knew full well that it remained unfinished. It was just a glimpse of her life story, that long and tragic story.

I finally said good-bye to Gita and left. As I was walking out the gate feeling heavy, she was waving at me. This time there was no smile on her face, only sadness. I could only imagine what might have been racing through her mind. She was no longer in my view, but her image lingered with me. The old taxi I was riding was zipping through those narrow and bumpy streets of Kathmandu, quite oblivious to the chilly breeze and auto horns blowing from different directions. A romantic Hindi movie song was blaring out of his scratchy cassette player. The taxi was loud and noisy and bouncing, but my mind was too occupied to feel its vibration. I was submerged in the motion of my own thoughts, wondering about Gita's life and future, how her story was going to play out at the end on the stage of prostitution, where her fate was ultimately going to lead her, and whether I would ever get to see or write the final chapter of her life. Before my thoughts had a chance to complete their journey, the taxi had come to a stop in front of my residence. Incomplete thoughts and an unfinished story!

The *kumari* and Gita, an interesting parallel between two damaged lives and unfinished stories. Their stories will never end even though their individual journey may one day reach the finish line, where more disgrace will likely greet them. Very few lives are probably more disgraced than that of an ex-prostitute. They have little value. Often poor, socially disowned, no longer desired by men, and totally stripped of their womanhood, most prostitutes become social destitutes. Unfortunately, their sad stories and slatternly legacies are lived and relived by those who are forced to follow their footsteps as the highway of cheap love continues to expand globally in a tentacle-like fashion. Prostitution appears to be an infinite continuum, like the cycles of the sun and the moon, reincarnating itself in different forms at different times and in different regional contexts.

GITA WITHIN A WIDER CONTEXT

Gita is no madam Heidi Fleiss, a high-class prostitute who catered to the sex-infatuated Hollywood moguls who did not want to go to clubs and hustle women or visit regular brothels. A 27-year-old daughter of a pediatrician, she did not have to resort to prostitution for money at all. It was entirely her decision and choice. Ms. Fleiss was not forced into prostitution by any pimp or because of social and financial circumstances (see Fleming and Ingrassia, 1993). Neither is Gita a street prostitute, one who prowls the streets in a city's red light district under the constant glare of her pimp, like some 7,000 poor Nepali hill village girls "sold each year to slave traders of the sweat-drenched brothels of Bombay" (Hornblower, 1993:45; also see Larmer & Roberts, 1994; Friedman, 1996).

Who can forget the scene in the movie *Salam Bombay,* the one in which a young Nepali girl is hauled down to Bombay and paraded in a brothel to be sold to the highest bidder, that virgin girl who brought the brothel owner a hefty profit? Margot Hornblower (1993:51) depicts the life of another Nepali prostitute trounced in Bombay. She writes:

With the fair skin and lovely slanted eyes of the Nepali, so exotic to Indian men, she attracts an average of seven customers a day. Her fee:

$1 each—of which the brothel owner, a squat, brutal woman, takes
more than half... Manju, 20, radiates an odd school-girlish innocence,
accentuated by the big white bow that adorns her hair.... Her story is
typical. Daughter of a poor farmer..., Manju was 12 when her mother
died. Unable to cope with three children, her father handed her over
a few months later to two strangers: she thought she was going to
Bombay to work as a house-maid. When the two men sold her to a
pimp for $1,000, `there was nothing I could do,' she says. She is
never allowed to set foot outside the brothel. Moreover, she is expected to repay her full purchase price.... Helpless, Manju, like many in
her profession, is resigned to her fate.

Friedman (1996:12) provides a similar description of Mira from
Nepal who now works in Bombay as a prostitute. One common deno-
minator of almost all of these Nepali prostitutes in Bombay and other
Indian cities is that they all come from very poor families.

Neither does Gita suffer the same fate as the Vadi women in the
western Tarai of Nepal, who have in recent years been forced to resort
to low-class prostitution in Nepalganj, a town located near the India
border. The Vadis constitute a small ethnic group whose traditional occupation used to be live entertainment. In a fairly recent study conducted
in Nepalganj, Surendra Pandey (1993) interviewed 33 Vadi women.
Except for a few elderly ones, all of them were engaged in prostitution.
Pandey reveals that out of some 500 Vadi people living in the survey
enclave, 100-150 Vadi women are involved in selling their bodies. Some
of these women are local and others are brought down to Nepalganj from
nearby villages, especially during the winter months when the traffic to
prostitutes' doors is much heavier because of increased seasonal migration to the town. Most prostitutes are infected with venereal diseases.
There is little doubt that in the near future the Vadis, who constitute a
very small number in Nepal's total population, will find a whole new
generation of them infected with sexual diseases unless some drastic
measures are taken to stem the tide. They might even face the possibility
of total physical extinction to parallel their cultural extirpation, the
obituary of which is already posted on the wall.

In addition, Pandey's study shows that while there were always a
few prostitutes among Vadi women, their mass practice of prostitution
is a fairly recent phenomenon. Before the advent of cinemas and television programs and VCRs which are all obviously glorified as artifacts
of modernization, Vadi women were an important source of live enter-

tainment. That was their trade or profession. Sometimes they even traveled to distant places in order to stage their rustic dancing and singing performances and thereby earn their living. As a boy, I would occasionally see Vadi women in Pokhara during the winter months. And I even recall going to their performances.

Explosion of Hindi movies and the recent invasion of TVs and VCRs have dramatically transformed the landscapes and norms of entertainment throughout Nepal, including its western Tarai region. These days few find Vadi singing and dancing performances entertaining; many actually think they are archaic and embarrassing customs. While so-called cultural modernization has rendered their trade obsolete and even defunct, thus wiping out their traditional base of income, there are few reliable alternative means of survival available to them. In addition to basic survival needs, new wants have been created as a result of growing consumerism and development, a situation which has only intensified their lack of resources and poverty. Western Nepal's changing cultural and development landscapes have consequently driven many Vadi women to chart a new course of entertainment, extending their cultural boundaries into the realm of prostitution. While development has proven to be a marvelous boon for some, it has crushed many, including the Vadi women and their families who are having to survive with little economic means and social dignity.

Not only have Vadi women lost track of the roots of their own cultural trade and professional skills, but they have been forced to abdicate control of their bodies and souls, virtually to anybody who wants to hire them for momentary pleasure. This is what development has done: decimated local skills, knowledge, and cultural resources, and replaced them with the hollow rhetoric of poverty alleviation. And in the meantime class biases and differences have intensified.

Gita, without doubt, is much better off than most other Nepali prostitutes. She makes a lot more money than they do, and does not have to share her income with any pimp. Gita was not sold into prostitution like those thousands of Nepali girls in Bombay. Nor does she have to display herself sleazily, without any dignity, like the Vadi women standing by the doors in the stench-filled town of Nepalganj to attract lowly paid hill migrants (and Indians from across the border) to spend their hard-earned monies on their skin and flesh rather than sending earnings home to their wives and children, who are compelled to endure the pain of both hunger and their husbands' and fathers' absence. In other words, victimization reaches beyond the doors of prostitutes to include the wives and children of those who seek sexual service, not to mention the service seekers themselves.

So Gita, although nothing flashy like Heidi Fleiss, certainly is better off. Yet, in terms of broad social consequences, such a comparison is artificial. It is futile and meaningless, for it does little to alter the fundamental contours of prostitution on its sociocultural map. As far as Gita is concerned, she is still a prostitute, socially condemned to the lowest status in society like millions of prostitutes in Asia and across the world. Gita is an echo of countless silent voices, endlessly tortured and taunted in one form or another, voices that reflect a myriad of social backgrounds and geographical regions. She is a living symbol of their collective plight and damaged lives. As Hornblower (1993:51) captures it, "Along the highway of cheap love that now circles the globe, the cost in destroyed lives has become a blight to rival any of the depredation mankind has inflicted on itself."

As illuminating and moving as the story of Gita's damaged life is, it would leave a nagging gap if this chapter fails to touch, at somewhat of a broader level, on the historical as well as contemporary dimensions of prostitution. With this premise, this chapter now shifts its focus to a discourse on the religious-feudal (historical) and development-tourism (contemporary) nexuses of prostitution. It is these nexuses that have played critical roles not only in defining both female sexuality and prostitution, but also in situating women in a position of powerlessness.

RELIGIOUS-FEUDAL NEXUS OF
FEMALE SEXUALITY AND PROSTITUTION

One common theme running through all institutionalized religions seems to be their obsession with virginity. Similar to the Hindu tradition of *kumari* worship, Christianity has created its own fantastically powerful image in the Virgin Mary and her immaculate conception of Jesus. The notion of Mary being a virgin mother is curious but contradictory. Yet it is presented cleverly in that only a virgin, presumably free of original sin, could conceive the son of the Holy Spirit and give birth to him. As related in the parable, this is how it goes. Mary was pledged to be married to Joseph, but before they had any physical relations she was found to be pregnant. When Joseph discovered this, he had second thoughts about the prearranged marriage commitment, but an angel appeared to him in a dream and said, "Joseph, do not be afraid to take Mary home as your wife, because what is conceived in her is from the Holy Spirit.... The virgin will be with child and will give birth to a son" (*NIV Pictorial Bible*, 1981:924). Given such a simple but divine scenario, who would ever dare question the possibility that Mary might have gotten pregnant as a result of an affair with another person or even a rape.

Once again, virginity is back in the picture, particularly among Christian fundamentalists. As Kaufman (1994) shows in his short piece, "Virgins for Christ," there is a campaign underway to preserve the "purity" of virginity. The campaign began as part of the 1993 Southern Baptist convention and its sex education program. Known as the "True Love Waits" campaign, its purpose is to ask the American youth to take the pledge of chastity that they would remain "sexually pure" until the day they entered a covenant marriage relationship.

What the organizers of the "True Love Waits" campaign are advocating is, of course, nothing new. The issue of virginity in Christianity is as old as the religion itself. In truth, the movement appears to be an attempt to reclaim lost virginity in the United Sates where dropping the robe of virginity before reaching the age of 15 is almost as common as sucking lollipops. According to a report in *Congressional Quarterly Researcher* (1993:420), the proportion of girls in the 15-19 age group who have had premarital sex has been consistently rising, from 29 percent in 1970 to 52 percent in 1988. This figure does not take into account girls under 15 who have had sex, including those who have been abused and molested. Since virginity is regarded as a question of religious morality, it is not surprising that some Christian leaders are obsessed with it.

As an observer, who has transgressed the borders of two different societies rooted in two distinct religious traditions—Hinduism and Christianity—I find it ironic that the reverence for female virginity has done little to arrest the proliferation of child pornography and outright defilement of children for sexual thrills, regularly in the hands of priests and preachers. While they preach against the sins of the flesh, their practice sometimes reveal their warped obsession with it. Many of them have been caught committing the sins of the flesh. Sexual abuse of young girls and women has thus become a regular event, almost like Sunday prayers, right within the church hierarchies, under the piercing stare of the Cross. When it comes to sex, the actual words and deeds of many so-called Christian religious leaders are no closer than the moral distance between heaven and hell. They remain prisoners of their own inner demon.

While there has been a media eruption in the United States about the sexual abuse of children—both girls and boys—in the hands of Catholic priests, non-Catholic ministers have so far managed to deflect such attention to their sexual abuse and exploits (*Newsweek*, 1993). It is true that the contradiction between Catholic priests' vow of celibacy and their sexual practice makes them an easy media target. But, in all likelihood, the problem is equally severe within the non-Catholic hierarchies. When Jimmy Swaggart, a TV evangelical (fundamentalist) minister, was caught sleeping with a prostitute, it made national headlines. The overall picture indicates that no matter how loudly Christian priests and preachers pontificate about the virtues of virginity, pledge to abstain from sex, and take the pledges of young people in the sanctuaries of Church halls to maintain their sexual purity, many of them continue to break the secret walls of virginity for the sake of their own personal sexual gratification and power.

Lust for virgin sex—irrespective of her puberty status—is not new, however. Nor is it confined to any geographical or religious borders, for pedophiles and pederasts are omnipresent. When it comes to deviant sexual behaviors, human ability to reason has failed countless men to set them apart from dogs.

In Hinduism, old men marrying young and pre-puberty girls, with little understanding of sexuality, is quite prevalent. One may claim that Hinduism has ratified sex with young children as religious decrees. The tradition of what is commonly known as *kanyadan* (*kanya*=young virgin girl often of pre-puberty age and *dan*=giving or offering; in this case, giving in marriage) is presented as an honorable religious act, an act deserving of divinely merit. As Mazumdar (1992) points out, *The Manu Smrti* or *The Laws of Manu*, a principal text of Hindu polity, declares that "The father who does not give away his daughter in marriage at the proper time is censurable (i.e., at the age before a girl reached puberty and felt the first stirrings of sexuality)." As a further elaboration of this dictate, later in the 16th century Mukundaram stated, "Blessed is the girl given in marriage at the age of seven... If at the age of nine a daughter is given according to proper rites to a bride-groom, the water offered by her son ensures a place in heaven (for her father)" (both quoted in Mazumdar, 1992:3). One principal reason for marrying young girls is, of course, to insure brides' virginity. In addition, from a behavioral angle young wives are much easier to tame and control than those who get married during their adulthood. Logically then, maturity is not seen as a sexual and social virtue, but as a potential threat to male domination and fantasy.

The tradition of *kanyadan* is most explicitly highlighted in one of the stories contained in one popular Hindu devotional text: *Swasthani*. The story is about a 70-year old man marrying a 7-year old girl named Goma. In this story Lord Shiva takes the form of a frail 70-year old man and then in a deceptive way compels 7-year old Goma's parents to let him marry her. The newlywed couple leaves her parents' house and goes to his place. One day, the old husband (Shiva) leaves pregnant Goma in destitution to return to his other wife, Parbati. This is a sad story, but one that is presented as a virtuous tale with a high moral overtone, glorifying girl child marriage, virginity, polygamy, and husband devotion, all in the same breath. What is so interesting is that when Shiva returns, Parbati, despite full knowledge of his philanderous flight with virgin Goma, worships him instead of hurling anger at him. On the other side, Goma, as expected, never wavers on her devotion to her old, departed husband even under the most adverse circumstances, thus depriving herself of the biological dictate of her sexuality. The moral of the story, ironically, reveals a twisted sense of morality: sacrifice your own personal needs and be like Parbati and Goma, utterly devoted to their husband despite his sexually flagitious behavior.

The nakedness of women's subordination and sexual suffocation is obvious in the Hindu expectation that a wife—no matter how young or old—remain chaste and faithful to her husband even after his death. The higher the rank in the caste hierarchy, the more exacting the demand for chastity. Female chastity has played an integral part in the religious value system of the high caste groups. Women were regarded as naturally libidinous, as a source of temptation. High caste and class families, therefore, imposed restriction on their female members' (daughters') outward mobility, normally keeping them confined in their houses as a way of controlling their sexuality.[2]

Mazumdar (1992:3) contends that, "Historically, then, it was the control of a woman's life and her body that formed the core of brahmanical ideological practice and underlined caste status." In essence, female sexuality was defined strictly through the prism of *pativrata* (devotion to the husband). The inventors of such myths went so far as to institute what is known as the *sati pratha*, a tradition of ritualistic self-immolation of the wife on her husband's funeral pyre. This tradition was practiced particularly among the upper echelon of the high caste groups, including the nobility (see Majupuria, 1985).

Although no longer in practice, the *sati* tradition was prescribed so the dead man's family would not have to worry about his wife losing her chastity and consequently blocking his place in heaven. This is the religious interpretation. Besides this, there is a social catch. It was also prescribed for high-caste, high-class families to avert potential social disgrace and humiliation that could result from the widow going out with another man. Becoming a *sati* (a true woman) was thus heralded as the ultimate symbol of *pativrata*, the final negation of not only her sexuality, but her right to life, so she could preserve the face and image of her husband's family. All of this goes to prove a wife's chastity and devotion to her husband, as well as to secure herself good karma, a better life in her next reincarnation (being born a female itself is considered bad karma). *Pativrata* is, therefore, her most important act of *dharma* (duties, both religious and social). There was, however, no imposition of such tradition on low-caste and low-class women as they were generally free to deviate from both *sati* and *pativrata* practices. Since they were thought to be intellectually and socioculturally inferior, mainly born to serve others, they were seen as a primary source of labor. As such, they had to be both allowed to live (so no *sati*) and work, and remarry (so no *pativrata* after becoming a widow) to bear children and hence produce future labor.

Then, of course, there is the so-called "heroic" story of stoic Sita, the wife of Lord (King) Rama. Sita is perhaps the most idealized and idolized female character in Hindu societies. Her unyielding defense of her chastity against her abductor Ravana is most eloquently and pas-sionately narrated in one of the all-time favorite classic Hindu epics, *The Ramayana*. After being rescued, Sita encountered a bitter-sweet moment when her beloved husband Rama, who at that time was living in exile, uttered that no honorable man would accept his wife back after she passed some time in another man's house. Sita was forced to undergo a fire test to prove her chastity before she was allowed to return to him. That was not the end of challenges to Sita's chastity.

From the exile, they returned to Ayodhya, the capital of the King-dom of Kausala, where Rama was crowned as the new king. One day, Rama overheard one of his subjects accuse Sita of being an unchaste wife (queen). Upon overhearing that slander Rama, widely acclaimed by the Hindus as the kindest and most benevolent of the Hindu rulers, whose rule, *Rama Rajya*, was proclaimed to be India's Golden Age, did not defend his wife and her chastity. Instead, he became most cruel. It made little difference to Rama that Sita had passed the fire test. He decided at once to banish pregnant and defenseless Sita into a wild, dense jungle for the upkeep of the religious and social principles. Rama announced to his brothers that to keep Sita in the palace would amount to a slur on their exalted dynasty and that he had got to save it from that slur. That's exactly right: in order to save his patriarchal dynastic face and to protect his (male) honor and royal power, Rama exiled his innocent, pregnant wife to the jungle.

On the other side, despite being unjustifiably mistreated and banished into the jungle, Sita remained totally devoted to her husband Rama till her death. Not surprisingly, her fidelity is exalted on the Hindu cultural map of female sexuality and powerlessness as a golden example of how a woman ought to behave: be totally submissive. The message drilled over and over in every female mind from very early on in her life cycle is that a true woman ought to demonstrate the qualities which Sita possessed—chastity, morality, and husbandly devotion at all costs—and that her own personal needs have no value unless they match those of her husband's.

All of this goes to demonstrate how male-female relations, or more specifically, how a woman's life and sexuality are governed in a country like Nepal with a deep root in its oppressive feudal-religious traditions. These relations are not only unequal, but also nauseatingly one-sided. While so-called modernization has brought about some cosmetic changes, the real situation with respect to the male behaviors and attitudes toward females remains more or less intact. To be sure, the contemporary Nepali conjugal law can impose fines upon a man marrying a second wife during the life of his first wife, but polygamy is still common and fully sanctioned by the Hindu social and religious codes. The social and religious history of Hindu societies is replete with examples of polygamy and male adultery. For instance, in the kingdom of Kausala (North India), the ancient king Dasharath, the father of Rama, had three wives. Virtually, every Nepali king, with the exception of the current one, had two or more wives.

One interesting side note about King Dasharath is that he had no children, let alone sons. Desperate and worried that his dynasty might cease to exist because of the absence of any heir, Dasharath sought advice from a sage who instructed him to perform a specific ritual. Upon the completion of that ritual, the King was given a pot full of rice pudding blessed by the Fire God; it was for his three queens to eat. After eating the pudding all three queens became pregnant and eventually bore him four sons, Rama being the first. Such a ritualistic process of impregnating the queens was portrayed as an act of divine intervention, a Hindu equivalent of Virgin Mary's immaculate conception, I suppose. There is little indication in the story that what was projected as a divine intervention could, in fact, have been some ancient form of artificial insemination.

Nowhere in the story is there any hint that King Dasharath was most likely infertile. Such a glaring omission of any suspicion about male infertility clearly typifies the nature and degree of entrenched male bias and insecurity in Hindu cultural ethos. Male infertility was rarely suspected. Even today, if a couple fails to produce any child, it is always the wife who is automatically tarnished with the image of being barren. She is accused of being a cursed woman. Also ridiculous is the practice that if no pregnancy occurs within reasonable time ensuing marriage, the wife is encouraged to worship the *linga* (phallus), an important symbol of Shiva, but never the *yoni* (vagina), the symbol of Shakti who is one of Shiva's female counterparts. The *linga* thus symbolizes the god of fertility. If she fails to become pregnant after exhausting all the avenues, she is expected to encourage her husband to marry another woman.

To carry this discussion a step further, it is noted that for a married woman, having at least one son is equally critical from her own personal viewpoint because the son not only opens for her the gate to heaven, but also represents a vital source of her clout, status, security, and power within the family. In Nepal, a woman's status is intrinsically tied to a male figure during every phase of her life cycle: to her father as a daughter, to her husband as a wife, and to her son as a mother. As a wife, if a woman bears sons to her husband, her status in the family climbs. She would have fewer reasons to fear (although there is no assurance) that her husband might marry another woman. So a mother's womanhood rests on her son(s).

To a Hindu woman, marriage is thus more than a biological function; it is a key sociocultural event to bear heirs, specifically sons, in order to insure the continuation of her husband's family lineage as well as her own security and status. Unfortunately, given the prevailing social contours of male-female relations, marriage also writes the final epitaph of her total submission to the male authority and sexual oppression because, for a woman, her husband is the highest male authority and dictator of her sexuality.

Returning to the issue of virginity, it is believed that in some Hindu communities a bridegroom was encouraged to go so far as to spread a white sheet on the bed during his first intercourse with his bride. This was done to insure the virginity of the bride, meaning if the white sheet was stained with blood then the bride would pass the test. The belief had it that every woman bled during her first sexual intercourse. This is an example of how far the ruling myths can veer from the axis of physiological reality or how deranged they can be in erecting a pillar of sexual morality. While unstimulated young or pre-puberty girls may indeed experience vaginal bleeding as a result of tissues being torn in the course of penile penetration, not all grown up teenagers and women bleed, especially if they are aroused during copulation. Yet the bride who failed this test of virginity would face the grim possibility of being insulted, mistreated, or even driven out of her husband's house on the ground of not being able to prove her virginity.

What is so hypocritical or ironic is that the same religious-feudal order that imposed such a strict rein over female sexuality induced, almost openly, prostitution. A brief look into the past shows that while most institutionalized religions condemned female fornication and even second marriage following widowhood, they openly, as previously mentioned, sanctioned both polygamy and their royal patrons' keeping of concubines, a practice which constitutes institutionalized prostitution. Concubines were royal prostitutes. The same religious morals as well as social laws were also ignored when village landlords forcefully imposed their sexual will on their tenants' young wives and daughters. Both royal concubinage and village landlords' sexual practices forced many of the abused women and girls into prostitution. Since the social-religious system made outcasts of defiled women, most of those removed from the royal concubinage and discarded by landlords generally ended up joining the ranks of prostitutes. That is, the religious-feudal codes of conduct with regard to female sexuality have often, directly and indirectly, promoted as well as perpetuated prostitution.

In order to further illustrate how the religious-feudal nexus has played a paramount role in controlling women's sexuality and subsequently inducing prostitution, let me refer to the ancient Hindu text, *The*

Kama Sutra of Vatsyayana(1963:174),[3] generally thought to be the oldest treaty on human sex and sexual relations. In the chapter entitled "About the Love of Persons in Authority for the Wives of Other Men," Vatsyayana provided an elaborate discussion of the different methods a king, village chief or landlord could use to obtain the wives of men below them. The same tactics could, of course, be applied to sexually subjugate daughters of any citizens under his authority. If none of the many methods of cajolement and indirect pressure worked, Vatsyayana went so far as to recommend the outright seizure of the woman of his desire. He wrote:

> Lastly, if the woman desired by the king be living with some person..., then the king should cause her to be arrested, and having made her a slave, on account of her crime, should place her in the harem. Or the king should cause his ambassador to quarrel with the husband of the woman desired by him, and should then imprison her as the wife of an enemy of the king, and by this means should place her in the harem.

In essence, Vatsyayana's prescription constitutes a recipe for the sexual violence against women based on authority and power relations, precisely the kind of vile and violent methods to which Europeans (masters) resorted in raping black women during the days of slavery as well as the women of their colonies across the world. Such is the Hindu religious-feudal nexus of female sexual oppression and prostitution.

DEVELOPMENT-TOURISM NEXUS
AND THE GLOBALIZATION OF PROSTITUTION

In the mid-1970s, the time when the feminist movement was spreading in the United States like a raging fire, I was a doctoral student at Indiana University. Although I cannot claim to have been swept by this fiery movement, it certainly had some influence on my thinking. As a transplant from Nepal, a country saddled with its repressive past and where feminism was an alien concept, I was quite curious about the movement. It was a new experience for me and for most Americans as well, I suppose, as the current of feminism began to spawn noticeable changes in the terms of debate over female sexuality (Firestone, 1971; Weeks, 1991). New parameters and definitions of male-female relations were being charted. The *Ms* magazine which made its debut in 1972 was leading the way as a major voice in this new wave of feminism. Those were interesting times in America. As a result of my growing curiosity about the movement, I occasionally browsed through feminist periodicals.

One day in the mid-1970s, I read an article that bluntly claimed: "Fucking is work." The assumption was that sex performed by women for male enjoyment is work, and as such it should have a price tag. Few would question the analytical content of this feminist perspective on prostitution. However, in societies where capital exercises dominance over labor and where profit is king and forms the basis of economic life and social order, such a strict market-based view places women dangerously in a position of being dehumanized. Furthermore, this market-based argument ironically extends the boundary of the religious-feudal rights accorded to men to control and abuse female sexuality into the territory of capitalist rights granted to so-called entrepreneurs of the skin trade to exploit female sexual labor for profits. As a result, prostitution becomes a capitalist business enterprise, whether officially sanctioned or not.

In the entrepreneurial spirit of capitalism, exploitation of female sexual labor as work is thus justified, no matter how dehumanizing it is, as long as prostitutes are paid for their services. Since the basic capitalist principle dictates that labor as a commodity is to be exploited for profits, female sexual labor exploitation is just one more feather in the crown of capitalism. So logically then, the only question that remains is: are women serving sex to men paid a fair market value for their labor, however determined? If they are paid fair market wages for their services, then, technically in the world of capitalism, there is no exploitation of prostitutes. This means we have reached the finish line of the debate over prostitution or female sexuality. This is the danger of the strictly market-based perspective on prostitution. Although radical in some respect, it obfuscates the issues concerning prostitutes and prostitution. The cries and voices of protest against female sexual labor exploitation become drowned unless, of course, the circumference of such protests is stretched to encompass labor struggles against the whole capitalist system. In other words, if we submit to the capitalistic logic that prostitution is a form of work without carefully assessing its nature and multifaceted implications, the struggle against female sexual labor exploitation will be fuzzy, and eventually lost (Firestone, 1971).

As the source of sexual labor, women are commodified. They are bodies without souls as they are expected to perform without any emotional attachment to their sexual act. Once physically used up, prostitutes are normally discarded like a piece of worthless carcass. After all, within the framework of capitalist economic logic, labor is only as good as its productive value, invariably measured against the marginality of its returns. As soon as sexual labor benefit (profit) dips below its cost, women are devalued. Their value rapidly slides down the diminishing return curve because prostitutes are highly vulnerable to market fluctuations in tastes. It is also very much age-based. Their economic value (demand) peaks fast and drops faster. As more and more buyers of sexual service gravitate toward younger and younger girls (virgins), prostitution becomes intensely competitive, much more so than most other forms of labor services. As commodities, therefore, prostitutes face a short life span and are used up fast as they are driven away by younger and fresher faces.

Interestingly, one can observe in this depressing drama of prostitution a convergence between the two seemingly antagonistic forces of feudal-religious dogmas and capitalist imperatives, both leading to a firm control of female sexuality, the former to keep female virginity in check for men's social gratification and the latter to make profits from selling female bodies. Paradoxically, it is the very virginity (young girls) that religious traditions so passionately covet, that commands the highest demand and hence the highest price tag on the capitalist global market of female flesh. Furthermore, so downgraded are the social value and status of girls (women) within the religious-feudal tradition that they are routinely sold into sexual servitude without any compunction, simply to make some money.

Prostitution certainly existed in the past as it is known as the oldest profession in the world. But it remained localized. Under today's deepening capitalist development, it has become highly commodified, commanding a global market where both prostitutes and their customers cross national borders, reaching virtually every corner of the world to sell and buy that ubiquitous commodity: sex. And Nepal is no exception as it is incorporated into the ever expanding global web of prostitution.

How did prostitution become global?

At the core of the globalization of skin trade lies the massive growth of tourism worldwide, mainly sex tourism. Increased affluence in Western countries and Japan, especially since the 1960s, has bred almost insatiable demands for leisure, entertainment activities, including travels, both domestic and foreign (more in Chapter 6). These activities were highly promoted in the name of tourist industrial development by the consortium of airlines companies, hotels, travel agencies, and tour organizers (Truong, 1990). They were all vying to capitalize on the enormous profit potential of the tourism sector. And there were plenty of large international banks, including the World Bank, ready to loan money to many underdeveloped countries to develop their tourism, along with the infrastructure necessary for it (see Tanzer, 1995). The huge demands generated by these affluent leisure seekers and travelers, however, explain only partially the rapid growth of the tourist industry, along with sex tourism, in the underdeveloped countries of Asia. The other part of the explanatory equation is directly related to the domestic policy of economic development pursued by these countries.

As already discussed in Chapter 3, many underdeveloped countries, following their emergence from colonialism, were madly driven by their desire to develop their economies, pillaged for decades by Europeans. In this pursuit, these countries not only maintained close relations with their former colonial masters, but also received financial and technical aid from them, as well as from the United States (Chapter 3). In their pursuit of economic development, most Asian countries gave a big push to the tourist industry in the 1960s and 1970s as an expedient way to earn hard currencies. With the help of foreign loans they embarked, at a grandiose scale, on the construction of tourist industrial infrastructure such as fancy hotels, resorts, large airports, and roads. As discussed in Chapter 6, Nepal was no exception as it too was swept by this new tourism development tempest (see Zurick, 1994). High class as well as low budget hotels sprouted throughout Kathmandu which now has almost as many hotels as ancient temples, often standing in close proximity as distinguished monuments of capitalist modernism and theocratic feuda-lism.

The combined forces of international recreation demands and the domestic emphasis on tourism development magnified the market for sex tourism as a natural subsidiary to the tourist industry. Networks to supply prostitutes and call girls were established. Since its genesis in the 1960s, sex tourism has proliferated and played a key role in generating hard currencies for many Asian countries (Friedman, 1996; Hinds, 1989). Matsui (1983) points out, for instance, how the government of South Korea acted, in the name of development, like a national pimp, pushing for the expansion of sex tourism. Matsui quotes Korean female tour guides telling Japanese tourists: "In our country the sanitation of *kisaeng* has been insured by a special Presidential order." A decree issued by the South Korean Ministry of Education reads: "The sincerity of girls who have contributed (with their cunts) to their fatherland's economic development is indeed praiseworthy" (quoted in Matsui, 1983:68; parenthetical phrase in original).

As a precursor to foreign tourists' sexual demands, the presence of American military forces in several Asian countries (e.g., Japan, South Korea, the Philippines, and South Vietnam) was a catalyst in engendering prostitution throughout the region. For instance, the American military helped to turn prostitution into an important economic sector of South Vietnam, transforming its capital city Saigon (now Ho Chi Minh City) into the largest sex center in Asia. Of course, Saigon's skin-trade market was obliterated, almost overnight, as soon as the US Military withdrew its forces in 1975. Reports filtering from Vietnam, however, indicate that since its reopening to capitalism around 1990, accompanied by tourism development activities, the sex trade is once again making a fast ascent in Saigon. Such a rapid comeback of prostitution gives a clear impression that the sexual vestiges left behind first by the French colonizers and later by the American military forces is well and alive. Its dormancy under the doctrine of communist purity to which Vietnam adhered until recently was merely a temporary hiatus in its continued growth. In addition, economic growth riding on the globally ever-expansive wings of capitalism and its off-shoot tourist and entertainment industry is inherently instrumental in spurring prostitution. These two phenomena go hand in hand, a fact that is further corroborated by the experience of Eastern Europe and China, another Asian adherent of communist purity until the late 1970s.

Since the early 1980s, when the Chinese government encouraged the market economy by inviting foreign companies to operate in the country, there has been a widespread resurgence of prostitution according to one tour guide with whom I spent three days in Beijing. In every hotel I stayed, massage parlors were prominently featured; customized room services were readily available to any visitor who wanted to have sex with Chinese girls, often stereotyped as silky "China dolls." Since Japanese are a major target, in many hotels one can observe signs in Japanese about massage services, a code phrase for sex. The signs are most conveniently posted right next to room telephones.

Wherever Westernism and Westerners (and now Japanese) penetrate, prostitution grows exponentially and develops a global connection. Truong (1990) reveals an overarching influence the US military presence in Vietnam had on the massive growth of prostitution in the region, especially in Thailand. In the mid-1960s, the time when the size of the American troops in Vietnam was peaking, Saigon alone could not satisfy the sexual demands of sex-hungry American GIs. Bangkok had already begun to capture this spillover market. But the city received an additional boost. Under the rubric of economic and tourism development, the sexual service industry was officially promoted after 1967 when "a treaty was signed between the Thai government and the US military to allow US soldiers stationed in Vietnam to come on `Rest and Recreation' leave..." (Truong, 1990:161).

On the heel of the American military pullout from Vietnam in 1975, Saigon became a ghost town for prostitutes, forfeiting its dubious status as the number one sex capital in Asia. Saigon's downfall proved to be a boon for Bangkok. With its already well-developed prostitute supply networks and tourist infrastructure, the city was fully poised and suited to instantly fill the void, replacing Saigon as Asia's Disneyland of sex. To this day, sex remains the most heart-throbbing allure of Bangkok, the most popular "Rest and Recreation" (R&R) center for all those Western and Japanese expatriates living in South and Southeast Asia, as well as for millions of tourists pouring into Thailand every year. Lillian Robinson (1993:496) pointedly writes:

It was in 1971, while the war in Southeast Asia raged, that the World Bank recommended the development of mass tourism in Thailand. (The bank at that time was headed by Robert McNamara, who had been U.S. Secretary of Defense when the R&R contract with Thailand was signed). The economic initiatives consequent on the bank's report led to what is routinely described today as a $4-billion-a-year business involving fraternal relationships among airlines, tour operators and the masters of the sex industry. In this sense, sex tourism is like any other multinational industry, extracting enormous profits from grotesquely underpaid local labor and situating the immediate experience of the individual worker—what happens to the body of a 15-year-old from a village in Northeast Thailand—in the context of global economic policy. From the perspective of First World customers, the international inequities translate into a great bargain, while their personal experiences of cut-rate ecstasy combine to make up those totals in the billions.

Traditional discussion of imperialism turn on the exploitation of labor and natural resources in the colonized territory. The neocolonialist leisure industry tends to identify the two. In a public speech in 1980, Thailand's vice premier asked all provincial governors `to consider the natural scenery in your provinces, together with...forms of entertainment that some of you might consider disgusting and shameful, because we have to consider the jobs that will be created.' Landscape, sexual entertainment and labor thus converge in a single economic image of Thailand.

Two attractive aspects of the sexual voyage to Bangkok (or any other Asian cities) are as follows. First, Thai (or Asian) women pose little threat to the Western male ego and sexual prowess. In the West, it seems that the excessively demonstrative and omnipresent images of sexual ecstasy or the incredulous Hollywood imageries of sex, many beyond one's ability or even fantasy, generally threaten men's sexual egos, particularly those of middle class white men who seem to be caught in the social limbo of human sexuality. They seem to be neither free from the lack of sexual hang-ups among the poor and blue-collar working class men, nor shielded from the social and sexual insularity of the wealthy elites who enjoy their women's docility. Middle class white males are often haunted by the perception (myth) of being sexually deficient. As previously argued, myths are powerful and tend to determine human behavior (Firestone, 1971).

Given the myth of middle class white males' sexual deficiency, it is quite likely that a large number of these men see their women as too aggressive, inattentive, self-centered, and too demanding of their personal sexual pleasure and satisfaction. In addition, the expanding realm of feminism that is most prevalent among middle class women and that continues to challenge and shatter many of the traditional preserves and bases of male power and authority has further deflated the already shrinking male ego of many men. That many middle class white women are no longer confined to home and dependent on their husbands for economic survival may have also contributed to the corrosion of middle class men's control over their wives and their sexuality. After all, in a relational context women's freedom from economic dependence on men often translates into their freedom from sexual subservience to men. When combined, all these factors play an important role in exacerbating their sense of insecurity, be it sexual, social, political, or economic.

But sex with prostitutes gives them a sense of power and control over women, along with sexual satisfaction, without any hang-ups, without feeling the pressure to perform well in bed to keep their women happy. In such sexual transactions, there is virtually no threat to their sexual machismo, for prostitutes never demand personal pleasure; they only deliver it. Hence, with prostitutes these men feel secure about their sexual and economic power because they are paying for their service. After all, prostitution is a buyers' market. In the case of Asian prostitutes, the blanket of sexual security becomes even thicker as they are, from the very childhood, coaxed and even indoctrinated to master the value of self-sacrifice and submissiveness to male authority and power as if the sole purpose of their existence is to serve men.

The second attraction is directly linked to Thai (Asian) women's exotic charm and inordinate attention to their sexual customers, something about these qualities that obviously tickle men's sexual fancy. For some reason, Western men, as Gita alluded to, appear either deprived of female attentiveness or simply crave for female compliance and intimacy. Lillian Robinson (1993:497) observes that "What the customer is buying, in addition to this unimaginative but unproblematic experience, is the woman's undivided attention. His overnight companion will also bargain with the cabdriver, work the unfamiliar pay phone and order food. I have no way of verifying how this social submission translates into an erotic vocabulary. But nights...start with sexual exhibitions, where women demonstrate remarkable control of the vaginal sphincter—`smoking' cigarettes and catching ping-pong balls with their genitals or extracting strings of razor blades from them..."

A Swiss tour operator describes Thai girls as "slim, sun-burnt and sweet...masters of the art of making love by nature." Keeping up with its colonial tradition, a Dutch agency depicts them as "little *slaves* who give real Thai warmth" (emphasis mine). On top of all of this, observes Robinson (1993:496), white men "are lured by an appealing conflation of natural, social and cultural forces, while they themselves are represented as inherently desirable." They are repeatedly reminded that Thai girls "love the white man in an erotic and devoted way." And they get all of this at a rate that is very low by any Western standard. So it is a jackpot, and who can beat that? It is quite common to see Western expatriates living in South and Southeast Asia routinely take short trips to Bangkok and Manilla to be serviced—sexually, of course. I have met several Americans living in Kathmandu, who regularly take such trips.

To summarize, what the expanding market of rapacious sex trade has created is a confluence of wealthy Western buyers and poor Eastern body sellers. The net is cast so wide that not even one sexual demand goes unmet. There is a mechanism set in motion to serve even those consumers who are unable to travel to distant sex capitals. Thousands of young girls from many poor, underdeveloped countries are transplanted in the fleshpots of Tokyo, Berlin, Brussels, Paris, Rome, New York, London and even Seoul and Singapore, or wherever the demand for them exists. When it comes to the skin trade, national boundaries rarely pose a hindrance.

In the past several years, a new trend has surfaced in the international traffic of young girls. Large numbers of them are exported from poor Asian countries to their prosperous neighbors and to wealthy Middle Eastern countries. In a newspaper report, "Slavery Thrives in Asia," Schmetzer (1991) writes that one million or more Asian women and children are sold, auctioned or lured into slavery.

> From Tokyo to Riyadh and from China to the South Seas, roving agents, ruthless pimps, kidnap gangs and cross-border syndicates have turned the flesh trade into one of Asia's most profitable multinational enterprises... `Slavery now is more sophisticated, more globalized and more technologized than ever. Women can be recruited for domestic jobs and end up as prostitutes in Japan and the Middle East. Slavery is now integrated into our countries' economies,' said Aurora Javate de Dios, a leading Philippine expert on the subject... The governments of Asia—Thailand, the Philippines, Burma, Bangladesh, Sri Lanka, India and others—generally turn a blind eye to the blatant enslavement of millions of their citizens at home or abroad (Schmetzer, 1991:1).

While there is a fairly receptive, though socially pernicious, market for these female guest workers (maids) in the importing countries such as Japan, Singapore, South Korea, and Taiwan, many foreign maids are coerced to do extra physical work, to become sex servants without any additional pay. If they refuse to oblige, their employers may abuse them or simply deport them. They have virtually no legal rights or recourse. This kind of sexual slavery has become increasingly common in prosperous Asian countries such as Japan, Singapore, and South Korea. In many cases, it simultaneously victimizes both the wife and the maid. Given the degree of social and cultural repression of women in East Asian societies, the wife is subjected to an emotional torture of knowing that her husband is having an affair with her own maid. On the other hand, the maid is kept as a sexual slave (house prostitute) until the day she is literally tossed out by her female master (assuming that she has the nerve to face her husband's likely wrath). During my visit to Singapore, one of my former Chinese students told me that such incidents are quite common in the country. He mentioned one case in which a neighbor beat his wife severely because she had literally kicked their foreign maid out. Her husband, the wife discovered, was having an affair with the maid.

In the case of South Korea, the general perception is that prostitution has intensified greatly since the outset of the American military presence after the Korean War. According to one intellectual Korean woman I met during my stay in the country as a Fulbright scholar, South Koreans justifiably believe that the presence of almost 40,000 sex-hungry American service men on the Korean soil, together with the swelling floods of other Westerners, has spawned tremendous demands for prostitutes. The booming business of prostitution has attracted young women to Seoul from all parts of the country. There is no denying that the presence of American troops has played a vital role in this business. It was quite evident at an American military commissary complex in Seoul, where I observed so many young Korean women hanging around American service men, looking and acting cheaper than most prostitutes in the flimsy corners of Reno, Nevada.

Then, of course, there are Japanese sex tourists, contributing to the prostitution boom in South Korea. Hotels are well-stocked with a bountiful crop of young Korean women (and even Filipino women), all ripe and ready to be harvested by Japanese sex tourists. Late in the evening, hotel corridors and elevators come alive with Japanese men of all ages openly escorting young Korean women into their rooms. Since everybody knows what everybody else is doing, there is no attempt to conceal their behavior.

One particularly popular destination for Japanese *kisaeng* tourists in South Korea (*kisaeng* in Korean means a professional female entertainer, equivalent to a *geisha* in Japan) is Cheju, a subtropical island located off the southern tip of the Korean peninsula. Cheju's reputation for its youthful-looking beautiful women makes it a magnetic destination for Japanese sex tourists. The *kisaeng* tours to Cheju are often disguised as golf tours as most Japanese tourists mix golf games with sex plays. The information offered by my two informants was corroborated by my own personal observations during a visit to Cheju.

In her article, "Why I Oppose the *Kisaeng* Tours," Yayori Matsui (1983), a Japanese author, explains why South Korea has become a sexual paradise for both American military men and Japanese sex tourists. No doubt, South Korea's geographical proximity to Japan reduces travel costs, thus enhancing the former's attractiveness as a popular sexland for the Japanese. The fact that many Koreans can speak at least some Japanese due to their colonial past adds further appeal. Moreover, the prostitution market in South Korea is much better than the one in Japan. "You can't find a decent *geisha* in Japan, even at a hot springs resort. They are not very friendly and a rip-off, too. South Korea's much better," declares one Japanese man. "In South Korea the spirit of rendering oneself completely to a man still exists among the women, and their exhaustive service is irresistible," claims another Japanese man, his eyes glistening (quoted in Matsui 1983:66). Matsui further points out that previously when Japan colonized the Korean peninsula and pillaged it for 35 years (1910-1945), some 200,000 Korean women were raped and forced into sexual slavery to service Japanese soldiers as "comfort girls." Now they return to the same land as sex tourists and disgrace her women again, this time by flaunting their money rather than their military might.

When the spotlight is beamed down on the globalization of prostitution, one can see a direct correlation between economic development (modernization) and the growth in the number of prostitutes. As sex tourists from developed countries roam the globe in search of young flesh, globalization deepens. This growing global trade of female bodies has prompted some to characterize it as international sexual slavery (Barry et. al., 1983). It clearly shows that as long as male sexual desire has a cash value, the profiteering spirit of capitalism will spare no corners of the globe in its incessant commodification of female bodies and souls. This is the height of sexual consumerism. So all of this leaves little doubt that money is the prime lubricant in the commodification of women's bodies and sexuality. Prostitution is a money-making machine, a truly multinational enterprise.

There is no end in sight to this most reprehensible and dehumanizing capitalist enterprise of prostitution as its relentless tentacles continue to grow deeper and wider, encompassing the whole world. As men hop around the world, from one sex haven to another, in search of virgin bodies, young girls become the biggest victims of prostitution. In the case of Thailand, *The New Paper* (October 9, 1993), a daily newspaper published in Singapore, argues that one of the scariest emerging crises of child prostitution epidemic is the swelling tide of HIV (human immuno-deficiency virus) positive cases, thus making them prime candidates for AIDS (acquired immune deficiency syndrome). The main reason why child prostitutes are so susceptible to HIV is because of their physical immaturity. Since most of them are not biologically ready for sex, during intercourse they suffer vaginal rupture and bleeding that makes them vulnerable to HIV infection. *The New Paper* estimates that 50 percent of Thai child prostitutes are HIV positive. Most of these cases will no doubt transpire into full-blown AIDS cases. Given the degree of poverty and the fact that AIDS patients are ostracized, few victims report to doctors, let alone receive proper medical care. Consequently, one whole generation of Thai prostitutes will face the likely horror of decimation. Eventually the whole society will suffer, in every respect: socially, culturally, economically, and medically.

Unfortunately, Thailand is not the only country facing the pending horror of AIDS. With the globalization of prostitution has come the globalization of AIDS. Its specter is already beginning to stalk Nepal. A recent report asserts:

> Though Nepal has only an estimated 5,000 HIV-positive cases today, medical experts figure that there could be more than 100,000 cases within five years. An outbreak would be disastrous in Nepal, where, in rural areas, there is one doctor per 52,000 residents. `It is a national threat,' says Dr. Daniel Tarantola, a Harvard University expert on the spread of AIDS. `A whole program of societal reconstruction is needed.' ...There are an estimated 5,000 prostitutes in Kathmandu, and 25,000 roadside *bhatti* houses throughout Nepal—drinking establishments where the matron often supplements her meager income with prostitution. In addition, some 200,000 Nepalese prostitutes work in the brothels of India's largest cities, and 300,000 migrant workers travel back and forth to India (Larmer & Roberts, 1994:23).

While some may argue that, compared to Thailand, AIDS is still in its infancy in Nepal, it is beginning to spread rapidly through three main vectors. First, Nepal's geographical proximity to India, where the raging epidemic of AIDS has already affected more than one million victims, poses a serious threat. As the Nepali prostitutes infected with AIDS are repatriated to Nepal by India and as cross-border migrants spread AIDS, the number of victims will surely soar. Second, the internal diffusion of AIDS through sexual exchanges with infected partners will produce more victims. The third vector is associated with the increased frequency of travels between Kathmandu and Bangkok (also Hong Kong and Singapore). As the Westerners living in Nepal journey back and forth between these cities to quench their sexual thirst, the chances of them acting as agents of AIDS diffusion will increase. There have also been a few HIV-positive cases in Kathmandu, spread by high-class Nepali men who come back from Bangkok and Hong Kong infected with AIDS (Upreti, 1994).

This impending public health crisis may play some role in curbing the growth of prostitution. Yet this is not necessarily comforting in that it takes a medical horror like AIDS to arrest the social horror of prostitution. Even then, the skin trade may not stop or even slow down; on the supply side, many prostitutes are faced with a cruel choice between grinding poverty that pushes them into prostitution and the deadly virus that ultimately ushers them from the sex bed to their death bed. Unfortunately, in this battle between the daily reality of poverty and the looming ghost of AIDS, poverty will most likely have an upper hand, mainly because the poor are more concerned with their immediate survival than future health. As a result, it is unlikely that many prostitutes will abdicate prostitution in spite of the deadly danger of AIDS. In the final analysis, I am not sure if it makes any difference whether AIDS wins or prostitution wins because eventually prostitutes lose. They are too powerless to fight either battle, let alone win it.

On the demand side, the spread of AIDS will extend the frontier of prostitution—geographically as well as demographically. That is, if the skin trade market in such renowned sex havens like Bangkok and Manila dries up as a consequence of AIDS epidemic, sex tourists from Western and other developed countries will simply move on to new territories and plow more fertile grounds, e.g., Kathmandu which is already well-known for its exotic and mystic appeal. As this process intensifies, it will become the 4th vector of AIDS explosion in places like Nepal. There is no indication that the sprawling market demand for skin trade will shrink soon. Rather the AIDS scare, to repeat, is ironically bound to further intensify the globalization of prostitution and the demand for virgin girls to minimize the probability of HIV infection. This means countless budding virgin Gitas will be lined up for open bidding in the global market of skin trade. More lives will be damaged, disgraced, and doomed even before they have a chance to fully bloom.

CONCLUDING REMARKS

Every phase of development has its own phase of prostitution. Under capitalist development, especially when tourism is promoted as a leading sector, prostitution reaches its highest phase, taking on a commercial form. By openly commodifying women's skin and flesh, prostitution takes away their dignity and degrades their sexuality as human objects of male sexual play and pleasure. But, generally, as a sexual commodity with a short life span, the value of female sexuality depreciates fast.

Prostitution not only constitutes a sexual betrayal of women, but also proves their absolute powerlessness, transcending religious, geographical, sociocultural, and class spectrums. Both historically and in the contemporary context, the roots of prostitution are complex. Yet it is clear that its religious-feudal nexus has been further aggravated by its development-tourism nexus, mainly because of the growth of the tourism industry, catering to tourists from America, Europe, and Japan. In other words, no matter how one dissects it, capitalist development and prostitution go hand in hand. The rise and fall of international sex meccas is, therefore, directly contingent on the constant flows of large numbers of foreigners seeking sexual thrills in exotic corners of the world—be it Bangkok or Bombay, Saigon or Singapore, prudish Kuala Lumpur or Kathmandu.

The globalization of sexual slavery has created a multibillion-dollar business, riding on the tender bodies of young women. To be sure, money is the engine that turns the wheels of the global prostitution business. But prostitution is more than a matter of money; it is more than simply work, providing slave work for poor girls and women. It is largely a manifestation and direct product of sexual power relations, relations in which men are dominant and women debased. As women's bodies and souls become increasingly commodified under the ravaging pace of capitalistic development that has been going on in Nepal and other Asian countries, their subservient position sinks even deeper.

Forced to live in poverty and lured and coerced by organized sex traders with close links to the tourist and brothel industries, countless families throughout Asia have taken advantage of their girls. Historically seen as an economic liability or wasted property, there is now a new twist in the contemporary karmic configuration of young girls' lives. In certain parts of Nepal, a growing number of families are beginning to view their daughters' lives in a completely different economic light. They have suddenly discovered their pecuniary values on the flesh-trade market. Given that Nepal's religious-feudal tradition has historically condemned women as male properties, many parents apparently have little compunction about selling their daughters as capitalist commodities into sexual servitude or subjecting them to their new sex role as prostitutes (Friedman, 1996; Hornblower, 1993).

For instance, some families in Sindhupalchok, a district located to the northeast of Kathmandu, have pushed their daughters into prostitution to make money. In fact, a place called Helambu in Sindhupalchok has long been renowned in Nepal as a major source of pretty girls. A friend recently informed me that Helambu girls were in the past used as sexual objects by members of the Rana ruling class. Even today, the district supplies a large number of girls to be exported to the brothels of Bombay and for the tourist hotels in Kathmandu.

Notwithstanding a few scattered cases of family prosperity resulting from their earnings, the vast majority of prostitutes and their families have witnessed little abatement of their poverty. This is largely because most of the money earned by prostitutes is disproportionately garnered by pimps, brothel owners, and hotel managers. This sad fact reveals that foreign tourists have indeed brought lots of money into many Asian countries, including Nepal as exemplified by its booming tourism-based hotel industry, casino operation, and other related activities. But with their money has also come plenty of misery for those who are already strapped to the bottom of the development pit.

True, prostitution has produced jobs for many poor girls, but that is hardly the kind of employment one can sustain on a long-term basis. In fact, for many, prostitution is no employment at all as it often turns into sheer sexual servitude. While a few have, to repeat, gained some financial security through prostitution, countless continue to rot along this path of social and economic servitude. They live like social outcasts, always undignified and degraded. And they die like an animal deserted by its herd; unable to fend for themselves, they die a lonely and painful death. Nobody sheds any tears or expresses any sorrow when they eventually pass away. As such, prostitution is simply another face of poverty, very taxing and tormenting. So what is good or gainful about sex tourism and prostitution for those who provide the actual service? Together they only produce trails of countless victims, victims whose lives are defiled and destroyed; they are simply buried alive. As

Hornblower (1993:45) succinctly states, the impact of prostitution "...is most devastating on an individual level... Souls do not count, only bodies, debased over and over, unmindful of social cost or disease."

> There were poor girls whom fortune failed in need:
> They sold their charms and threw their youth away.
> Old age caught them alone and desolate—
> Unmarried, childless, where could they seek help?
> How sorrowful is women's destiny.
> Who can explain why they are born to grief?
>
> (Nguyen Du quoted in Truong, 1990:131)

NOTES

1. Nowadays, in Nepal, the word American is commonly used as a generic term to denote to virtually all white people regardless of their geographical origins. Until the early 1960s, we used the term *Angreji* or *Belayati,* which literally means English (or British), for all white people. In other words, the word American has now replaced the word English as a more popular symbol of Western power or the white man's continued hegemonic domination of the globe.

2. It is generally believed that this type of excessive spatial confinement of daughters induced incestuous relations within the compounds of Nepal's royal and noble families. Such relations are known to have been particularly common among the Ranas, who ruled Nepal for 104 years between 1946 and 1950. Typically characteristic of their feudalistic tradition, the Ranas were notorious not only for their social and political oppression, but also for their sexual tyranny. That is, if a Rana man saw a girl and wanted to have sex with her, there was not much that anybody could do to prevent him from imposing his sexual will over her. Moreover, such spatial confinement of high caste and class women was partially intended to keep them from too much sun exposure and thus to maintain or augment their fair complexion, generally considered to be more beautiful and desirable.

3. All references to the *Kama Sutra* in this book are based on its 1963 edition published by G.P. Putnam's Sons.

Kumari—the living goddess

6

POT GOES POP ON
KATHMANDU'S FREAK STREET

Sir, sir, want to buy hash?

— A young Nepali boy

Kathmandu is a paradigm of pollution, pollution of the urban environment as well as mind and body. It is a parasite that devours everything.
In his article, "The Bagmati Scorned," Dixit (1992:25) writes: "Sand
from its riverbed, hydro-power from Sundarijal, drinking water from
Budhanilkantha and Sundarijal, and irrigation water throughout its
length—metropolitan Kathmandu takes all these from the Bagmati River.
Does the city give anything in return? It does—raw sewage generated by
hundreds of thousands (of people), untreated effluent from industrial
estates, hospital wastes, toxic chemicals and acid from `carpet washing'
plants, pesticides and chemical fertiliser leaching from fields, the detritus
of cremation *ghats.*" No doubt, Kathmandu stinks—like a toilet pit.

NATURE OF PHYSICAL POLLUTION: PAST TO PRESENT

Situated in the central hills of Nepal, Kathmandu has a long history
of being a very dirty, stinky city. More than anything else, it was the
ubiquitous rubbish that struck me most about Kathmandu during my first
visit to the city almost 30 years ago, in 1968. There was defecation and
urination, even right outside the entrance doors of their homes. Every
little open space was used as a place for defecation. Nothing was safe,
not even temple grounds where they went virtually every morning to
worship their favorite gods and goddesses. It was very difficult for me

to fathom how they could so callously defile the very temple ground that they regarded as being most sacred. There was little physical separation between the temples and the toilets. Contradictions have been the high points of Kathmandu.

So streets were littered with human excrements and garbage. They looked like garbage dump yards. The whole city stunk like a rotten carcass. Yet Kathmandu residents were absolutely nonchalant about such poor sanitation. The whole scene was beyond my imagination. To those from outside the Valley, taking a trip to Kathmandu was seen almost as a voyage to the world of civilization, far removed from mundane rural life. To many, it was the center of the world; in fact, Kathmandu was Nepal, a whole different world. When asked where they were going, many people on their way to Kathmandu used to say routinely they were going to Nepal. Such was the imaginary allure of Kathmandu. But, to me, it turned out to be anything but the world of civilization. If that's how the world of civilization looked, then I didn't want to have anything to do with it. That's how I felt. Blasted by all those layers of filth spewing foul smell, I almost vomited, literally. It was quite a scene, very different from my home town of Pokhara. I stayed with some college students from Pokhara, who had rented a room in a house located in the central business district of Kathmandu, where, unlike in American cities, the rich and poor shared the same space or neighborhoods. In other words, at that time there was little spatial segregation by class or social status. This particular neighborhood was (is) called Makhan Tol. It was a very accessible location, but the surroundings were extremely dirty.

Kathmandu's heavy population, I am certain, had quite a bit to do with the city's filthy condition. But it was largely the mentality of the city's residents that, I believe, was the biggest problem. They simply did not seem to give a hoot about waste disposal. People would throw garbage, including children's feces, out the window into the streets without any concern for pedestrians. My friends used to warn me regularly not to walk in the middle of the streets in order to avoid being hit by the garbage tossed out the windows. They advised me to walk close to the houses in order to minimize the chances of such incidents. Every so many houses shared a small courtyard-like space, filled with every foul object one could imagine. The house in which my friends lived also shared such a courtyard facility, more appropriately a filth disposal site. The stench originating from that courtyard was so obnoxious that we would rarely leave the room window open for any extended period of time. The whole scene was so obscene that, initially, I had difficulty adjusting to that environment. My mind and body were reacting to that foul condition so adversely that at one point I developed constipation. I sometimes wondered how people could live in such a condition. They must have developed total mental immunity against it, I suppose.

I am not suggesting that Pokhara was a very clean town. It too was dirty, but nothing like Kathmandu. Certainly, there were signs of defecation along some of its back roads and a few rotten garbage items scattered here and there. But main streets rarely served as open latrines like in Kathmandu. Pokhara's low population density and open space were, I assume, contributing factors in keeping it cleaner than Kathmandu. Almost everybody in Pokhara used open fields, quite a distance away from their homes, for defecation. Most household garbage was disposed into a compost pit to be used later as fertilizer for farming. Since the vast majority of people were engaged in farming, household garbage was considered a valuable source of compost manure. Very few objects were discarded randomly or wasted. Such was not the case in Kathmandu where almost every street served as a open waste disposal pit.

Although defecation along the streets and throwing the trash out the window are less common today, the problem still persists in many parts of the city, especially along those streets and areas where the volume of morning traffic is relatively light. At the aggregate level, Kathmandu's solid waste disposal problem has actually worsened. This is largely attributed to so-called modernization. There are piles and piles of trash everywhere, in fact more omnipresent than the countless temples. While the temples dot the city's cultural landscape, garbage piles stand as the mighty mounds of modernization. The city can be metaphorically described as one huge landfill. Yet one cannot help but wonder how something like this could happen in the capital city, the tourist hub of the country (see *Himal*, 1992, 5:1, Special Issue on Kathmandu).

As far as the question of why the volume of solid waste has increased exponentially over the past two decades, there is no mystery. Certainly, the city's population growth over the years has contributed to the increased volume of garbage. In reality, however, the problem goes far beyond the numerical increase in Kathmandu's population. The real culprit is the capitalist culture of consumerism which is running amuck in the wake of growing affluence of the elites. Per capita consumption has increased many times over during the past few years: consumption simply for the sake of consumption. As a symbol of social status, it is often defined not only by how much people consume, but also by what and in what form they consume. The form of consumption has changed. There has been a tremendous rise in the consumption of prepackaged goods and commodities.

Almost lost in all of this is the tradition of recycling. Nepali people were, until recently, far ahead of most Western societies in their practice of recycling although it was done largely out of necessity, meaning most people could not afford new or fancy things. Besides being economically out of reach, most of the consumer objects which are readily available today were difficult to find in the past. There was less to consume. As a result, even the rich were limited in their overall consumption. Given such a reality, recycling was common and vigorous across all classes. This situation has taken a dramatic turn over the past two decades. With the declining level of recycling has come the increasing amount of garbage production.

Since the rich can now easily obtain manufactured and packaged goods, they see little need for recycling. Even the poor are increasingly abandoning their traditional practice of recycling as they seek to avoid all manifestations of their poverty. There is a totally new definition and perception of development being created in Nepal (Chapter 3). Wasteful consumption or riding the tidal wave of consumerism has become synonymous with modern values and development. Pressure to hide their poverty bears heavily on the poor, forcing them to give up many of their traditional practices of survival, and instead to live in pretenses in order to project the aura of being modernized. This is what I call the pumpkin syndrome: a pumpkin usually looks good on the outside no matter how rotten it may be on the inside. One cannot always tell it is rotten until it drops and breaks. To be sure, there has always been some level of pumpkin syndrome in Nepal, particularly in Kathmandu, but the consumer culture has now spread the syndrome far and wide.

What is so ironic about all of this is that while Western societies, particularly their well-to-do citizens, are actively pushing to promote the practice of recycling, Nepali people are regrettably pushing it aside. Gone are the days of recycling. Until a decade or so ago, merchants diligently saved old newspapers and magazines and later used them as wrappers or made small paper bags out of them for their customers' use. Old bottles, tin cans, and other containers were used and reused time and again. Today, not only are they routinely discarded as waste, thus adding to the volume of trash, but they are replaced by non-biodegradable plastic bags with a high level of toxic content. So what was once recycled is now an additional piece of solid waste on a sidewalk. As one garbage collector, who works for the Kathmandu municipality described about its residents, "...they produce too much garbage. Just ten years ago I used to collect half a tractor-load of garbage from Kasthmandap (an area near the center of the city) every morning. These days, I have to make two, sometimes three, trips. It is becoming impossible to keep this place clean" (quoted in Basnet, 1992:26).

In essence, the old habit of throwing garbage out the window without any regard for pedestrians has now been replaced by the random disposal of everything people cannot or do not consume directly. As the total volume of consumption goes up, so does the production of solid waste. Even for a very underdeveloped society, Kathmandu produces a tremendous volume of garbage. The three sister cities of the Valley—Kathmandu, Lalitpur, and Bhaktapur—currently house approximately 700,000 people, that is, not counting those living in the surrounding areas. Assuming that each individual on average produces 2 pounds of solid waste on a daily basis—and this is a very conservative estimate—the total would amount to almost 1.5 million pounds (or roughly 700,000 kilograms). That is a lot of solid waste for a valley with few operational sewer lines and waste disposal facilities. Streets have unfortunately become the most obvious and accessible garbage disposal sites, all free and unencumbered. That is why virtually every street in Kathmandu and its sister cities is filled with filth. So, in a way, nothing has changed as Kathmandu residents' overall sanitational practice seems to be frozen in time.

A few years ago, a garbage pickup and disposal project was launched. Like all other projects, this too was initiated by foreigners and financed through foreign aid which came from what was then called West Germany. Large garbage bins were stationed in different parts of the city. They are overfilled and rarely picked up on a timely basis. Anyway the novelty of those garbage bins has long worn out. Today, they stand as unsightly landmarks, a timeless feature of Kathmandu's abhorrent sanitational past as well as contemporary pollution. They are also ominous of the city's pending future decays, both environmentally and in human terms.

This is not the end of the story, however.

Kathmandu has lately earned a dubious distinction as one of the most polluted cities in Asia (*Himal*, 1992). The level of air pollution is very high. In 1994, I was back in the country two times, once in the summer and once in the winter. Every time I went out, my shirt would get practically all dirty, particularly around its collar where I could see a heavy dark layer of dirt from smoke caused by vehicle emission, not to mention the dust. The hair would feel heavy and greasy in a matter of just a few hours of exposure to the city's physical environment. It was an amazing experience, something that seemed quite remote until just a few years back. Dust has always been a problem in Kathmandu, but the pollution problem associated with toxic fuel emission is a recent phenomenon.

The high level of Kathmandu's air pollution is not surprising given its bowl-shaped valley location surrounded by mountains and given the heavy use of very old vehicles running on diesel and leaded gas with no emission controls. In June 1994, I met on an airplane a Kathmandu merchant who deals in motor vehicle parts. We had an opportunity to discuss the city's air pollution problem. He asserted that besides the numerical explosion of motor vehicles, there are two other factors choking the city's air quality: the use of petrol mixed with kerosene (which dealers use to boost their profits) and the overloading of most commercial vehicles, namely buses, trucks, and tempos (three-wheeled passenger vehicles). This problem is exacerbated by the city's undulated terrain, a geographical factor that places additional pressure on the already overloaded engines. Whenever they climb even a slightly elevated slope, one can observe those vehicles belching out so much dark smoke that it temporarily obstructs the visibility.

While air pollution appears to be getting out of control, there has been little control over the numerical explosion of motor vehicles in the past few years. Even those neighborhoods which were once considered quiet and sleepy are experiencing a traffic uproar. One report noted that there were 60,000 motorized vehicles in 1992 (currently estimated to be nearly 75,000). The same report said, "Exhaust from about 30,000 vehicles alone amounts to 22,000 tonnes per year of carbon dioxide, 22,000 tonnes of carbon monoxide..." (*Himal*, 1992:30). Simply expressed, the problem of air pollution is getting very serious. Here is one depressing remark made by Brian Whyte, a long-time observer of Nepali tourism. "November," he said, "used to be the month for mountain watching, once the morning fog lifted. This past November, there was not a day when the mountains were absolutely clear" (quoted in Shrestha, 1992:20).

POLLUTION OF THE MIND:
A DOPE TANGO ON FREAK STREET

There is another type of pollution endemic to Kathmandu: the pollution of both mind and body stemming from the diffusion of what can be characterized as the pot (dope) culture, one that is no less insidious and injurious to the overall health of Nepal than environmental pollution described above.

Since the early 1950s Nepal has served as an attractive destination for Westerners for three main reasons or simply characterized as 3 p's: *peaks* (towering Himalayan mountains), *pot* (marijuana and hashish), and *poverty* (marginal life chances of the Nepali poor). While the peaks attracted mountain climbers and pot brought hordes of hippies, poverty caught the attention of "development missionaries." Although we can now add a fourth "p"—*poker* (growing casino gambling)—the focus here is primarily on the spread of the pot culture, along with a contextual reference to peaks and their initial role in preparing the groundwork for tourism development.

When the country was first officially opened to the world in the early 1950s, Western mountaineers were attracted to Nepal because of its majestic Himalayan peaks. After all, Nepal contains many of the world's tallest peaks, including Mt. Everest. The first conquest of Mt. Everest by Tenzing Norge and Sir Edmund Hillary in 1953 symbolized the power and passion of human courage and technology—a feat that clearly demonstrated human ability to subdue even the imposing height of snow-clad mountains. In addition, their achievement heightened the attractiveness as well as stature of Nepal as the most preferred destination for serious Western mountaineers. As they began to flock to the country, this gave further impetus for tourism development. From the economic and cultural perspective the impact of the mountaineering enterprise was so profound that it can be described as the forerunner in tourism development in Nepal. In essence, it opened the door for the subsequent invasion of Nepal by Westerners whose numbers have consistently grown over the years. By 1990, the total number of tourists in Nepal had reached 255,000, almost 75 percent of them coming from advanced countries (CBS, 1992).

Then came the 1960s, when Nepal's tourism industry took off. The 1960s proved to be a thunderbolt as Nepal was suddenly jolted out of its relative calm and tranquility, and swept over with a new wave of

Westerners. That was actually the second wave of Western invasion. This phase was, in some respects, associated with the US Peace Corps operation in Nepal which started in the early 1960s. Specifically, it cracked the door open for the growing hippie movement—and its pot culture—to infiltrate Nepal. With the diffusion of the pot culture, Nepal was put on the cultural map of hippiedom as one of the most desired places for the hippies to loiter freely. Totally confused about the cultural value system, most hippies suffered from a crisis of identity. They viewed pot as an escape route and as the prime source of happiness. Such a view was, of course, based on their distorted understanding of the East and its culture, often interpreted as the land of Shangrila, filled with mystic beauty and inner peace. I distinctly remember a comment made by an American Peace Corps friend in the mid-1960s. He asked, "Nanda, do you know why the Nepali people are always so happy and smiling?" I thought that was a rather silly question. But he was not asking me a question; it was a definitive statement as he added, "I know why they are always happy. They smoke marijuana; that's why they are always happy." That was one of the most ridiculous observations I had ever heard about Nepal and Nepalis as it was fraught with misconception and misinterpretation. But I had no idea at that time what the basis of such a laughable assertion was.

Of course, I have never analyzed the Nepali society and its people from a phenomenological angle to discover why they are happy (or sad for that matter). But to think that marijuana smoking was the cause of their happiness is totally bizarre. Marijuana generally makes smokers feel high, but I am not sure if it necessarily makes them feel happy unless one equates feeling high with happiness. Furthermore, only a small number of Nepali people smoke marijuana, normally those who are over 45 or 50-years old. Also included among the marijuana smokers are those who have renounced (or pretend to have renounced) the earthly world and its many material trappings; they are often called a sadhu or *jogi* (Nepalese variation of the term *yogi*). These *jogis* are presumably the followers of Bhola Nath (or Shankar), one of the many manifestations of Lord Shiva. In his Bhola Nath form, Shiva has freed himself from such material temptations. He is high and intoxicated from smoking marijuana, hashish, or opium. In essence, Hinduism has a long cultural history of marijuana smoking, transmitting a sense of transcendental beauty, inner peace, and ultimate freedom. It was perhaps this image of the East, filled with mysticism, that seemed to have captivated the Westerners immersed in the hippie movement.

Yes, in my own family, my father smoked marijuana with his friends on a regular basis. For him, it was a form of socialization as well as a means of relaxation. I have no doubt he felt high and calm when he smoked marijuana. Now one of my older brothers does it, one who is in his 60s and acts like a half-*jogi*. Yet, growing up in Pokhara, I rarely saw any young men smoking marijuana. As far as I am aware, smoking pot was a social activity, mainly associated with people's life cycle, but rarely with happiness.

Regardless of one's interpretation, the hippie movement had not only arrived, but also gripped Nepal. It symbolized the Western pot culture that had gone pop (become popular). While smoking marijuana could certainly be considered part of the Nepali culture, it was never a cultural movement. But now suddenly, Nepal was thrust into this rapidly unfolding dope dance performed by the hippies. As countless hippies poured into Nepal, they played a big role in tourism development.

The new wave of budget tourists coming to Kathmandu in search of dope and happiness continued to swell throughout the 1960s and 1970s. The spread of the pot culture and the influx of dollar-a-day tourists had tremendous influence on the emerging cultural and development mindset of Nepal. Local merchants and youths quickly assessed what the low-budget tourists were looking for. Cheap hotels and restaurants as well as other low-budget services sprouted everywhere to capitalize on the hippie demand. Most of those operations were set up haphazardly. In addition, Nepali youths seized on the opportunity to sell marijuana and its much more potent derivative, hashish, to the hippies. Their attention was diverted from studies as they were attracted by the possibility of making instant money by selling dope and other tourist objects. Many subsequently became drug pushers although there was little evidence of the kind of tightly organized drug business found in the West.

In general, hippie activities initially centered around the core of Kathmandu, specifically along the narrow street called Jhochen. Because Jhochen was the hub of the Western hippie freaks, it soon became popularly known as the *Freak Street*. It was even identified as such on several tourist maps. And the Freak Street had indeed become freaky. No question about it. Although Jhochen has witnessed a quiet death in the last 10-15 years due to the shift of the primary locus of low-budget tourists to Thamel, a neighborhood located across from the royal palace, the historical role of Freak Street in transforming the cultural mindset of Kathmandu cannot be underestimated. The allure of hippiedom might be subsiding, but its derelict influence has already begun to haunt the Nepali youths in a hideous form.

By the late 1960s, Nepal had come to be heralded as one of the pristine meccas of marijuana, a pot cultural recreation center for the hippies. Although its contribution to the global drug trade was negligible, some hippies did introduce drug smuggling to Nepal. An American friend recently told me that her sister and her boy friend used to smuggle marijuana and hashish out of Nepal back in the 1970s. In a relatively short time, Nepal had traversed practically a whole new landscape, from the height of mountain peaks to the trough of marijuana pot. Nepal's popularity as the marijuana country was largely attributed to the fact that hippies could immerse into the deepest depth of the pot culture without having to face any moral taboo and social prohibition. On top of that, drugs were legal. The price of marijuana was negligible, and in some cases even free, largely because it had not been commodified yet.

There was a time, in fact as late as the early 1980s, when people could freely pick marijuana while walking down any back roads. In the fall of 1979, a professor from America and I were walking down one of the streets in Kathmandu. We saw a marijuana plant growing along the street, and he picked a few small branches which he consumed later. Marijuana grows wildly almost everywhere, in backyards as well as in public places. Although marijuana plants are no longer as ubiquitous as they once were because of the disappearance of public places and the rapid expansion of the built environment, they can still be found quite widely in rural areas. During my visit to the western Tarai district of Bardiya in July 1994, I noticed patches after patches of marijuana plants growing wild, in some places so dense and lush that I initially thought they were commercially grown. In fact, in 1984 I discovered that some farmers in the eastern Tarai had embarked on the commercial farming of marijuana which is mostly exported to the harbors of Calcutta to be transhipped across the Indian ocean to European destinations.

Lamentably, although few low-budget tourists are "hippies" any more, the outcome of early hippie activities has not been too pretty. While the virulent growth of low-budget activities greatly helped to propel Nepal's nascent tourist industry into a prematurely developed phase, they also set the grand stage for the sustained moral disintegration of the country's sociocultural fabric. The whole society is coming apart.

For plenty of people residing in Kathmandu, serving Westerners has become the sole purpose of their existence.

Then came the 1980s. It was during this decade when some Nepali youths underwent a dramatic behavioral transformation, from selling dope to consuming it. As they began to emulate Westerners, the decadent culture of pot smoking which the hippies passionately espoused began to take over both their minds and bodies. Pot is no longer a fad. It has become an addiction. According to Bhandari (1989), there were at least 25,000 drug addicts in Nepal in 1989, and 15,000 of them in the Kathmandu Valley alone. They were the lost souls of Nepal. If the non-addict drug abusers are counted, the number climbs to as high as 90,000 in the Valley alone. Bhandari's estimate shows that the drug users spend 1.5 million Nepali rupees a day on drugs (close to $40,000 back then). Since 1989, it is likely that the total number of drug addicts has jumped to 30,000 (20,000 in Kathmandu). The number of addicts and the amount of expenditure on drugs both seem very small by the American standard, but not so for Nepal. Bhandari's findings suggest that heroin addicts came from all socioeconomic spectrums, rich and poor. Many quit their schools. Cultural implications aside, many of these addicts could not even afford to pursue such a lifestyle. Yet it mattered little to them. From a Nepali perspective, the pot culture has graduated to the final stage in its life cycle, from production and distribution to consumption and addiction.

Nepali youths have generally failed to recognize that they do not have the luxury that American hippies enjoyed. Americans could afford to indulge themselves in such a wasteful activity and lifestyle because most hippies came from relatively well-off families. Furthermore, low-budget tourists could buy a great deal of luxury for a few dollars because of the dollar's high value against the Nepali rupees. Back in the 1960s, if American hippies spent five dollars a day in Nepal, they could live very comfortably. For them, spending five dollars meant perhaps no more than 2 hours' income at that time in the United States. But, today, an average Nepali person can't earn five dollars, even if s/he works a whole day; for some it will take a week's work, perhaps more. What this means is that in order to buy the level of comfort that an American hippie enjoyed in the 1960s and 1970s, the average Nepali would have to spend one week's income. This comparative advantage that American tourists enjoyed in Nepal has not changed at all even though the overall cost has gone up significantly since the 1960s.

A comment by a white American female graduate student at the University of Wisconsin-Madison drives this point home even more explicitly. During a conversation in early 1994, she mentioned that she was going to be in Nepal for two years. When I asked why, she replied, "I can't afford not to be in Nepal as long as I can." What she meant by this comment was that she could live very comfortably in Nepal for only a fraction of the money she would have to fork out in Madison or any part of the United States.

The point is that the pot culture has left some deep scars on the Nepali cultural and economic map. A growing number of teenagers have fallen victim to this social illness, all because of their emulation of Western hippie habits. Unfortunately, their drug consumption is not limited to marijuana and hashish; they have gone so far as to consume manufactured, hard drugs, smuggled into the country from outside. Heroin, also commonly known in the market as smack or white powder, is the drug of choice as over 90 percent of the abusers prefer it to other drugs (Bhandari, 1989). One can regularly read in local newspapers reports about young drug users being found completely stoned.

Here is the irony about all of this deepening social illness: while it is no exaggeration that Western hippies were influenced by their perception of the East, Nepali youths have acquired their dope habit from the hippies. While the Westerners swarmed to Nepal in the 1960s and 1970s in search of marijuana and hashish, in the 1990s Nepali youths are after foreign drugs such as heroin. Kathmandu is now a drug importer. Ironic or not, the emerging trend speaks volumes about Nepali youths' Western orientation in their attitudes and behaviors. This is a case of what may be termed the reverse diffusion of pot smoking. Young Nepalis showed virtually no interest or desire in pot smoking when they observed only their parental generation do it. But when they were exposed to Western hippies and saw them getting high, drug consumption became chic and glamorous. Such a blind mimicking of Western habits and values, without any thought to their tragic consequences, is not only confined to growing drug abuse; it penetrates almost every facet of society and life. Emulation of all things Western has become hip.

DINESH: A PRODUCT OF THE POT CULTURE

Phewa Tal—or Lake Phewa as it is popularly called today in tourist parlance. Tucked away in the southwest corner of Pokhara, Phewa Tal is one of the most enchanting natural features that the valley has to offer for Western tourists. But now—it is a hippie haven, the focal point of the pot culture in Pokhara.

One early afternoon in 1980, a long-time friend from Pokhara and I were walking toward Phewa Tal, where I had spent many a Saturday, swimming and canoeing in the lake, as well as periodically having picnics with classmates. It used to be a very serene and peaceful lake; its natural beauty was beyond human description, especially early in the morning, when the reflection of Machhapuchhre (Fish Tail mountain) with a reddish golden face would gently ripple through the calm waters of the lake as if it was thoroughly drowned in a passionate kiss. The majestic mountain and the serene lake—they looked like two eternal lovers inseparable from one another. A truly breathtaking beauty, filled with a romantic vision! No wonder why Phewa Tal was the most popular recreational area for Pokhara's high school and college students! Because of the presence of the Barahi temple on its little isle, Phewa Tal was also one of the major religious centers in the town.

It was a prickly hot summer day. The sun was high above the head. To fend off the heat, I was wearing a hat and sun glasses—something I had learned to do in America. I must have looked like a tourist. My friend and I were walking at a relaxed pace, chatting about our old days in Pokhara. Totally submerged in the memories of the past—both sweet and bitter—we were both oblivious to our surroundings. After all, it was a very familiar foot path which we had walked hundreds of times in the past: the same vista and the same landmarks. We kept talking and walking without paying much attention to anything else.

Suddenly, we were both startled and awakened from our sublimity by a boyish voice, a voice coming from behind us. We turned around and saw a young boy walking toward us at a rapid pace. Short and slim-built, the boy had piercing eyes and jet black hair. There was something quite striking about him although I could not quite figure out what that was. He did not smile much. That was quite unusual for a Nepali boy. Nor did he make much eye contact. But his bony face looked shiny enough to radiate an aura of self-confidence.

"Hello sir," the boy said in English, "want to buy hash? A1 quality... A1!" My thoughts were silenced by that boy's question. It was obvious that he had mistaken me and my friend for foreign tourists. That was not the surprise though. What was shocking to me was the vivid reality of a young boy with a long life ahead of him becoming a drug pusher, at such a tender age. He had already lost his tenderness, along with the innocence and joy of his boyhood. He was a little young man in a boy frame. In the meantime, there was a scary thought haunting my mind: that boy could have been me! The thought kept repeating in my mind. After all, I was connected to many Peace Corps volunteers. I could have been pushing drugs to Western hippies just like him. Deep down in my heart I felt both a sigh of relief and sadness. A sigh of relief because I had somehow escaped from such an entrapment—a path of self-destruction—but sad because I was seeing a young boy walking down the very path that could have easily swallowed me up. Questions began to twirl in my mind: "How many other young boys have been seduced to become drug pushers as a result of tourist development? What has possessed Nepal? What has happened to Pokhara; how could it be so ruthlessly devalorized? Is this economic development or social vulgarization? How could a young, tender boy be led down a vulgar passage?" That boy's fate was a typical symptom of what had happened to Pokhara, once lovely and serene Pokhara! It looked all naked and sick, with all of its tranquility and beauty totally pealed off. It was no longer the same Pokhara where I grew up. It had been turned upside down. I deeply felt the fate of Nepal being tightly wrapped up in that boy's life with all of his innocence erased with one stroke of vulgar development.

Putting aside all of my wailing emotions and painful inner thoughts about ongoing social and cultural decadence, I decided to strike a conversation with the boy in order to find out more about his life, why and how he became a drug pusher. Since I knew well that revealing my true identity (i.e., my Nepali roots) would deter him from carrying on any serious conversation with us, I decided to act out the image that he had formed of us: Western tourists. So I spoke in English. "How much hashish do you have?"

Taking a ball of hashish out of his pocket, about one-half the size of a golf ball, the boy said, "This much. You want more? I get more for you tomorrow."

"Let me see it."

He gave me the hashish ball. I pretended to be interested in purchasing it. That was the only way, I thought, I could keep the boy talking to me. I played with the hashish. I sniffed it. It perhaps weighed about an ounce and a half. It was pure hashish. I was not sure what to do about the whole situation. On the one hand, I felt like scolding him for throwing his life away at such an early age. On the other hand, I felt a profound sense of sympathy for him. A tug-of-war was brewing within me. However, I continued to proceed with my conversation.

"How much do you want for this hashish?"

"20 dollars, only 20 dollars."

"20 dollars!" I sounded surprised. "That's a lot of money."

"Not for you. You very rich, sir. My hashish A1 quality. But I sell for 15 dollars, only for you, sir. You want more? I get more tomorrow, sir!"

He was getting quite serious about selling his hashish to me. He was pushing it hard. He was already switching his gear into a bargaining position. Little did he realize that I was only taking him on a wild goose chase. Before letting him continue to make his bargain pitches, I decided to change the nature of the conversation. "What is your name?"

"My name is Dinesh. What is your name, sir?"

I hesitated for a while and replied, "My name is Jose. Now tell me, Dinesh, how old you are."

"I am 12," said Dinesh.

"You're only 12! Don't you go to school?"

"I quit school, sir!"

"When?"

"Two years ago. In the 7th class, sir," Dinesh replied. But there seemed to be no remorse in his voice about quitting school, no hard feelings. His answer was quite indifferent, nonchalant.

"Were you a good student?"

"I always pass my class, sir!" replied Dinesh beamingly. That was the first time I saw a little smile on his face, a sense of pride. But it did not last very long.

"Why did you drop out of school, then?" That was a redundant question. I knew that. Born and raised in Nepal, I pretty much knew the answer. Family poverty is the primary reason why most children drop out of school in Nepal. In my own case, I had to quit school two times because of poverty before finally completing my high school in Pokhara. Going to school in Nepal is not an easy task. Many cannot simply afford to pay monthly fees and buy necessary books and supplies. For most poor children, there are additional impediments because they cannot afford to bypass numerous time-consuming family responsibilities such as looking after younger brothers and sisters, fetching fodder for animals, cleaning animal sheds, and doing other daily chores, or simply fighting the battle of survival day after day. Although the burden of household work normally falls much heavier on girls than on boys, the latter are not always spared of such responsibilities. Being poor is not easy.

"Because," said Dinesh hesitatingly with his head bent low and eyes cast down on his worn out thongs, "because..." He did not finish his sentence. He was silent. I put my hand around him and lifted his head. His eyes were all watery. He was fighting hard to hold back his tears. It was obvious that he was hurting inside. A few yards down the foot path, I gently stroked his head to comfort him, and then prodded him to answer my question: "Dinesh, tell me why you quit school."

Wiping his tears off and blowing his nose with his fingers, Dinesh lifted his head, looked up straight in my eyes, and started talking, very softly. "Four years ago," said Dinesh, "my sister dead. Sick and died. She was typist in government office. She earn money and bring home for my father and mother. She pay my fee and books. But she dead now, so no money. No money for my fee. No money for my books so no school for me."

"What about your parents? Don't they work? Don't they have land?"

"Yes, my father work. My father is office piun (the Nepali variation of the word peon). He earn little money, not enough for family. My mother sick many days. I can't go to school."

What Dinesh was telling me about his misfortune is a common story, much too common. They are so familiar and so similar, both in terms of its nature and impact; they sound the same. Such is the lot of most poor families and their children. Under the canopy of Nepal's ongoing development, poverty wears many faces and has many tentacles to keep the poor trapped in its constrictive grip. It does not always kill the poor, at least not immediately. As development in the form of medicine keeps them alive—one might say artificially—death is often postponed (Chapter 3). Under such circumstances, poverty only makes the poor suffer, almost endlessly, thus disgracing their existence. For most poor, poverty is thus like a torture chamber situated in the midst of hell, with few exit doors. For the poor and their children, there is always something that keeps them pinned down to the ground. In Dinesh's case, it is the death of his sister, the primary bread winner of the family, that nipped the bud of his hope for a better future at a tender age.

Although often drawn out, death does ultimately claims its victim. Death in the family is quite common. One quickly gets used to it from an early age and learns to cope with death. Nothing unusual about this type of experience. In this sense, the real long-term tragedy in most poor families is not the death *per se* or the one who died; for the dead, death actually spells freedom, freedom from the burden of life and living in poverty. Rather it is the death of a bread winner in the family that deals a disastrous blow to the survivors, those who remain chained to the yoke of survival. Often most poor families have one or two bread winners. Since they rarely earn more than a bare subsistence, the family's lot is like a teeter-totter, consistently swaying between hunger and starvation. When the primary bread winner in the family passes away or falls ill for an extended period of time, the foundation of family survival collapses. It is like being caught in a landslide: there is no stopping until one hits the bottom. When the family hits the bottom, there is no telling what may happen to it. Actually, it normally finds itself entirely buried under a pile of debris, buried so deep that there are few avenues to pull out of it. Perhaps the only thing the family can do is cry out for help, often to no avail.

I could easily identify myself with Dinesh's tragic situation as his mentioning of his sister's death and his parents' plight hit me hard, personally. When my oldest brother, the principal bread winner of the family, passed away, I was very young, only 5 or 6 years old. I vividly recall the trauma my family underwent. That was a devastating blow, and we were shattered. We suffered many hardships, some beyond imagination. A few days after my brother's death, I was shooting marbles in the front yard of a neighbor's house. I overheard the neighbor's wife make a piercing comment to another neighbor woman on my situation: "See, he is a smart boy, but he is an orphan now. I don't know what is going to happen to him. I feel bad about his situation." I have never forgotten that comment. It is still fresh in my memory as if it was uttered just yesterday.

Every time I think of that woman's comment, I realize what a poignant social observation that was about the nature of Nepal's poor and their poverty and about their children's future. It captured the whole panorama of poverty that infests countless lives in Nepal. The whole social reality of the life the poor have to live, day in and day out, was painted in one simple stroke. When that woman referred to me as an orphan, she was not saying it in a conventional sense. After all, my parents had not died; they were still alive. What she meant was that I was an economic orphan because my oldest brother, on whom the family relied, had died. He was only 28 at the time of his death. As I became disconnected from my economic support base, I was deprived of the potential opportunity to build my future. In the aftermath of his death, I had to take on a much greater level of family responsibility at home although I was barely 10. Like it or not, children have to mature fast, often at a premature age, for the sake of both family and personal survival. Such are the life chances for children born in poverty.

Poverty is a vicious chain, an intergenerational chain. I feel fortunate to have gotten a break, thanks to the help of a Peace Corps friend (see Chapter 3). In the meantime, I am fully aware that very few get such breaks to pry themselves free from the entrapment of poverty. Yet the game of blaming the victim, the poor, goes on.

I was not done with Dinesh yet. I continued my conversation with him while holding his hashish in my hand. "So you quit school after your sister died. I suppose you make some money by selling hashish to tourists and give that money to your parents. Right?"

"Yes, yes...," said Dinesh. But he seemed a little bit fidgety. Either he was bored with my questions or simply wanted to cut the deal and move on to the next pasture. Once again, he asked, "You want to buy hash? I go now." But this time he did not address me as "sir," a sign that he was probably losing his patience with me as a customer. Sensing his fidgetiness, I once again put my arm around him to calm him down. However, I skirted around his question instead of answering it: "What is the rush, Dinesh? Stay for a while," I said in a soft voice. "Before you go, let me ask you a few more questions. How much do you make in one day by selling hashish?"

Before he had a chance to answer my question we reached the lake. The conversation was temporarily halted. We all sat under a tree, in a shady area, in order to avoid the sun. Keeping up with the Nepali tradition, I ordered tea from a small restaurant right across from where we were sitting. No matter how hot the temperature is, Nepali people rarely shy away from a glass of hot tea which is a very common social drink. A couple of men sitting at the restaurant were teasing Dinesh in a joking way. Obviously, they knew him and his operation. In Nepali, they were saying, "Looks like you caught a big fish. Today must be your lucky day. Don't forget to throw a feast for all of us later on."

Dinesh offered no response to their comment, but did flash a big smile on his face. Sitting cross-legged on the grass and sipping hot tea, I asked Dinesh again to tell me how much he made in a day.

"Sometimes 20 rupees, sometimes 30 rupees, sometimes 50 rupees, sometimes nothing."

"How much money do you give to your parents?"

"Maybe, half."

"What do you do with the remaining half?"

"Spend. Food... cigarette."

"Do you like selling hashish?"

At first, Dinesh hesitated and then said, "Yes, it give me good money." Then, he added, "Tourists love hashish. They are crazy!"

"Do you love hashish?"

"I only sell hashish. I no smoke it, only cigarette." I was not surprised that he did not use hashish. As mentioned earlier, it was very rarely used by young people. In fact, even cigarette-smoking was not common among teenagers. Most children used to be told, repeatedly, by their parents that if they smoked (including cigarette) at a young age, their intestines would rot. Although cigarette (or tobacco) smoking is widespread among adults, such a ghastly portrayal of the adverse effect of smoking, I am sure, scared young children and kept them from smoking until they passed their teenage phase. This scare tactic seems to be breaking down, however, among teenagers as cigarette-smoking has become popular and cool.

"Are you going to go back to school in the future?"

"You take me America. Then I go to school and study hard." It was an unexpectedly witty answer; it threw me off balance. I clearly sensed that what he said was not a joking remark; he was actually serious. I am sure he was aware that Westerners had taken some Nepali children back to their countries either as adoptees or for study. Plus there are many Nepali youths who, as indicated in Chapter 3, dream about going to America as I did. If Nepal once evoked a mystifying image of the Eastern Shangrila for the American hippies, America exists in the geographical imagination of Nepali youths as the Western Shangrila embroidered in material glitter. Sometimes, inadvertently, Westerners give these youths a false hope that they might be able to help them achieve their Western Shangrila dream. Given this reality, I wanted to make sure that he did not get any such false impression from me just to be disappointed later on. So it was at that point that I decided to reveal my true Nepali identity. I spoke in Nepali and told him who I actually was.

Not surprisingly, Dinesh was shocked to find out that I was Nepali, and from Pokhara. His mouth almost fell open. He looked nervous and wanted to run away from me, but could not because I still had his hashish. I am sure he did not want to part with it, something that was his precious source of income. He asked me to return his hashish, which I did. Once he got his hashish back, he tried quickly to run away from me. I held his arm and asked him to stay. I said it firmly but gently so that he would not feel intimidated or scared. He sat down and we had another round of tea.

While sipping tea, I asked him, this time in Nepali, how he got involved in selling drugs. Dinesh spoke very quietly and said it happened accidently. He had no idea about selling drugs; nor did he ever think about doing it. He repeated that after his sister died, he quit school and started hanging around the lake. Since he lived in Baidam, a village situated only a few minutes' walk from the lake, it was quite easy for him to hang around the lake. Sometimes, he would do temporary jobs, for example, washing dishes in local restaurants if they needed extra help. Otherwise, he would just waste time doing nothing productive. That is how he used to pass his long and tedious days, sometimes catching flies, literally. Time seems infinite and treacherous when one has nothing productive to do; it is so difficult to pass.

Dinesh said he had seen many tourists around the lake, frequently smoking marijuana and hashish and getting stoned. That was nothing new. Dinesh also talked about some of them bathing in the lake naked and kissing and hugging in public, something Nepalis found very embarrassing and distasteful. In fact, local people would feel so embarrassed about their open sexual displays that they would simply turn their heads and walk away from the scene.

One day Dinesh was skipping pebbles in the lake to pass boredom. There was, he said, a tourist walking toward him, quite intoxicated. That tourist asked Dinesh if he had any marijuana to sell. When Dinesh gave him a negative answer, the tourist handed him a 10 rupees bill and asked him to bring some marijuana. At first, Dinesh did not know what to do, whether to get him marijuana or not. He had never sold marijuana; nor had he even contemplated such an option. But the money looked too tempting to pass it up; after all he could buy some food for his family with that money. Unlike nowadays, one could buy two days' ration with 10 rupees in those days. Dinesh, finally, made up his mind to keep the money and bring the tourist some marijuana. He rationalized that he was not cheating anybody to make that money. Leaving the tourist by the lake, he went looking for some marijuana plants. He had a good idea as to where he could find them. He broke off a few small branches of a marijuana plant and brought them back to the tourist. Upon his return, he found the tourist fast asleep. Instead of waking him up, Dinesh set the branches beside him and left. He went looking for the tourist the following day. Marijuana branches were gone and so was the tourist. Dinesh never saw him again.

That was his initiation into the emerging world of pot culture. With his appetite thus whetted, he had suddenly come to discover a path to making money, if not a whole lot, at least some money—by supplying hippie tourists with marijuana and hashish. He had found something to do in the short run, no matter how detrimental that path might prove to be in the long run. In essence, the opportunity to make money relatively easily by selling hippies such an abundant product like marijuana was too powerful a temptation for a poor and cash-starved boy like Dinesh to forgo. The expansion of the pot culture had created a market for marijuana which previously had only negligible commercial value.

The pot culture had reached Pokhara from its earliest hearth—Kathmandu's Freak Street. In his own way, Dinesh had fallen victim to this culture whether he realized it or not. To be sure, nobody could dispute Dinesh's vendor spirit, his ability to hawk pot to Western consumers and make some money to supplement his family income. No doubt, he was working as hard as he could. Selling drugs is work just like prostitution is work. Anything that one does to make a living is work, whether personally beneficial or detrimental in the long run, whether one approves it or not. So what Dinesh was doing was certainly admirable as he was making money the old fashioned way: earn it. Even more importantly, he was doing it to keep his family afloat. So how could one possibly see moral trepidation in his entrepreneurial spirit? Yet two crucial questions arise: (1) was he helping himself in terms of building a good future? (2) could he, as a young boy enmeshed in poverty, have pursued a better path, especially in a society like Nepal where economic opportunities are very limited? Then there is the question concerning the possibility of Dinesh moving through the pot culture's life cycle, namely graduating from its selling phase to its consumption phase when the seller becomes a consumer and hence self-destructive.

Few can answer the first question with any degree of certainty. However, the likelihood that, as a drug boy, Dinesh will be able to pull himself and his family out of poverty is not that great. Unlike in the West, there is not a whole lot of money that one can make in the drug business unless one manages to get plugged into the international drug traffic network. Dinesh said there was not a whole lot of options he could pursue except to follow Western tourists and try to sell them pot. That was his daily routine and he had gotten quite accustomed to it. Occasionally, he got together with his village friends, those with whom he used to go to school. The more we talked about his activity, the more he seemed to miss school. Yet he did not think he was ever going back to school. Not sure if he would ever quit selling drugs unless he could no longer find customers to buy them, he was resigned to his current fate. Additionally, he deeply felt the need and responsibility to support his parents. He was very concerned about his mother's health.

After a long talk, my friend and I parted Dinesh's company, with lots of questions and thoughts swirling in my mind. I did not offer any words of wisdom, any advice to Dinesh. Besides, I was not sure if my advice would have made any difference. I deeply felt that Dinesh had no long-term future in his drug selling activity. He was traveling down a damned path, leading him nowhere. Yet I could not tell him to quit it. How could I? How could I tell a poor boy to deprive himself of the only opportunity he had to make some money? That was his only income source, income to buy some food for his family, income to buy medicine for his ill mother, income to buy a few items for himself. How cruel!

While walking away from him, my heart felt heavy. I turned back to take one last glance at Dinesh. I caught him gazing at me almost motionless. He waved at me and I waved back. That was the first and last time I saw Dinesh, some 16 years ago. Our paths have not crossed since. I wonder what he is up to these days, whether he is still selling drugs to tourists or has himself become a drug addict. Perhaps, he got married and had children. I wonder if his children are having a little better life than he himself had as a young boy. While I fear that he might have suffered a terrible fate that most poor do, I maintain a glimmer of hope that his lot has improved.

CONCLUSIONS: MYTHS VS. REALITY

Dinesh is not just a young boy. He is a product of Nepal's social history and its spreading pot culture. As a product of social history living in poverty, he provides a peep hole through which to view how social forces, including education, operate and impact different segments of society. It is precisely through this hole that the second question posed above can be analyzed: could Dinesh have pursued a better alternative?

Admittedly, the above question is difficult to answer. Perhaps, it has no clear answer, especially given the fact that there are few gainful alternatives to which poor, undereducated Nepali youths can resort. Yet this is an important question because it sheds light on how one after another generation is lost to poverty or left teetering at the margin of both society and life. In providing a short discourse on this question, it is important to separate myths from reality, especially about education as a channel to developing personal human capital, so one can escape from poverty.

As suggested earlier, once trapped in poverty, there are few roads out of it. What is so inherently debilitating about poverty is that it invariably ends up being an intergenerational problem in that every succeeding generation inherits it from the preceding generation. With every succeeding generation, it becomes harder and harder to break the link of poverty's intergenerational chain. There is a mythical notion that almost anybody can break this link through hard work. It is true that few can tackle poverty without hard work, but hard work alone does not guarantee success. If it did, so many poor people, who work very hard day in and day out to make a living, would not be living in poverty. Accompanying this mythical notion is yet another myth that education is the passport out of poverty.

Education does help, but what often goes untold is that education itself has historically been biased along both class and caste lines as it has been the preserves of the high caste and well-to-do members of Nepal. The flip side of this fact is that the poor have been deprived of education. Rarely endowed with the opportunity to be educated, the poor usually couldn't even read or write. This class bias in education has not changed much over the years, for most poor children continue to encounter many barriers in their pursuit of education. Despite a few examples of educational success attained by students from poor families, it is no exaggeration that they are born with a built-in handicap in that most of their parents are uneducated. That is to say, in addition to many societal impediments, they are born into a family environment which is not always conducive to establishing a good educational foundation at their early age. Parents are the first teachers for most children. But given the parents' lack of formal education, children are denied the first opportunity to start on good footings. As a result, future educational aspirations are stunted. Furthermore, poor children are much more heavily loaded with domestic chores than their counterparts from well-to-do families. This means they have less time available to pay attention to their education. They often suffer from hunger and consequently poor physical condition. A hungry belly is rarely conducive to children's sound physical and cognitive development. It also has a tendency to obstruct one's concentration and stable life. Encumbered by one hurdle after another, every step of the way, from childhood to maturity, poor children are, in short, severely disadvantaged during their early formative years when good educational habits and foundation are firmly grounded. Education is, pure and simple, like constructing a house: without a solid foundation, a strong house can't be built. Since not too many poor historically had the opportunity to attain anything more than a few years of elementary education, they could not establish a solid educational foundation on which to build their children's educational future and legacy. So no education, no good jobs, and without a good job few can improve their lot and educate their children. It is a catch-22.

Especially deadly in this sociohistorical drama of education has been the combination of low class and low caste, a situation in which poor children are almost predestined to be doomed. During the time of Rana aristocracy, education was rarely accessible to the general public. For instance, the first high school established in Nepal was the Durbar High School (for a brief history of education in Nepal, see Sharma, 1990). Since the school was established primarily for palace children, it was given the name Durbar (palace). If people outside the Rana circle wanted to educate their children, they had to often send them to India—something that no poor could afford to do. Such a class bias in education has taken on a new dimension in recent years and has actually intensified in a very sinister manner.

In spite of persistent class and caste biases, some attempts were made during the 1960s to make education more accessible, and it was certainly more equal than today. While family-related barriers were still common, some of the sociohistorical impediments were beginning to come down—although very slowly, I might add. Unlike before, most schools operated more or less at the same level in that they were all public schools which admitted students regardless of their class or caste background. Even though the quality of instruction varied from one school to another—urban schools generally fared much better than rural schools—it was not by design. The concept of private schools was almost unknown: in all of Nepal there were only two private schools where only the rich could afford to send their children. They were St. Xavier's School and St. Mary's School, both English medium schools run by Western Christian missionaries. As indicated in Chapter 3, these two schools certainly played a leading role in transforming both the educational perception and process. It is true that these two missionary schools did open the educational door to non-Rana elites as long as they could afford the cost of their children's education. I believe they did offer a token number of scholarships for poor children, but that was no educational reprieve for the poor. As these two missionary schools popularized Western education, especially English as an instructional medium, they unfortunately sharpened both the class bias and class process in education, actually taking it to a new height. A good education was no longer good enough; it had to be English-based education, which meant sending children overseas if they could not be enrolled in these missionary schools within Nepal. Outside the immediate domain of these two missionary schools, schooling within Nepal generally remained relatively uniform and confined to public schools until the early 1970s.

Since the early 1970s, however, the foundation of public education has rapidly cracked. The quality of public education has reached a point where its real value is questionable. Viewed as second-rate, public schools are largely populated by children from relatively poor families who cannot afford the cost of private schooling. The accelerating demise of Nepal's public schools is mostly attributed to two major factors: disciplinary disintegration and proliferation of private schools. There has been a remarkable disciplinary breakdown among students and their respect for teachers, a process that started in the 1970s and intensified in the 1980s and early 1990s. In the past, next to parents, teachers garnered the most respect. Although some teachers were inclined to abuse their power and authority, subjecting students to corporal punishments, they invariably occupied a position of reverence. Teachers exercised full control of classrooms without any fear of reprisals from disgruntled students. That is no longer the case. These days teachers are routinely threatened and intimidated by students, in some cases even roughed up. Teachers are barely figure heads in the classroom. There is a great deal of gangster mentality pervading these schools. In fact, the gangster mentality has widely spread to private schools as well, where children from high class and powerful families openly exhibit obnoxious behaviors toward their teachers as well as peers from less powerful or well-to-do families.

The second factor in the downfall of public schools is the mushrooming of private schools. Since private schools have become extremely fashionable among the "upwardly mobile" families, they are in tremendous demand. And running such schools has emerged as a very profitable business enterprise. There are several interrelated reasons for the rapid growth in the demand and supply of private schools in Nepal. In other words, the 1970s witnessed an oppositional trend in educational demand and supply. At the same time English-based education was rapidly growing in demand, the Nepali government adopted a pseudo-nationalistic—some might call it Nepali-centric—education policy whereby public schools deemphasized English. Even scientific words and terms were translated into sanskritized Nepali, some of which sounded more foreign than English. Previously, English was introduced at the elementary school level, starting in the first or second grade. But now, following the new policy, it was not introduced until the sixth grade. Perhaps, there was nothing wrong with the policy itself, but what was so conspicuously contradictory about this policy change was that the very ruling elites who propounded it were not sending their children to public schools, thus effectively relegating the public schools and Nepali-based education to second-class status. The elites in general preferred English-based education for their own children, sending them overseas or to English medium schools in different parts of India such as Darjeeling and Dehradun. The whole policy exhibited the gruesome hypocrisy of the Nepali elites.

In addition to the ruling elites, other upwardly mobile families were demanding English-based education for their children because it was considered to be the language of *bikas* and hence superior. As such, it commanded a much higher level of respect than Nepali-based education offered in public schools. Moreover, English education was perceived as essential for joining the corps of *bikas*-minded elites. Those who could afford to send their children overseas for English education did so. But there existed a large local demand for such education among those families who were upwardly mobile and modern-minded but could not afford to send their children overseas for English education. In order to meet this rapidly growing void between demand and supply, many got involved in the private school business, and the growing need for private school teachers was largely met by an influx of India-born Nepalis from

Darjeeling, a northeastern part of India, where there is a large enclave of people of Nepali origin. They are not only fluent in Nepali—Darjeeling has for long been a leading center of Nepali literature—but also generally better educated and have a much greater command of English than locally educated Nepalis.

The overall outcome of this bifurcated educational system is that it has reinforced the previously existing social class division between the elites and ordinary citizens, between the rich and poor. Moreover, this two-tier system elevated private schools to a higher status while denigrating public schools to a level that is almost dysfunctional. As a result, two distinct educational standards have been established: higher standard private schooling for the rich and low quality public schooling for the poor. What this means is that a good private school is beyond the reach of perhaps 90-95 percent of the Nepali households. It is accessible only to those who can either afford it or hold high positions of power in the government. Incidentally, the question of affordability is not just a matter of being able to pay what can be considered very high tuition fees by Nepali standards. It is mostly a matter of being able to dole out at the time of admission thousands of rupees in donation to the school, easily 50,000 or higher, in some cases even more than 100,000, a sum of money very few Nepali households can afford. The greater the level of perceived prestige of the school, the higher the sum of initial donation, and the amount keeps increasing every year. Most cannot even imagine such a huge amount of money. Admission thus ends up becoming a donation bidding process or a matter of political clout as it is invariably based on one's financial position and power connection rather than academic ability. So those who are unable to participate in such a bidding process settle for less than prestigious private schools because of their higher status value (although many of them are only mediocre and hardly any better than public schools). They are all caught up in what can be described as a "keeping-up-with-the-Joneses" syndrome.

Both the culture and economics of education are adversarial to the poor and to the overall national interest. For the poor in general, the whole notion of education has turned out to be one gigantic delusion. It is a dream that has historically been deferred for the poor as few have been able to realize it. When the poor try to get an education, they can only afford to go to public schools. This means they receive an inferior quality education, a situation which rarely gives them an edge over those educated in private schools and those already plugged into a network of elite nepotism. The poor are hence caught in a no-win situation.

Given such a gloomy educational scenario, one can't help but wonder whether Dinesh—and many other young boys in the same predicament as Dinesh—could have pursued a better option, one that was more rewarding and productive, one that would have elevated him to the platform of progress.

To conclude, the class disparity in education has become so much greater and so much more wicked than before that there is little hope for the poor to close this gap and catch up with the rich. Consequently, there is little hope for somebody like Dinesh to escape from the vicious prison of poverty. Deprived of any sound educational opportunities and gainful employment, poor children are increasingly forced into a situation, in which their daily struggle for survival overrides virtually any other concerns in life and in society. In this daily struggle for survival, poor children have few choices but to do whatever they can to earn a living: be it selling drugs or prostituting themselves. Such is the saga of Nepal's social forces and educational system that leaves countless Dineshes in a ditch, in a state of permanent disadvantage and deprivation. But it is the stories like this that have unfortunately become the integral pieces of Nepal's development collage.

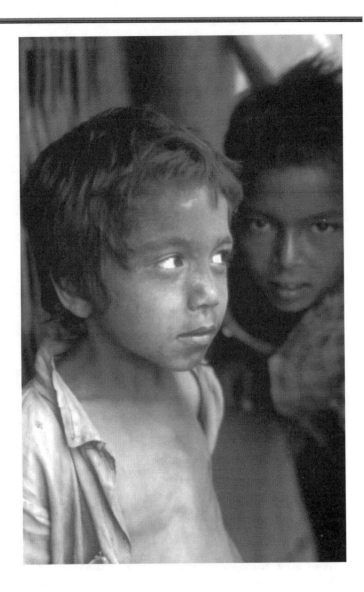

Young boys hanging around

Young girls doing household chores

7

WHERE HAS
ALL THE FURY GONE?

If there is no struggle there is no progress. Those who profess to favor freedom and yet depreciate agitation are men who want crops without plowing up the ground, they want rain without thunder and lightning. They want the ocean without the awful roar of its many waters. This struggle may be a moral one, or it may be a physical one, and it may be both moral and physical, but it must be a struggle. Power concedes nothing without a demand. It never did and it never will. Find out just what any people will quietly submit to and you have found out the exact measure of injustice and wrong which will be imposed upon them, and these will continue till they are resisted with either words or blows, or both. The limits of tyrants are prescribed by the endurance of those whom they oppress... If we ever get free from all the oppressions and wrongs heaped upon us, we must pay for their removal. We must do this by labor, by suffering, by sacrifice, and, if needs be, by our lives and the lives of others.

— Frederick Douglas, 1857
(Foner, 1950:437)

Contemporary development is a war, a class war, pitting the rich against the poor, the powerful against the powerless, and human beings against nature. Like every war, it has produced its own victors and victims. While its bounty has greatly enriched a few coffers, its hardships have befallen many.

This war rages on every day, yet it has no battlefield. It has no physical weapons. It is all silent, yet it poses a virulent threat to the dignified survival of Nepal's poor and downtrodden. There is injustice and deprivation everywhere, yet there is no visible outrage to awaken the masses to action. Anger runs deep, yet there is no social eruption; the arteries are too dry to pump any blood into the veins of those who are angry. Everything seems muted. There is utter silence. And there is something eery about this silent war.

The poor are being increasingly encircled in this silent war.

THE CHANGING NATURE OF CLASS RELATIONS

I recently received a letter from a very highly educated member of the Nepali elite class, somebody I have known for a long time. He is a development advocate, who works for and with Western aid agencies on a contract basis. He is doing very well, all thanks to development, of course.

In his letter, he identified population growth as a major problem facing Nepal today. No surprise here because everybody thinks that way. What attracted my attention about his letter is the way he articulated his views on poverty and democracy and why he thought the poor were the national menace. Although his views are characteristically symptomatic of the general elite thinking on population and the poor, I had never heard any member of the Nepali elite class contextualize it quite in that manner. When I read his letter, I could vividly imagine Thomas Malthus suddenly coming alive from his British grave and performing a tango with his mind. There was a striking resemblance between his letter and Malthus' blame-the-poor social theory of population. Here are some of the key points from the letter that I have translated and summarized:

1. The rich and educated are making a conscious decision to have fewer children by adopting family planning whereas the poor recklessly breed like pigs.

2. This situation does not bode well for nascent democracy in Nepal. Since democracy means one person one vote, the poor will end up having more votes and hence holding the decision-making power because of their sheer number. (One assumption of his logic seems to be that the poor are uneducated and irrational; they are not capable of making correct decisions so why give them a voice and allow them to vote? Or perhaps his thinking is a clear reflection of his class analysis of democracy

that it may not serve the elite interest, for the poor may actually grab the leverage of power through elections. Quite a curious notion of democracy or one might say what a supreme example of elite chauvinism or paranoia!).

3. The poor are landless, destroy forests, and encroach on forest lands.

4. They occupy open streets, create filth all over, and let their children play in the streets without any supervision. If something happens to their children, they quickly blame the others and hurl insults at them.

5. What is more, political leaders and power brokers make impossible promises to these "careless lazy masses" (he wrote this phrase in English) in terms of various benefits for the poor if they are elected.

6. Whatever resources the government has, the poor want to utilize them for their benefits. They grab so many of the limited resources that they threaten the rich. On top of that they have to be subsidized.

Given all these factors, there is little incentive for the poor to have fewer children, he surmised. There is no respect for performance and ability, he complained bitterly. The notion of rewarding people according to their ability and performance remains foreign to Nepal, he claimed. Then he asked: why should the government take care of the poor lazy masses? When he talked about ability and performance, he was explicitly referring to the hollow notion of meritocracy, meaning the elites are always more meritorious than the poor, and hence they deserve more. It is obvious that he does not think the poor do have any ability or work hard to earn their living or deserve any merit.

I don't know whether he is so blind or so ideologically biased that he can't see the reality of the poor being shafted from every angle. He must have a different measure of merit and performance. Given his profession, his criteria of hard work is perhaps based on paper work, i.e., churning out development project feasibility studies and project evaluation reports for the Western agencies financing these projects, reports which are very heavy in word counts but light in contents. Since development consultants like him are given contracts by their Western patrons to prepare these reports, they do a whitewash job, routinely providing a rationale for foreign aid projects, basically saying what foreign agencies want them to say, so they can continue to receive such contracts.

In his heart he knows—and almost everybody within the development establishment knows whether they are willing to admit or not—consultants like him are subordinate players with little power or say. They are simply high-class lackeys to Western agencies and agents. He also knows that not even 2 percent of the consultants do any hard work. Their only merit is their education, not their work or work ethics. They are the biggest parasites of society, reaping the benefits of others' blood and sweat. They mostly spend their time in meeting rooms, behind their fancy desks, and at parties in five star hotels, totally drowned in foreign booze and cigarettes. Who said the truth matters and the reality cannot be refracted like a stick plunged in a clear glass of water?

What I also found appalling about the letter is his point about the utilization of limited development resources. Not only does he entirely misrepresent the truth about the use and abuse of development resources, including foreign monies, but he absolves the rich of their naked irresponsibility. It is agonizing to see a highly educated individual make such a baseless accusation about the poor. Virtually everybody, who lives and works in Nepal, knows that most resources are sucked up by the ruling elites—all at the expense of the poor. This is a fact that most foreign agencies have openly acknowledged time and again.

Furthermore, it is not the poor who are responsible for deforestation and other natural resource depletion as he charged in his letter. Deforestation of commercially valuable trees is the handiwork of commercial loggers, who operate both legally and illegally (Shrestha and Conway, 1996). It is the elites and wealthy who are responsible for reckless, excessive resource use and abuse. It is no overstatement that on average they probably use at least 10-15 times more forest and other resources—and in a much more destructive fashion—than the poor.

Consider, for example, the consumption of tremendous amounts of timber and bricks when the rich build fancy bungalows and accumulate a wide array of furniture items. Their consumption of timber products is many times greater than the total consumption by the poor. As the number of palatial buildings continues to grow at a fairly rapid rate, the demand for timber soars. Forests are randomly cleared to produce timber for the rich. Not only are the forest resources used, but they are completely destroyed without making any provision for reforestation. When the poor use forest resources, they essentially collect firewood and extract whatever they need without ever completely taking the life away from the trees and forests. Their use is based strictly on their survival needs rather than frivolous and ostentatious activities.

Likewise, in the process of brick production, some of the most productive lands in the Kathmandu valley have been, and continue to be, totally stripped, not to mention the lands that are removed from agricultural use to build fancy houses and motorable roads to connect them with main roads and market centers, all for the convenience and benefits of the elites (and Westerners). Many rich people erect not just one house, but several houses to be rented to foreigners. These houses are invariably surrounded by flower gardens rather than vegetable plots. Every piece of land used for flower gardening is a piece of land taken away from the production of basic necessities, e.g., vegetables. So no matter how one cuts it, the rich are the primary culprits of natural resource depletion, be it forests or farm lands or something else. Let me shed, but not to be gross, some light on a simple but important amenity of modern life that the rich savor. I am speaking of flush toilets. Almost every one of these houses has three or four such toilets. What's the big deal about it? One may ask. Oh, it is a big deal, mainly in Kathmandu where there is a severe shortage of water. Water is one of the most basic resources in every respect. Every time they flush one of those toilets, they drain some three gallons of water, compared to one quart of water an average poor person uses when s/he goes to the latrine. While the public is suffering from the severe shortage of water, the rich waste 12 times as much water. And what about all the toilet paper? That is also a form of resource that the rich waste, but not the poor, who clean themselves with water—again that one quart of water plus another half a quart to clean the hands.

When the poor construct their dwellings, they use small plots, just a few hundred square feet, and use the remaining lands for growing vegetables. Regarding house construction materials, they mostly use forest by-products such as tree branches and thatch in a non-depletable fashion. They possess virtually no furniture made of felled trees. Brick and cement use is also minimal.

There are many other areas of production and consumption that can be discussed, in which there are tremendous disparities between the rich and poor. One such area is beer production and consumption. Beer production has experienced phenomenal growth over the past 20 years, both in terms of volume and the number of breweries, all affiliated with foreign companies. Production of local beer, commonly known as *jand* or *chhang,* has always been quite popular in Nepal, but nothing like what is occurring in the arena of commercial beer. *Chhang* did not have the mass appeal that commercial beer has because the latter is associated with modernization or Western tastes. Drinking beer is a status symbol while *chhang* is now a low-class beverage. Since *chhang* production was localized and limited in volume, the amount of food grains used to produce it was also limited. In other words, not much grain was siphoned away from its direct consumption. It did not have any noxious pollution effect because virtually all of its by-products were either fed to animals or composted to produce manure. On the other hand, commercial beer production, which is mostly targeted to the tourists and the domestic rich, has adverse effects. In addition to contributing to environmental pollution, the multi-fold growth of the beer industry has led to increased demands for certain food grains, thus reducing their public availability for direction consumption. As a result, their prices have gone up, thus squeezing the poor even harder. Simply put, the rich are consuming almost twice as much grains as the poor, first in the form of solid grains and then in the form of beer. This does not even take into account the fact their overall food consumption is much higher than not only that of the poor, but also what they need to sustain their physical health. It is, therefore, no coincidence that there is a direct correlation between being rich and being fat and overweight while the poor suffer from malnutrition and hunger.

Yet the rich have the audacity to blame the poor for excessive resource consumption and depletion. How obscene! They are the ultimate cause of forest depletion, but blame the poor. They are the ones who produce most of the non-biodegradable waste, but blame the poor. The rich blame the poor for virtually everything while they are the primary roots of most of the social ills facing the nation, from price inflation to resource depletion which hurt the poor most. Such is the nature of the vile attitude the rich have developed toward the poor.

In other words, not only do the rich no longer share any of the burden of poverty that is ravaging the poor masses, but they are now openly hostile toward the poor. Their hostility is directly related to the breakdown of the patron-client relations that were mutually dependent, although unequal. As far as the rich are concerned, the poor are no longer an integral part of their daily life and existence, something that used to be so common. The symbiotic relationship that existed between the rich and poor is gone, particularly in the urban context, where the rich have few reasons to directly interact with the poor. For example, when the rich need food these days, they can get it from the market; they don't have to depend on the poor to till their lands to produce foods. If they need clothes or shoes or anything else, they no longer rely on the traditional craftsmen and occupational groups such as the Kamis (iron-smiths), Sarkis (leather-workers), and Damais (tailors). There are plenty of imported, ready-made products available in the market. If they want to have entertainment, there are plenty of video stores, Western television shows, and movie theaters.

Based on the tone and nature of their reaction, the rich now see the poor as both the cases of personal failures (basket cases) and class enemy. In short, the class relations in Nepal have undergone a fundamental metamorphosis, from being unequal but interdependent to those of open hostility toward the poor. It matters little that the poor are the ones who are directly and indirectly shouldering the cost of the self-indulgent life-styles and decadent behaviors of the rich. The poor are the ones who are paying the price of development while the rich reap its benefits.

No, being poor has never been pleasant. But now it is worse, much worse, as they are not only having to fight the battle of daily survival, but also face outright humiliation and indignity. They are being treated like a bunch of felons whose only crime is being poor, and even that mostly due to antagonistic social forces. The poor are, to repeat, being closed in from all directions, yet there is no visible outrage.

Where has all the fury gone?

Is the age of revolution over? Or has it simply taken a back seat to greed and apathy, a sense of resignation and dejection? Or is it just a temporary lull, a short hiatus, before the political cyclone sweeps across the national landscape with a massive force?

Basically, the question, once again, is: what can be done about the whole situation? One common answer that the social history of different countries reveals appears to be a social revolution. With the premise that a revolution may indeed be inevitable in Nepal despite its seemingly gloomy prospects, let me first provide a quick glimpse of the historical trend with respect to its outcomes.

REVOLUTIONARY FORCES AND COUNTER-FORCES

"There are, all around us, signs of social, cultural, and moral disintegration," writes Barrington Moore (1987:124) in his book, *Authority and Inequality under Capitalism and Socialism*. "They exist in both the capitalist and socialist camps... There is no reason to expect social, cultural, and moral decay to be self-limiting or self-reversing. Death and collapse may be an equally likely outcome." Then he concludes on a somber note: "If humanity is to work its way out of its current plight— and I am far from sure that it can—there will have to be leaders at all levels who can turn their backs on political glamour and work hard for feasible goals rather than glamorous ones. All this is quite unexciting and in fact totally uninspiring. For that very reason it may be exactly what we need."

This is a very gloomy assessment, but a very real and poignant one. Humanity seems to be fated to suffer. Referring to both the capitalist (United States) and communist (former Soviet Union and China) regimes, Moore (1987:13) continues, "With the apparent failure of their secular solutions to political and economic misery, and the alleged moral and intellectual failures of modern science, there has been a return to religion. Despite some contrary trends there has been a marked growth of chauvinist fundamentalism in many parts of the world. It is as obvious in the United States as in Islamic countries or India."

Moore's overall argument implies that it is not the political system—be it capitalism or socialism—that offers solutions to human misery and injustice in society. If we are to tackle human misery and injustice forthrightly, what is needed is the leadership rooted in decency, fairness, and selflessness, one with a simple and sustainable development agenda instead of grandiose and glamorous plans which are neither feasible nor desirable for national needs. So the question of leadership is critical. The leadership must offer a genuine alternative to the current mode of development, one that is not only indigenous, but also capable of fundamentally challenging the national infatuation with what E.J. Mishan (1970:4) calls growthmania—a situation in which the ruling motto is that the faster the economic growth the better it is. As Mishan continues, men have, for much too long, become the victims of their faith in mechanistic development. Virtually every politician, planner, policymaker, and even an ordinary citizen is "impatient to acquire a reputation for economic sagacity and no-nonsense realism is busy shouting giddy-up in several of two-score different ways." Nepal is no exception to this giddy-up mentality. Following Nehru's line of argument, the late king Mahendra of Nepal declared that Nepal has to achieve in 20 years what Europe did in 200 years.

Furthermore, if a society fails to rectify its growing oppressive inequalities and injustices, sooner or later it will be rife with political turmoil, most likely accompanied by violence. No justice, no peace. Mishan argues that revolutions from below break out not when material circumstances are oppressive but when they are improving and hope of a better life is in the air. So long as toil and hardships were the most integral part of the mass of humanity over countless centuries and so long as economic activity was viewed as a daily struggle against the niggardliness of nature, when human disparities were limited, people were resigned to eke out a living by their blood and sweat untroubled by the mouth-watering visions of plenty. But the situation has changed.

As previously stated, the images of economic growth and development heighten expectations of a better life, and unmet expectations are a simmering source of disappointments with their fuse connected to flickering sparks waiting to ignite a prairie fire. When people find themselves going hungry while the plates on the other side of the table are overflowing with foods, a sense of injustice will deepen. Consequently, the deprived will perceive (or realize) that while their basic survival rights are threatened, the elites' material pie continues to get bigger. Simply put, rising expectations when unmet and combined with the deprivation of basic survival rights in the face of grotesque inequalities and injustices could plow a fertile ground to breed what Moore calls "chauvinist fundamentalism" and "political glamour" (i.e., politically glamorous revolutions), often transfused with violent acts.

One example of chauvinist fundamentalism is the Khomeini-led revolution in Iran which overthrew the Shah (Pahlevi) regime in the late 1970s. This Iranian case offers a highly illuminating example of how diverse forces converge to ignite a revolution as it attracted not only Islamic fundamentalists but also the working class, the poor, the educated, the petty bourgeoisie, and even communists, all factions coming together against the common enemy: the Shah. On the one hand, the Shah's modernization attempts and close Western ties symbolized a

growing erosion of fundamental Islamic values and hence moral decadence. On the other hand, his failures to redistribute the country's
massive wealth, along with political oppression, signified deepening
inequality and injustice in a country where the expectations were rising
high in the wake of oil boom. For many, the hopes of material advancement were dashed. The outcome: massive political discontent and a
fundamentalist revolution.

Other examples include the Philippines and Nicaragua. Although the
overthrow of the Marcos regime in the Philippines and the Somoza
regime in Nicaragua was largely politically-driven, these cases also offer
powerful examples of how diverse forces come together to ignite a
political fire against a common enemy when a system of injustice
reaches a point where it becomes unbearable. In Nepal too a similar
revolution occurred in 1990 when the students, the workers, the activists
from different political parties, and even some peasants joined forces to
oppose the existing Panchayat system that functioned under the tutelage
of the king's absolute rule. The revolution was successful in terms of
overthrowing the Panchayat system and reducing the king's absolute
power to constitutional monarchy, at least on paper.

Unfortunately, success of any revolution cannot be judged solely on
its ability to bring down a regime and handing over the power to the
revolutionaries. Nor is it always the change of ruling hands or the
perfunctory transfer of power that defines its success. Its success should
be judged on the ground of what the new rulers or revolutionaries
achieve afterwards and how the masses fare under their rule, along with
those who served at the front line as well as the back line: the rock-
throwers, the flag-carriers, the political graffiti artists, the poster-
painters, the silent marchers and distant supporters, the barricade-
builders and tire-burners, those who suffered the beatings and shed their
blood, those who sacrificed their limbs and gave their lives, those who
refused to budge when the police ordered them to move.

While revolutions have throughout history engendered much political
glamour and high hopes, their socioeconomic outcome has not always
been too glamorous. Once again, Nepal is no exception. The so-called
revolutionary leaders of the 1990 revolution were not fighting with any
resolve to uplift the masses; they were fighting for the spoils of power.
They were not true revolutionaries; they were merely a different faction
of the same class that had, for too long, been left out of power, and
hence denied an opportunity to dip their long arms into the spoils of

power. That is why, the 1990 revolution has simply turned out to be a factional feud within the same class. So, in this respect, it was no revolution; it was rather a periodic blood-letting ritual between different factions of the ruling class. While it is invariably the masses who are sacrificed on the altar of this blood-letting ritual, benefits accrue to the new ruling faction. As aptly characterized by Kuber P. Sharma in his letter of resignation from the Nepali Congress Party, power has certainly changed hands as a result of the so-called 1990 revolution, but not the policy and patterns of corruption or personal gains at the expense of the masses:

> I was granted the membership of the party after I pledged my faith in and allegiance to `Nationalism, Democracy and Socialism"—the proclaimed objectives of Nepali Congress. After having won the general election in 1991, the party formed the government.... Nepali Congress has now been reduced to a party for leaders who are more inclined to cling to power, satiate their lust for material affluence and arrogance.... We the party-workers are helpless witness to immoral, unscrupulous and illegitimate acts such as rampant abuse of authority, embezzlement of public revenue and resources by party functionaries.... (Fairly recently, Finance Minister Dr. Ram Sharan Mahat was found to have deposited about 45,000 dollars in a New York bank[1]). Leaders and party functionaries, oblivious of the past commitments and trust reposed on them by the people, carved maddeningly for power and adopted lavish lifestyles at the expense of Nepal, Nepali people and hard-won democracy.... Those who could not pay rent yesterday have today become owners of palatial buildings. The new generation of leaders are driving fancy cars and dreaming of taking over the mantle of Nepali Congress leadership. The spirit of co-existence has been replaced by conspiratorial `Kill your comrade' tendency (extracted from *The Nepal Digest* on the internet, December 9, 1996; parenthetical sentence mine).

One possible exception to this common history of revolutionary failures to improve the socioeconomic condition of the masses, although Moore would disagree, is Mao's China, a period that spanned more than a quarter century (1949-1976). To be sure, Chinese people experienced many hardships under Mao. Human atrocities were committed. China's physical environment suffered. Despite all these, under him the security of people's subsistence was number one priority. The long and torturous history of Chinese poverty was brought under control as peasants and workers fared better than they ever had. Mao was keen on the need to guard China's independence—both political and economic—from foreign powers, including the former Soviet Union (Schram, 1974). It is this vision of independence that led him to adhere unshakably to the principle of self-reliance, which he defined as "regeneration through one's own strength" (also see Tang, 1993; Hinton, 1993). He firmly believed in the principle of balanced development which he termed "walking on two legs."

Mao's model of self-reliant and balanced development was not glamorous. Although China's economic growth under Mao was never spectacular, certainly nothing like its current annual economic growth rate of over 10 percent, almost everybody had a fair economic share and security of employment. However, the notion of employment was configured differently in Mao's model than it is in the capitalist model of development. To most Western eyes, employment is normally inter-preted in terms of so-called labor productivity rather than labor utili-zation. During my visit to China with a group of American geographers, we had an occasion to visit a geography center. There, in the front lawn of that center, we observed four or five Chinese women methodically weeding grass with their bare hands.

Some of the group members were apparently appalled by that scene of seeming labor inefficiency, but I was not surprised by their reaction. Weeding lawns with bare hands certainly looked "primitive" to Western eyes used to fancy lawn mowers. They only see workers as a commo-dity, invariably viewed in cost-benefit terms. They rarely see them as a vital resource with human needs of their own, i.e., as integral members of society who need to be employed so they can remain productive as well as support their families, who need to have a sense of purpose in life. But my North American group members could not fathom this human dimension of life and society. In addition, they were being quite naive about one basic aspect of economic production. Classical Econo-mics dictates that of the three basic means of production—land, labor, and capital—whichever is available in abundance should be employed to the highest degree possible (see Lewis, 1954). In the case of China, labor is obviously the most ubiquitous and hence least expensive means of production. Employment is more than a source of income and an act of getting a given task done; it is a vital source of self-dignity and pride for people.

But Mao's primacy of politics (social needs) over economics (growth) has now been replaced by a new Chinese policy which places economic growth above mass security. Mao's revolutionary zeal and vision of building a society based on economic security and justice for all now stand as a nostalgic memory as today's China is infatuated with capitalist modernization and driven by growthmania. The so-called "capitalist roaders" whom Mao simultaneously reviled and feared have come alive once again. After more than two decades of Mao's self-reliant development, in the early 1980s China thrust itself upon the economic landscape of what is euphemistically termed "market socialism," a convenient cover for the deepening roots of capitalism (Weil, 1994, 1995; Toporowski, 1995). No question, under Deng Xiaoping's open-door policy China has posted an enviable economic growth rate. Most capitalist advocates gleefully point this out as an indisputable evidence of the miraculous power of capitalism (DuRand, 1990). Yet they conveniently brush aside the immense plight this very economic miracle has heaved upon some 200 million people of China, a number that is close to 80 percent of the total U.S. population. Lindorff (1994:742) writes:

> More than 100 million rural workers and peasants are now unemployed migrants, wandering from city to city looking for day labor. By one account, total unemployment in China may now top 200 million, but that is only one of many troubles. The American managing director of a firm financing a new joint-venture office tower in Shanghai tells of flying from Hong Kong to China's largest city for a ground-breaking ceremony. Standing at the site and flanked by city officials, he realized that he was actually celebrating the eviction of a whole block of tenants who had lived there for decades.

I wonder if these Chinese unemployed workers and peasants and evicted residents, who have seen their economic security and residential quarters vanquished by the miracle of capitalism, wish Mao were still alive to deliver them from such living hell (Weil, 1995). Despite some glimmer of hopes that Mao's China presented for peasants and workers (Hinton, 1994; Hsu and Ching, 1991), communism has not proven to be the answer to human miseries that it was projected to be, at least not in its current form. The only solace is that its counter force, capitalism, is worse (Miliband, 1991). Both in praxis and theory, capitalism is a cut-throat system devoid of any moral axis. As Paul Sweezy (1994) argues in one of his recent essays, if the current trend of financial capital continues, its magnificent ability to increase capital accumulation without generating jobs for the growing number of unemployed masses may prove to be self-destructive to all encompassing capitalism: the true Midas touch so miraculous and yet so self-destructive. Greed is good: this is the motto of capitalism, and this is what is being peddled as a panacea to poverty throughout the underdeveloped world, including Nepal. How could greed ever cure poverty?! It is beyond my comprehension. Dialectically, it is impossible because they are antithetical.

Today, communism exists in China only in name, not because of its moral authority. Gone are the days of Mao's relentless emphasis on self-reliance. Whatever moral authority there existed in Mao's China has almost completely decayed. It has totally lost its social and economic zeal, its goals, and its vitality. It is just a matter of time before Chinese communism crumbles like a house of cards, creating massive clouds of chaos and confusion, along with tremendous blood-letting. If the bloodshed was bad during China's revolutionary days, it is bound to be much worse during its almost pending dissolution in the hands of capitalism. Now Vietnam is being shoved down the same path by the global forces of capitalism. And then Cuba and North Korea will most likely follow suit. Almost everywhere socialism is under siege (Wallis, 1996).

These holdover countries are obvious battlefields as they represent the isolated communist ghosts lurking in the shadow of capitalism. They are the nagging gnats. The war waged by capitalism against communism is actually an economic war carried out on a political front. The ongoing trend suggests that the whole era of communist revolutions will soon come to an unsavory end, finally allowing global capitalism to raise its victory flag in every corner of the world. It looks like socialist revolutions will all be a chapter in the political history of the world.

In fact, with respect to the avalanche-like downfall of socialism, it can be argued that the socialist regimes' mindless pursuit of techno-material growth mastered under the capitalist mode of production affirmed the supremacy of capitalism. As Victor Wallis (1992:5) thoughtfully argues, "...the socialist bloc was never able to distance itself from capitalist criteria of success." So the development story of socialism goes deep. What socialism gained in terms of its political victory, it lost in terms of its economic development focus by trying to play a capitalist game in the world already firmly controlled by capital. Playing such a game from the position of weakness has proven to be a very costly and foolish game, a game it had little chance of winning. Competing against capitalism on material terms was a poor strategy, one that was bound to bring defeat on both fronts of the battle.

In other words, by blindly accepting the materialistic development model, the socialist regimes not only elevated capitalism to a superior position, but also dropped the guillotine on non-capitalist cultures, value systems, and economic modes of existence, seeing them through the same prism that colonial masters used: as backward and hence antithetical to development. By doing so, *socialism practically forsook its most fundamental mission and moral authority*, thus setting the stage for its own eventual downfall. This is the same fate that now, to repeat, hovers over China like a vulture ready to descend on a dying cow.

Despite all this, it is still premature to write the final obituary of "socialist revolutions," no matter how bleak their prospects may seem at the present time. A new wave of such revolutions can never be ruled out, especially in light of the fact that history tends to be cyclical and that poverty and social injustice have always provided a potent breeding ground for communism. As Jameson (1996) remarks, its appeal will not wither away as long as capitalism exists.

Yet I can't help but recognize that the task of any revolutionary anywhere in the world is not getting any easier in the face of the seductive power that the counter-forces of capitalism or Westernization have unleashed against non-Western societies. I call them the "wild golden goose," and it is a formidable counter-force. In the past, especially during the colonial days, national revolutionary movements were generally engaged in a one-front battle, i.e., against one enemy. Nowadays a true social revolution involves a battle on two fronts: one against the tidal wave of Western materialism that global capitalism and its corollary popular culture have spread all over the globe, and the other against the national ruling elites who essentially act as the domestic agents of global capital as well as the internal class enemy.

As much as these capitalist counter-forces have generated currents of class resentment in various countries, they have also stifled sustained political participation and protests by engendering false hopes that everybody, including the disenfranchised and downtrodden, can strike gold if they ride the waves of the global march of capitalism. In other words, as more and more people—rich and poor—chase the wild golden goose in a lake where many can't even swim, they lose sight of the depth of the problem facing Nepal. The number of potential participants in a revolutionary march diminishes, the outcome being that the march either never gets off the ground or suffers a premature death. In short, the wild golden goose has become the modern-day opium of not only the elites, but also the masses, keeping them from lighting the fire of genuine social movements.

In dangling the hypnotic charm of the wild golden goose that Westernized development represents, the avant-garde gurus of development show little remorse about any of its adverse consequences except to prescribe more bogus development recipes to an underdeveloped country like Nepal that has long been drained of its indigenous ideas and self-reliant abilities, especially among the ruling elites. Commenting on Samuel Huntington's (1993) "The Clash of Civilizations?" article, Robert Bartley (1993:16-17), editor of *The Wall Street Journal*, loudly proclaimed that Western values are an artifact of development (or vice versa). "The world's language is English. Even the standard-bearers of `the rest' were largely educated in the West.... Development creates a middle class that wants a say in its own future, that cares about the progress and freedom of its sons and daughters. Since economic progress depends on this same group...this desire can be suppressed only at the expense of development." Gerard Piel (1993:25-26), chairman emeritus of Scientific American Inc., goes even further, confidently declaring that "The West is best" and "other" cultures, which he calls "ghostly civilizations," don't exist. As all of the developing countries look upon the West as a model to emulate and are "still engaged in the conquest of the material world, (they)... progressively embrace the Western ideas of individualism... (and) liberalism."

Indeed!

As disturbing and irritating as these comments sound, it is mostly true. And that is the problem, a powerful obstacle to any social revolution. And this is exactly how capitalism has managed to triumph over socialism and other alternative and indigenous modes of life. That is why, it is difficult to write those comments off as merely arrogant or loony and ludicrous. Pursuit of Western values and material goals reigns supreme almost everywhere. Nepal is no exception in this galloping material race. It has even gone so far as to unleash a current of casino gambling in Kathmandu, all in the name of development. With four casinos presently operating in its fanciest hotels, all managed by Richard Tuttle, an American casino king of Nepal (virtually all of the fancy hotels are, by the way, directly connected to the royal palace), Kathmandu can now boast its dubious status as "the Las Vegas of South Asia"—a phrase that Joe Manickavasagam of the World Bank has coined to describe this medieval city. Casino gambling! This is the pinnacle of modernization, the latest chapter in the sweeping triumph of free-market liberalism. In his article published in *The Milwaukee Journal* (Jan. 30, 1994), Thomas Wagner declares that this is "...the best economic news for the poor nation since it became a democracy four years ago and began reforming its socialist economy." (I don't know where Wagner got the notion that Nepal ever had a socialist economy). Growth of gambling as the best economic news for Nepal: what an obscene thought! What price my motherland has been willing to pay, all in the name of so-called democracy and development!

Best economic news or not, *poker* has now become Nepal's latest tourist attraction (Chapter 6).

Bartley is right when he claimed that development creates a middle class with its own future in mind. The case of Nepal proves him right.

Casino gambling and various other forms of contemporary development have certainly created in Nepal a "middle class," a fat middle class, both financially and figuratively (being fat, as noted above, is generally a most visible physical index of being rich). Though small in size, perhaps 10 percent of the total population, it is a powerful group; they are the elites who include planners and politicians, bureaucrats and businessmen. They are the standard-bearers and trend-setters. They hold the mantle of power with the military backing it.

Piel is right too, when he said that non-Western societies and their citizens are furiously engaged in the conquest of the material world and that they have embraced the Western values and ideas of individualism and liberalism. At least Nepal has proven him right as its ruling elites have adopted these ideas as their gospel and forsaken their previously professed allegiance to nationalism. To put it another way, it is this middle class, mostly composed of Nepali elites, that has become the *middlemen* devoid of any scruples and commitment to collective upliftment, or national identity and dignity. To them as well as to the young generation in general, money has become the sole measure of man (and woman) and his power and status. It has become the single most defining character of success, the most important attribute of economic progress. It seems to matter little as to how one makes money as long as s/he makes it or acquires it. For instance, it is absolutely baffling that middle class sons and daughters go to North America, Europe, Japan, South Korea, Taiwan, Saudi Arabia, and many other countries to work, most of them illegally without work permits. In their destination countries, they are generally hired to do menial work, characterized by three D's—dirty, dangerous, and demeaning—jobs that the local people avoid. Some work in slaughter houses and others in warehouses and mines. Some work in restaurants as dishwashers and others clean public places and bathrooms. Some work as nannies and housemaids and others as prostitutes.

This is why Robert Bartley's and Gerard Piel's comments ring so frighteningly true. Under such a formidable tide of material values, one of the most potent forces of political activism—the urban and educated youths—is lost to the chase of the wild golden goose. Without political activists, it is difficult to keep the revolutionary flame burning. They have little concern or time for genuine political activism and collective progress. This is a dangerous trend for a country like Nepal suffering from growing social injustices and economic inequalities, both at the local and national levels. In other words, for these Nepali youths slaughtering chickens in foreign countries is far more appealing than serving as members of revolutionary cadres; they find digging mines in foreign countries a lot easier than digging a revolutionary path in their own country. As one black civil-rights activist, currently an executive officer of a large American beer company, said, selling a case beer or Coca-Cola is much easier than selling the cause of social justice and equality. No revolution is easy to sell or launch.

Once again the question is: what can be done to establish a just society where it can free itself from the shackles of Westernized development, where one's honor, dignity, and happiness are not measured by material acquisition, where social, economic, and environmental harmonies prevail over greed and destruction, where one segment of humanity is not subjected to the whims of another, where objects are defined based on their use value rather than exchange value, or where, to quote Miliband (1991:23), there is "...a progressive decommodification of life, the removal of the cash nexus as the core social relations."

REVOLUTION LIVES ON?

It is precisely the above question that I was discussing two years ago with a Nepali friend, somebody who is well-educated and has long been involved in political activism. For the past several years, he has been working for a foreign non-governmental organization (NGO) doing some rural development work in Nepal. We were in a local restaurant in Kathmandu, sipping Nepali beer and having some snack. I was basically expressing my depressed feelings about the tragic saga of Nepal's contemporary development and wondering what the Nepali poor could do to improve their overall conditions. After some serious discussion, he said, "What we need is a true revolution."

Nothing unusual about that statement. What shocked me was when he said, "We should first terrorize Kathmandu's Western community." And he was not joking although I didn't think he was ready to explode.

It was a radical thought to which I could not respond. I was quiet, but he continued, "If we start terrorizing them in an organized fashion, we can immediately mobilize a large force of activists, particularly college and university students. Nobody makes a better common enemy than Western agents and agencies. If we use Westerners as a target, the nationalist blood will start flowing among the students. Students act as a powerful mobile force in any revolution. Once they light the fire, it will spread quite fast across the nation. And it isn't that hard to terrorize them in Kathmandu. We can terrorize them emotionally. We can launch a hit-and-run attack on their properties."

He seemed serious about his views. His logic was that "Once we start terrorizing them, they will pack up and leave Nepal. That's what we need. You know what that will do? That will clip both wings of the ruling class. That will shatter them. You know what happened when the British left India, right? The Ranas lost their British support, and four years later we had a successful revolution that kicked them out of power. When Westerners leave, the ruling class will lose its biggest allies, the linchpin of their political as well as economic power. They will be isolated and their money pipe will be dry pretty fast. Without westerners' help, many of them won't be able to function well. They don't have any resiliency and endurance like the poor. Then we can hit them hard in their bellies, as well as break their legs, and kick them out of power."

Although my friend certainly had a point, it sounded too harsh. Despite my disagreement with his approach, a social revolution cannot be ruled out, however, not always because of its inherent desirability, but because it tends to have an almost natural mass appeal to raw rage secreted in most human nerves. In addition, it generally has a larger social and geographical support base than most localized movements. As

Barrington Moore (1987:124), a leading authority on the history of the peasantry and peasant revolutions, concedes, "In some circumstances, to be sure, political glamour may be the only ingredient that will get desirable results, i.e. a reduction in human suffering."

I said to him that my own preference would be first to explore a peaceful solution to the socioeconomic problem, terrorizing Nepal and its masses. Certainly, the most desirable remedy would be a structural change through a non-violent means, a kind of Gandhian political struggle and economic vision. *Politically,* a non-violent revolution is less costly in terms of both human lives and resources necessary to launch a protracted battle against the ruling class and its state apparatus, especially the military.

Economically too, the Gandhian model is most appropriate for a resource-poor country like Nepal. One invaluable wisdom of Barrington Moore's observation is the dire need, as previously noted, to pursue feasible goals of development, goals that are suitable for both local human needs and resource base, goals that are self-reliant rather than externally dependent, and goals that are simple rather than grandiose and monumental. The principal goal of such a simple model should be, I added, to preserve and insure the sanctity of nature and the survival of humanity, all humanity, not just a select few. A revolutionary movement should have at the core of its economic philosophy an indigenous development paradigm capable of offering a clear alternative to the dysfunctional material value system of capitalism, as well as to the form of socialism applied in the former Soviet Union or currently practiced in China.

My friend said, "No, no, the Gandhian model is not possible. It's not that I disagree with you; it just is not possible."

"Why not?"

"Because the ruling class will not allow us to have a peaceful revolution. They are too intoxicated with political power and control to abdicate it. With political power comes all kinds of economic advantages and social status. They have no tolerance for any form of revolutionary activities—whether violent or peaceful. Violence in the name of peace and order is their primary language and method to suppress the voices of opposition. Now, you see why they will not allow any revolution to remain non-violent. They will do everything in their power to make sure that our revolution takes a violent turn so they can readily justify deploying their military forces against us. The ruling class will not give up its power unless it is defeated."

"But what about the Gandhian type of economic vision?"

"That's a different matter. I agree with you," he said. "But you know you can't implement an economic model unless you have the political power to do so. Politics has to come first, before economics."

However, I stressed to him the need to pursue a simple development path. True, such a paradigm may conjure up in many minds the images of simple living, a society grounded in the reciprocity of grace. It evokes an image of life and living that one can discern from E.F. Schumacher's book, *Small is Beautiful*, which too is rooted in the Gandhian economic model. Obviously, such a vision goes against the currency of today's development ideology, so passionately advocated and carefully mapped out over the past 50 years by both Marxists and the World Bank, the institution sitting at the helm of the capitalist ship as its captain.

Yet Nepal needs, in my view, something diagonally opposite of the prevailing development ideology. It is precisely for this reason that the Gandhian vision of self-reliant development, in addition to being truly sustainable, is most suitable to the soil of Nepal, i.e., to its needs and resource base. The moral basis of the model can be essentially depicted in a simple sentence that Gandhi uttered, almost in a saintly manner, that there is enough for everybody's need, but not for everybody's greed. After having analyzed various development models, both from a historical and theoretical perspective, I believe that the Gandhian model is the most feasible one if Nepal is to arrest its ongoing development victimization, as well as to remove the social basis of its massive poverty and injustice and uplift the masses. This is the best way Nepal can avoid the same fate that visited and destroyed Soviet socialism and is about to complete its destruction of China. In other words, the true success of any future social revolution in Nepal will depend on its pursuit of a simple path to development that can be charted from within, with local resources—without any foreign aid.

Without directly responding to my point, my friend reiterated: "That's why we need a revolution, to remove the existing ruling class. The essence of my argument is that there is a fundamental need for change in the leadership from those with vested interests to those whose only vested interest is that of restoring and preserving the national honor and serving the masses. And we have to drive the Westerners and their foreign aid out of this country to cripple the ruling class, so we can succeed."

Foreign Aid and Foreign Agents: One More Look

After my friend and I parted each other's company, what he said kept ringing in my head. Can Westerners actually become the common enemy for a revolutionary cause in Nepal? How much damage have Western aid and agents done to the Nepali psyche. Will the Nepali ruling class weaken and eventually fall in the absence of foreign aid as my friend concluded? Is there enough rage left to mobilize the masses to participate in a revolution? These are the questions that kept gnawing at me.

It has already been pointed out that foreign aid has been the mainstay of the Nepali economy and ruling elites. Every ruling faction of Nepal since 1950, including the main communist party that ruled the country as a minority government for about a year in 1994-1995, has bilked foreign aid as a milch cow to fulfill its vested interests. In 1994, there were 302 foreign-aid projects under way in Nepal, and 80 percent of the total outlay for these projects came from foreign countries (*Nepal Press Digest*, January 17, 1994). This clearly reveals how entrenched foreign aid is in Nepal. Despite its entrenchment, however, most of the foreign aid money goes right back to aid-giving countries in various forms. In fact, recently, the United States Agency for International Development (USAID) "distributed fat folders of documents showing that nearly 80 percent of its budget is recycled back to the United States" (*Newsweek*, May 29, 1995:50). This pattern holds true in Nepal as well. Of the remaining 20 percent, very little trickles down to the poor (Shrestha, 1990).

There is nothing new in this regard about foreign aid. What is often left out of the discussion on the politics of foreign aid, however, is related to my friend's argument. First, it is not always the begging country's ruling elites who are the sole culprits of Nepal's growing foreign aid dependency. Western donors are equally guilty in this game. They are so eager to give foreign aid that they will go to any length to insure aid-receiving countries' acceptance of their aid package and projects. Since high-level government officials are fully cognizant of their impatience to launch foreign aid projects in Nepal, they sometimes hold out on purpose as long as they can before approving such projects.

They know their delay is not going to make foreign agencies withdraw their proposals.

Both parties know why the holdout occurs. It is a political ploy to extract certain personal benefits from foreign aid agencies, including non-governmental organizations and project contractors. To avoid such holdouts, foreign aid agencies routinely bribe appropriate government officials to get proposed foreign aid projects and packages approved. Virtually every aid package involves some type of bribe, one common form being scholarships or similar deals for their children and relatives to study in the United States or England. Sometimes a bribe can be offered in the form of high-paying employment for sons, daughters, or other relatives. For example, one Nepali ambassador to the United States had his daughter hired by an American development consultant company which had been awarded a contract for a USAID project in Nepal. Sometimes foreign agencies can extract necessary approval of their projects quite cheaply, by throwing an elaborate party for concerned Nepali government officials in a fancy hotel or by presenting them with a couple of bottles of brand name scotch such as *Black Label* and a few cases of American or British cigarettes.

One may wonder why Western agents possess corruptive behaviors and willingly participate in corruption despite their self-righteous pontification against it. As suggested in Chapter 2, they do it because, in addition to buying influence, foreign aid acts as a great source of employment for Western development agents with questionable credentials. Many times, as Hancock (1989) reveals, their only qualification is their white face. Additionally, it offers fat checks and luxurious lifestyles. Any wonder now why 80 percent of the foreign aid money goes right back to donor countries? Aid money is used to employ their own kind at the salary rates that are invariably higher than their own domestic rates. This is why they are eager to give foreign aid and bribe Nepali government officials to get the proposed projects approved. Through such mutually corruptive practices, Western donor agents keep themselves employed and the domestic ruling elites in control of Nepal's power leverage. Western donors are vehemently opposed to any social revolution that threatens their *de facto* internal control of a country like Nepal. By controlling the elites, they control the country.

The second aspect of foreign aid that is rarely discussed deals with Western agents themselves and their colonial attitudes toward the native people. While my friend was talking about the Western expatriates in

Nepal, I was thinking, all along, about my own personal encounters with various American development advisors and experts in Nepal. One particularly disturbing encounter occurred with an American advisor named Rex. It was this experience that revealed to me, for the first time, how the Nepali elites have learned to suppress their rage and act subordinate to Westerners in their own country, and by doing so how they have subverted the potential for a mass revolution, all for the sake of their own material benefits and hollow privileges.

Once again, back in Rampur, that little dusty town in Chitwan (see Chapter 1). That is where I first met Rex who was there as the team leader of an USAID project at the College of Agricultural and Animal Sciences. A couple of days after moving into his quarters, Paul introduced me to Rex. Paul told him that I was a Ph.D. student at Indiana University and was doing fieldwork in Rampur. Paul also mentioned that I was staying with him. As soon as he found out my living arrangements in Rampur, Rex suddenly appeared cold and hesitant to shake my hand. Although I found that to be a strange behavior, I did not make much of it.

Based on what I could observe, Rex was an interesting character. I did not know how he passed most of his time in Rampur. He did not seem to have much to do. Rex and other American advisors were posted to Nepal to work with the Nepali people to help them improve their quality of life, but there was little evidence that he had done anything of substance to achieve this goal. During my whole time in Rampur, some eight months, I rarely saw him interact with any Nepali workers or venture out of the college compound to spend time with the local farmers or even visit the Rampur bazaar, perhaps no more than 500 yards away from his quarters. A couple of people informed me that his (American) predecessor, George, used to describe Rampur as a place with no civilization (by implication a town surrounded by barbarians). When he returned to the United States, he said, "I am finally back in the world of civilization." Perhaps, Rex felt the same way about Rampur and the people there.

His activities in Rampur were confined to his office and quarters. His dealings were almost strictly limited to his Nepali workers and administrators at the college. Such a behavior was totally strange to put it mildly, especially considering the fact that he was in charge of a project that was specifically designed to help rural folks, namely farmers, improve their lives. The project was directly affiliated with the college, the mission of which was to play a leading role in the modernization of farming. Its immediate role was to prepare agricultural extension agents, good in both theory and practice, who could relate to farmers. With the kind of disdain he displayed toward the local people in general, it was difficult for me to imagine how Rex could achieve the project mission of preparing effective agricultural extension agents and bettering farmers' lives.

The only time I saw Rex venture out of the compound was when he was on his way to Kathmandu or when he occasionally went to a nearby town called Narayanghat, about 20 miles away from Rampur, to buy some fresh vegetables. Even this task of purchasing fresh vegetables was mostly done by his Nepali maids. Most of their food and other household supplies came directly from the American commissary in Kathmandu. He and his family regularly went to Kathmandu, the closest place to the world of civilization, to which he was accustomed. Rex was not an isolated case, however. He was typical of most Western advisors' behavior and attitude toward the native people which Hancock (1989) vividly captures in his book, *Lords of Poverty*. Hancock (1989:124) writes:

> In one recent and unfortunately typical USAID mission, a senior official based in the Indonesian capital of Jakarta went `up country'—supposedly to learn about a project for mothers of malnourished children in a remote rural area. On arrival the visitor was greeted by a large group of mums and kids. They had dressed in their best clothes and had prepared, in the words of one observer, `a big table groaning with food...they were poor, but they wanted to honour this guy.' The USAID man, however, refused to leave the protection of his vehicle and insisted that `under no circumstances' would he eat with `such people.' Asked by junior colleague if he would at least take a cup of tea he again refused and suggested: `You could tell them that the important American was just too busy.' All in all, although three full days were spent driving out to the project and then driving back to Jakarta, less than half an hour was spent at the project site itself (and none of the local people were talked to).

The above quotation could easily have been written to characterize Rex's attitude and behavior. Hancock also writes about how possessive Western advisors become of certain material objects made available for a given development project and how they react if the local staff try to make use of those objects for project-related purposes. "A Western consultant heading one rural scheme," states Hancock (1989:118), "complained bitterly that locally hired staff seemed to feel they had a `right' to make use of project vehicles, and admitted that this issue was `souring the atmosphere of co-operation;' the vehicles, he said, were intended for the expatriate advisers only." That Western consultant's attitude clearly shows how Western advisors view and value the native people, how they establish dominant-subordinate power relations, a double standard between themselves and the natives. Theirs is a typically colonial thinking: how could the local barbarians dare claim that they too have the right to use project vehicles; what makes them think that they deserve the same amenities of life that Western "masters" enjoy?

To these Western advisors, it matters little that the whole project was supposedly meant for the local people. It is interesting to note that foreign aid projects are invariably advertised as international partnership for progress. But, in practice, there is very little partnership, a concept that assumes mutual respect and equality between partners. Western advisors act dominant in terms of both actions and attitudes. They are too wedded to the culture of colonialism to free themselves from it and be able to see native people as equal. No wonder why they constantly devalue native lives and their worth. Since such devaluation is so widespread, it is neither funny nor puzzling any more. Rex is a living example of how the vile culture of colonialism has been revived in an equally viral neo-colonial form.

So Rex is simply one of those countless American (Western) advisors in Nepal who refuse to see native people as complete human beings. His hostility toward me was on the rise. Mindful that any misstep on my part might put Paul in an awkward situation with Rex, I continued to be polite toward him. But my precautionary measures did not pay off. The relationship between Paul and Rex went totally sour. Damage had already been done, I found out later. Rex had already launched a smear campaign against Paul, undercutting him and his professional integrity among other American expatriates in Kathmandu. Paul was regarded as a pariah, somebody who had betrayed his own kind and the sacredness of American advisors' self-asserted superiority and exclusionary practices. He obviously evoked an image of an expatriate gone native.

Paul had been completely isolated from the vast majority of American expatriates in Nepal. This I found out later from another American advisor named Bill. While Bill worked as a rural development expert for the USAID, his main qualification for the job was that he had once been a Peace Corps volunteer in Nepal. It was clear that Bill himself did not want to have any professional or personal ties with Paul. I surmised that by treating me as equal and letting me share his USAID-provided quarters, and by regularly commingling with the Nepali people, both inside and outside the campus, Paul had failed to live up to the glorious image of that Little America, carefully guarded inside the Fort Durbar (Chapter 2). His behavior was "abnormal" and outright different from the rest of the Americans.

In view of the tense reality, I tried to avoid Rex, but that was not always easy because the campus was small. One day our paths crossed. Since I refused to be openly rude to Rex, I said hello to him. He did not respond. That did not surprise me because he had ignored me before. Instead he gave me a look filled with hate without uttering a word about his hatred toward me. That shocked me. I was enraged deeply. Yet I bit my tongue hard, once again, and suppressed my rage. Without saying a word, I walked away in the opposite direction. While walking away, I felt my veins shaking and my heart pulsating rapidly.

As my internal rage slowly subsided, I kept asking: how could he try to demean me in my own country (territory)? He was let into my territory as a guest, but now he was acting like a master. My rage was not just personal. Nor was it an isolated incident. It is a common experience. Rex and I were simply two manifestations, two opposite embodiments of the broader pattern of debasement and demonization of the native population in the dominant-subordinate relations between Westerners and natives. One can clearly discern from Rex's colonial behavior that no native people are insulated from being mistreated by Westerners like colonial subjects forced into some form of servitude. So, for most Nepalis, not even their high education and national territorial boundaries are enough to protect their dignity and integrity. Their nationality is their curse and disgrace while, for the Westerners, their white skin served as the source of their power and privileges. If American advisors like Rex blatantly mistreat a US educated Nepali for no reason, somebody who could return to Nepal, occupy a high-level government post, and actually determine the fate of foreign aid projects like the one he himself was directing, it is not difficult to imagine how they treat other Nepalis, especially those who are less educated and directly work for them. In fact, one does not even have to imagine; any casual observer of the power relations between Westerners and natives can notice the degree of humiliation and indignity Westerners inflict on

In the name of development

the Nepali people on a regular basis. Rex is just one personification of this live drama of colonial culture, being played out in the world of Western aid and development.

Rex's behavior also raises a serious question: how can Westerners help the very people they so despise? It is plainly inconceivable that they could or would. Every Nepali ought to ponder this question seriously: Western money, Western projects, and Western advisors at what cost and to what end? Who are they really serving when they act like masters of our destiny and our country? It is the reality like this that makes my friend's point about Westerners relevant, the point about viewing them as a common enemy to be forced out of the country.

After I returned to my room, I, once again, felt the rage engulfing me. This time, I was more incensed with myself than with Rex because I chose not to challenge his colonial attitude and behavior. Speaking of the cruelty of slavery, Frederick Douglass remarked, "A slave to-day, to-morrow, next year, all the years of my life—my manhood denied, ignored, despised—this being eternally shut up to a single condition, no outgoing, no progress, no future, this is more terrible, more distressing than the whip" (quoted in Burke, 1996:36). That is exactly how I felt. It was not the hateful stare of Rex that bothered me most. Rather it was the fear that Nepalis might be doomed to the fate of perpetual degradation and dehumanization by Westerners in their own country that was choking me. That was the most terrifying thought racing through my mind. I found my lack of any response to Rex reprehensible.

"...[A] man who will not fight for himself, when he has the means of doing so, is not worth being fought for by others... For a man who does not value freedom for himself will never value it for others, nor put himself to any inconvenience to gain it for others. Such a man, the world says, may lie down until he has sense enough to stand up," warned Frederick Douglass (Foner, 1950:435). I had become precisely that man that Douglass described—a gutless man who had failed to value his freedom and the freedom for others, who had failed to exercise his right to defend his dignity and the dignity of his fellow Nepalis. I had become a prisoner of my own distorted sense of civility, trying to protect my elite status and privileges at the expense of my manhood. I despised myself for acting like a defeated dog. I had become a true middleman. The whole quarter suddenly looked like a ghostly castle, where I was alone and being haunted by my own shameful act.

I wished I had heeded to what one of my high school teachers in Pokhara used to say: "A life lived in indignity dies a thousand deaths, whereas a life lived in dignity dies only once." At that time, I never fully grasped the moral underlying this statement. But now it was teasing me. When individuals are willing to live an undignified life, the only value that they command is the value somebody places on them. They have aborted their birth right to determine their own value. My decision not to express my rage by confronting Rex essentially signaled my first death. That was when I fully realized that I had succumbed to the culture of colonialism and developed the kind of behavior that is typical of a colonized mind (see Chapter 3).

Suddenly I began to miss my old days back in Pokhara when my sense of national pride and anti-colonial sentiments were much deeper and more responsive, when I used to react spontaneously to my thoughts, when I was more concerned about the issues than my own status. I specifically remembered the time when we vehemently opposed British Christian missionary activities in Pokhara. The British were the living symbol of Western domination and colonial culture. They were the ones who annexed about one-half of Nepal's pre-Anglo war territory (1814-16) to the British raj. They were the ones who kept Nepal within the sphere of their imperial control. I did not mind them coming to Nepal as long as they did not engage in proselytization. Those missionaries were demonizing our traditions and practices and proselytizing Nepali into Christianity. Not that I was a Hindu fundamentalist zealot, concerned about preserving the integrity of Hinduism. That was not my concern.

To me as well as to my friends in the group, the issue was bigger. Correctly or incorrectly, we viewed missionaries as colonialists who came in as docile and harmless mice, but emerged as hungry and harmful lions. Those British missionaries in Pokhara were not doing God's job. They were doing colonial masters' dirty fieldwork in order to maintain their domination over us through Christianity. When we felt that those missionaries were acting like witches, taking control of Nepali bodies and minds, one by one, and thus gradually planting the seeds of Nepali inferiority and the demise of their self-dignity and self-respect, we decided to take action.

We organized many students, mobilizing their individual raw rage into a collective force, into a mini social movement against Christian missionaries in Pokhara. We used to snoop around to find out where they would be holding their Sunday prayers and conversion meetings and then periodically disrupt their meetings. They would look very frightened like little dogs bitten to submission. Fearful that we might harm them (which, by the way, was never our intention; nor did we ever attempt to do so), they would huddle together. Almost motionless, they would look pale and timid as if begging for mercy. We never thought that our disruptive act would scare them to timidity and submission, as though clinging on to their dear lives. That was the first time I observed Westerners in a submissive position as if we were holding their fate in our fists. Colonial masters crouched together in fear in front of us, whom they treated as colonial subjects. That was quite a scene! We felt tremendous power in our collective force as if there was nothing we could not achieve against those British missionaries. We could have crushed them and we could have kicked them out of our land. That was our mini revolt, a successful revolt, that went on for several weeks until we finally decided to give up after they agreed not to hold prayer meetings outside their Shining Hospital quarters.

The table of power relations between them and us had been turned completely upside down, at least for a few weeks. I wonder if those Westerners ever imagined how the colonized people must have felt when they tossed them into ditches begging for mercy, life, and dignity.

The point of this story is not to suggest that my friends and I were not cowards and muted voices back then. The point is that the rage is there, a big reserve of rage, simmering underneath and waiting to be drilled. It exists even among the elites as already remarked. With proper drilling, it can still be channeled into a collective fury and action. What is needed to release this rage into a collective force is a group of dedicated organizers, informed and disciplined rebels willing to light the fire. In fact, I could have done the same thing in Rampur against the development missionaries like Rex that we did in Pokhara against the British Christian missionaries—organize a group of students and challenge Rex. Organizing a group of Chitwan students would not have been that difficult because Westerners with a dubious reputation, like Rex, always serves as a good target. Plus there were (are) many Nepali youths in Chitwan (and across Nepal) who harbored enough hostility toward Americans because of their condescending attitudes and behaviors. I personally knew several people in those villages who were fed up with many of those American advisors in Rampur.

Any such open challenge would have brought Rex down to his fickle knees and made him heel like a tamed dog with a simple command. He would have rather sacrificed his dignity and acted like those British missionaries in Pokhara than stood up to me if I had only chosen to defy my colonized mind and organize a group of students to challenge him. He would have probably never again mistreated any Nepali. Anybody who acts like a master to others and denies them their dignity when occupying a position of power has no self-dignity and always lives in fear, shivering like a beaten dog, when his power-hold is broken.

But I failed to do that as if my fury had all died out. My failure also reflects the failure of the Nepali elites as a class to confront the prevailing Western colonial mentality head-on in order to restore Nepal's national integrity as well as embark on the path of indigenous development. Before we succumbed to the Western material culture of *bikas* or foreign aid in general, we had not surrendered our national pride and dignity. Even in our apparent defeat to the British during the war of 1814-16, we held our heads high and fiercely protected our national integrity. But in our vain pursuit of dependent development we have completely subordinated our dignity and national integrity. It is precisely this subordination that defines today's Nepali elites who are too wedded to Western aid for personal material benefits to challenge Westerners even when they degrade our dignity—both openly and subtly. These elites are too consumed by their own personal agenda rather than driven by national goals.

While Westerners may not fathom the power we can still unleash through the collective force of our raw rage to drive them out of our country (if we so choose), most of them are keenly aware of the degree of our dependency on their money called foreign aid. They know full well that foreign aid is the ultimate leverage of our material destiny as well as power base. And they control this leverage. It is no wonder why Western aid has managed to maintain a tight grip on Nepal's ruling elites. No wonder why the domestic ruling elites are the ones at the front line battling against any internal forces opposed to Western domination in all spheres of national life. They are the local collaborators and agents of foreign domination. No wonder why most Westerners operating within Nepal refuse to shed their arrogant colonial mentality and deranged sense of superiority. No wonder why even a low-ranking Westerner in Nepal occupies a higher status in public eyes than a high-ranking Nepali. So widespread is this public perception that it can be considered fully socialized among the general populace. They have fully accepted the presumed notion of Western superiority (and, by implication, their own inferiority), virtually in every respect.

A REFLECTIVE NOTE ON NEPAL'S FUTURE

Nepal is definitely facing difficult times. Everywhere there is social and moral disintegration. As I have said before, agrarian life is resilient, but its resiliency is now being put to a fire test. Hardened by the daily grind of survival, the poor possess enormous abilities to endure many hardships of life, but their endurance may now be reaching a breaking point. For the countless masses, life is simply getting harder and harder to live; it has turned into an uphill battle, a Sisyphian task. No matter how hard they try, life never seems to get better. It only deteriorates. Hunger is more frequent than ever; it is more widespread than ever. Frustration is mounting as the pressure of survival increases on the poor, especially in the face of deteriorating life chances.

Such is the entrenched reality of contemporary life in Nepal. It is not a pretty scene.

I still firmly believe that the best path for Nepal, under these circumstances, is a Gandhian vision of non-violent change and pursuit of simple and self-reliant development that I discussed earlier. Almost 50 years ago, in his seminal book, *The Great Transformation*, Polyani (1957) argued that, as development conquers habitat (the primary source of people's survival security), as it turns land and labor—the two most basic building blocks of family and society—into mere commodities, the economy acquires an existence of its own, driven by laws of its own, whether conceived in capitalist or Marxist terms. The capitalist dogma of a self-regulating market is nothing other than a prescription for disaster. "Such an institution," Polanyi proclaimed, "could not exist for any length of time without annihilating the human and natural substance of society." Stripped of social, cultural, and ecological systems, he continued, people will perish from hunger, pestilence, violence, and neglect. While Polanyi was obviously premature in dismissing the resiliency of capitalism, he was right on target in his analysis of the dangers inherent in the elevation of the capitalist, Westernized economy (existence) over all other aspects of human endeavor and modes of existence (also see Levitt, 1995).

As Polyani correctly pointed out, the individualistic behavior is not a natural tendency regardless of what the capitalist bible of today's mainstream economic establishment preaches. This is not how societies existed for centuries in the past before the advent of capitalism and its global domination. Communal existence was the norm, based on the principle of reciprocity and coexistence. It is precisely this form of social and economic life that remained dominant in Nepal until the 1950s, and even until the 1960s. As discussed in Chapter 4, life was simple with human wants limited and artificial scarcities rare. People instituted ways to manage or minimize misuse or abuse of resources, often in religious terms, so they would be widely practiced. In fact, communal institutional mechanisms were set up to assure that people, regardless of class positions, adhered to such practices. Even in the area of food consumption, moderation was actively promoted.

But none of this will be possible unless foreign aid is removed first. It has to go, for it is not designed to serve Nepal and its masses irrespective of its claims. As long as foreign aid exists, there can be no self-reliance, nor any simple development. It is destructive to both Nepali psyche and sovereignty, not so much politically, but from the viewpoint of national integrity and pride. Foreign aid is nothing more than neo-colonialism.

As much as I believe in simple and self-reliant development and in a non-violent path to societal change, I do not foresee much hope for them to materialize under the Westernized development ideology that grips Nepal, that its ruling elites have adopted as their new religion. Perhaps my friend is on target when he said without a social revolution no new policy, no matter how beneficent, can be implemented. Perhaps he is correct when he saw Westerners in Nepal as a shield, protecting the domestic elites, and talked about the need to break this shield first to cripple the ruling elites. Maybe a social revolution is necessary. Maybe violence is inevitable; maybe it is the last hope for a better future as Barrington Moore conceded. How ironic it will be to be engaged in a bloodbath to rectify a bloody situation in which Nepal is trapped!

Maybe, despite the irresistible allure of the wild golden goose, there are still enough people left in Nepal, like my friend, who deeply feel the rage and, at the same time, are ready to funnel their rage into a collective fury to embark on a revolutionary march which, if it ever occurs, is bound to be a long one, perhaps longer than Mao's epic march popularly known as the *Long March*. If there is ever any genuine mass revolution in Nepal, it will have to be waged, as previously indicated, on two powerful fronts: one against the external counter-forces of capitalism (Westernization) that is currently blazing across the globe, crushing every form of resistance along the way, and the other against the internal state and its ruling elites who are obviously shielded by Western aid and agencies.

The revolutionary forces will have to be particularly mindful of the counter-forces of global capitalism. Even if they manage to break the Western shield and defeat the domestic elites, it is not certain at this point that they will be able to keep the all-consuming and overarching counter-forces of capitalism at bay. It possesses many tentacles and many channels; it has its own guerilla tactics of encircling the enemy when it is weak and retreating when the enemy is advancing. It is like a mutant virus that can lie dormant or use many vectors of penetration to break down the immune system of any social revolution. To repeat, it has already humiliated the former Soviet Union and brought down the Berlin Wall, and is now moving fast to conquer the Great Wall (China, that is). Following its remarkable triumph in 1975 over America's military might, Vietnam was finally able to exorcise its capitalist ghost, first imposed by the French and later by the Americans. But that did not last too long as they are already back in Vietnam with a vengeance, once again like the masters that they were prior to 1975. This proves that if these countries, with all their ideological training and philosophical grounding and with a long history of opposition to colonial and capitalist forces, could not resist the counter-forces of global capitalism, there is no way any social revolution of Nepal can afford to treat these forces lightly. That is why the revolution, if it is to succeed and leave a lasting imprint, will have to be constantly watchful, day and night, of global capitalism's many means and powerful weapons, both military and economic.

But, again, all these points and arguments might be moot in view of what has recently transpired in different parts of Nepal. Since I completed the first draft of this chapter toward the end of 1995, a major political movement has occurred in the country. While I don't have any clue as to whether my friend—there has been no news from or about him since my last visit with him—is, in any way, involved in this new move-ment or not, his thoughts have remained with me and have constantly reminded me of the volatile nature of revolutionary marches. One day it may look completely dead and finished, and the next day it suddenly rises from its ashes. As I have expressed in this very book, I was not sure about any prospect of a revolutionary march taking place in Nepal, at least not in the near future. Then, all of a sudden, here it is, at the doorstep—a revolutionary fire spreading across the country. I had seen no signs of it coming down the chute, at least not with the magnitude of force and organizational base it has demonstrated so far. It is real and cannot be ignored.

Let me conclude this chapter and this book with a brief account of this new revolutionary movement which is commonly known as the "People's War." The movement is launched by the Maoist faction of the Communist Party of Nepal (CPN-Maoist). It is a relatively small faction which has an antagonistic relation with the major communist faction called the United Marxist-Leninist (UML) party. The revolution started on February 13, 1996, with an attack on several private and state entities in different parts of the country. According to the account provided in the latest CPN-Maoist publication called *The Worker* (June 1996), on February 13, they attacked seven targets in six districts: two in the west (Rukum and Rolpa), one in the east (Sindhuli), and three in central Nepal (Gorkha, Kathmandu, and Kabhre). In the district of Gorkha, where the present Shah dynasty had its origin, they blasted a liquor factory and took possession of the Small Farmer's Development Programme Office located in Chyangli village. They also attacked three local police outposts, one each in Rolpa, Rukum, and Sindhuli districts. The target in Kabhre was a feudal usurer whose house was raided at night. In the capital city of Kathmandu, the activists' target was a soft-drink bottling factory owned by a multinational company. A portion of the factory building was torched.

The selection of the seven targets and their strategic geographical distribution in six districts in three different regions of the country provide a glimpse of not only the specificities of the people's war, but also its popular support and organizational strength. "The targets clearly symbolise the principal enemy classes, namely feudalism and comprador and bureaucratic capitalism, and their state power. The forms of actions resorted to in this initiation process are clearly seen to include guerilla actions, sabotage and propaganda actions.... And the political intent of the armed actions has been declared and emphasized from the very beginning to give a correct political orientation and to check possible distortions and disinformation by the reactionaries" (*The Worker*, 1996: 5).

Within three weeks following the onset of the people's war, the party had, through its local supporters and activists, distributed leaflets

In the name of development

about the war activities in 65 of Nepal's 75 districts. Such sabotage actions as destruction and seizure of properties, and punitive actions against local goons, police informers, and other enemy elements were carried out in three additional districts: Jajarkot and Sallyan in the west and Sindhupalchok in the east. So during the first three weeks, the radical forms of actions were concentrated in nine districts although propaganda activities were scattered throughout the country. Again, most of the radical actions revolved around the destruction and seizure of properties owned by those considered to be local "feudal tyrants and comprador and bureaucratic capitalists." In addition to a soft-drink bottling factory in Kathmandu, the only other entity with foreign affiliation that has come under attack is the locally-staffed field Office of Save the Children, which is an international non-governmental organization based in the United States (*The Worker*, 1996). I have seen no report of any attack on any foreigners or the entities directly run by foreigners.

According to the list included in *The Worker* (1996), a total of 30 party workers have been, as of June 1996, reported killed by the state forces, mostly police operations. In addition, the state has already launched a counter-offensive, randomly arresting and imprisoning hundreds of innocent citizens, party-workers, and those suspected of assisting the people's war movement. The Maoist party claims that war actions "...were carried out in such large numbers in the first two weeks that the party had to issue a circular and make an appeal to slacken the speed and scale of actions so as not to (go)... beyond the resistance capacity of the people and the Party" (*The Worker*, 1996). Scaled back or not, the people's war appears to be deepening and expanding. According to various newspaper accounts, in its high-action forms it is now being waged in more than 10 districts (see Map).

The war is being fought in a typical guerilla warfare fashion: hit-and-run, advance-and-retreat as necessary. The party has declared that "In the present condition of the balance of forces, the enemy wants to drag us into a decisive war, but on our part we want to avoid it and prolong the war. The enemy uses the strategy of attack, but we use the strategy of defense. The enemy wants to incite us, but we want to harass the enemy, tire him out and attack him at his weak points at the time and place of our convenience.... This path will unfold by making uses of all forms of struggle in keeping with the historical stage of development of Nepal and principally, as we have been saying all along, according to the strategy of encircling the city from the countryside, with agrarian revolution as the axis and from the midst and in conjunction with the rural class struggle.... Our armed struggle will be conducted by relying on the labouring masses, particularly the poor peasants" (*The Worker*, 1996:11, 14, 18).

One notable feature of the ongoing people's war is that it is being fought most intensely in a cluster of four western hill districts in the Rapti Zone of Nepal: Jajarkot, Sallyan, Rolpa, and Rukum. It is these districts that form the party's stronghold or operational base. And this is also the very area where the United States Agency for International Development (USAID) has implemented its largest development project in Nepal (in fact, it is the largest such project funded by a Western donor agency). The project has been going on for the past 15 years, and its major emphasis has been on the promotion and adoption of commercial farming and other forms of micro-enterprising among small farmers, including the production of liquor from a variety of fruits such as apples. The fact that Rapti peasants are actively supporting the Maoist movement in the region in open defiance of the state and its police forces suggests that so-called development efforts have polarized the communities and that they have further aggravated poor peasants' overall socioeconomic conditions and, consequently, incited them to resort to violence or to fight back for their survival rights.

I cannot say whether or not the ongoing people's war is the right medium to wage a struggle against the ruling class to restore national integrity and social justice and to uplift the masses. I have no way to predict whether it will succeed, and what form and direction it will take if it does succeed. One thing I know for sure is that it is a torturous and long road, demanding immense endurance and sacrifice from those marching down this road. The victory will not come easy, nor quick. If it does beat the odds and emerges victorious after a long struggle, I deeply hope it does not repeat the same mistakes that many past revolutionaries have committed in the aftermath of their ascent to the position of power: more undue terror and atrocities inflicted on the masses in the name of masses. Regardless of the course of the current revolution, I hope one day the masses themselves will awaken to their own common cause and chart a common course that binds them together as one communal unit, sharing and working together, setting aside their personal differences and greed to build a good society where they can live in harmony, where justice and peace prevail, where one's life is not for sale just to survive, where trials and travails of human history don't repeat, so they can be fully emancipated from their misery and see the vision of the following words turn into a living reality.

> Lift your faces, you have a piercing need
> For this bright morning dawning for you.
> History, despite its wrenching pain,
> Cannot be unlived, but if faced
> With courage, need not be lived again.

> — Maya Angelou, 1993
> ("On the Pulse of Morning"
> read at President Clinton's 1993 inauguration)

NOTES

1.   Dr. Mahat has denied the charges. Although he resigned from his post after many questions were raised about his account, he was later reinstated to the same position. Despite his public denial and explanation about the account, it is curious that the deposit was made during his tenure as Nepal's Finance Minister.

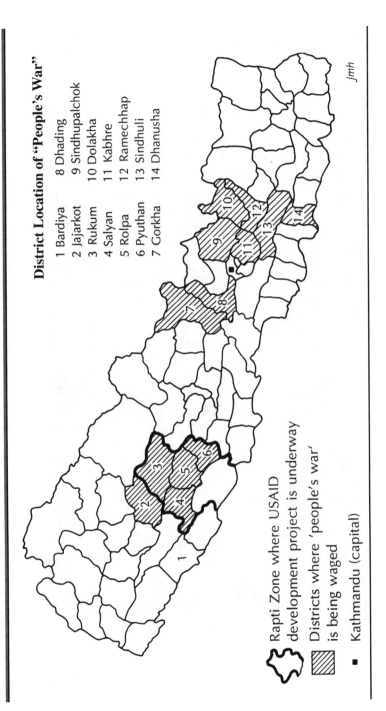

District Location of "People's War"

1 Bardiya   8 Dhading
2 Jajarkot   9 Sindhupalchok
3 Rukum   10 Dolakha
4 Salyan   11 Kabhre
5 Rolpa   12 Ramechhap
6 Pyuthan   13 Sindhuli
7 Gorkha   14 Dhanusha

Rapti Zone where USAID
development project is underway

Districts where 'people's war'
is being waged

Kathmandu (capital)

jmh

A typical house in the hills

REFERENCES

Acheson, Dean 1950 "Aid to Underdeveloped Areas as Measure of National Security" *The Department of State Bulletin*, April 3.

Amin, Samir 1976 *Unequal Development*. New York: Monthly Review Press.

___ 1993 "Can Environmental Problems Be Subject to Economic Calculations?" *Monthly Review*, 45:7.

ARTEP 1974 *A Challenge to Nepal: Growth and Employment*. Bangkok: ARTEP.

Baran, Paul A. 1973 *The Political Economy of Growth*. Middlesex: Penguin Books.

Barry, Kathleen, et. al. 1983 *International Feminism: Networking against Female Sexual Slavery*. New York: International Women's Tribune Center.

Bartley, Robert L. "The Case for Optimism: The West Should Believe in Itself" *Foreign Affairs,* 72:4.

Basnet, Suman 1992 "Urban Voices" *Himal,* January-February.

Bhandari, Bishnu 1989 "Drug Abuse in Nepal: A Case Study of the Kathmandu Valley" A paper presented at the 18th Annual Conference on South Asia, Madison, Wisconsin.

Bishop, Naomi 1993 "Circular Migration and Families: A Yolmo Sherpa Example" *South Asia Bulletin*, 13:1.

Blaut. James 1993 *The Colonizer's Model of the World: Diffusionism and Eurocentric History*. New York: Guilford Press.

Brass, Tom 1990 "Class Struggle and the Deproletarianisation of Agricultural Labour in Haryana (India)" *Journal of Peasant Studies,* 18:1.

___ 1991 "Moral Economists, Subalterns, New Social Movements, and the (re) Emergence of a (post-) Modernized (middle) Peasant" *The Journal of Peasant Studies*, 18:2.

Brass, Tom 1990 "Class Struggle and the Deproletarianisation of Agricultural Labour in Haryana (India)" *Journal of Peasant Studies,* 18:1.

___ 1991 "Moral Economists, Subalterns, New Social Movements, and the (re) Emergence of a (post-) Modernized (middle) Peasant" *The Journal of Peasant Studies,* 18:2.

Bridel, Renee 1983 "Traffic of Children" in Kathleen Barry et. al., *International Feminism: Networking Against Female Sexual Slavery.* New York: International Women's Tribune Center.

Broad, David 1995 "Globalization versus Labor" *Monthly Review,* 47:7.

Brower, Barbara 1992 *Sherpa of Khumbu: People, Livestock, and Landscape.* Delhi: Oxford University Press.

Burke, Ronald K. 1996 *Frederick Douglass: Crusading Orator for Human Rights.* New York: Garland Publishing.

Caplan, Lionel 1970 *Land and Social Change in East Nepal.* Berkeley: University of California Press.

CBS (Central Bureau of Statistics) 1992 *Statistical Pocketbook of Nepal.* Kathmandu: National Planning Commission.

Chatterjee, Pratap 1996 "Everything You Ever Wanted to Know about the World Bank (in South Asia)" *Himal,* July.

Congressional Quarterly Researcher 1993 "Preventing Teen Pregnancy" May 14.

Corbridge, Stuart 1986 *Capitalist World Development.* Totowa: Rowan and Littlefield.

Cose, Ellis 1993 *The Rage of a Privileged Class.* New York: HarperCollins.

Davidson, Basil 1992 "The Bones and Blood of Racism" *Race and Class* 33:3.

Department of Resettlement 1973 *Punarbas ra Abebasthit Basobas Niyantran Sambandhi Yojana ra Karyakram* (Resettlement and Control of Disorganized Settlement: A Policy and Plan of Action). Kathmandu: Department of Settlement, Government of Nepal.

Des Chene, Mary 1993 "Gurkhas as Diplomatic Currency" *South Asia Bulletin*, 13:1.

___ 1996 "Ethnography in the *Janajati-yug:* Lessons from Reading Rodhi and Other Tamu Writings" *Studies in Nepali History and Society,* 1:1.

Dixit, Ajaya 1992 "The Bagmati Scorned" *Himal,* January-February.

DuRand, Cliff "The Exhaustion of Developmental Socialism: Lessons from China" *Monthly Review,* 42:7.

The Economist 1984 "The World: Upside Down, Inside Out" December 22.

Engels, Frederick 1978 "Introduction" Karl Marx, *Wage Labour and Capital.* Peking: Foreign Languages Press.

Escobar, Arturo 1992 "Planning" in Wolfgang Sachs, ed. *The Development Dictionary: A Guide to Knowledge as Power.* London: Zed Books.

Esteva, Gustavo 1992 "Development" in Wolfgang Sachs, ed. *The Development Dictionary: A Guide to Knowledge as Power.* London: Zed Books.

Fanon, Frantz 1963 *The Wretched of the Earth.* New York: Grove Press.

Feuer, Lewis S. 1976 "Introduction" Karl Marx and Friedrich Engels, *Basic Writings on Politics and Philosophy.* Garden City, NJ: Anchor Books.

Firestone, Shulamith 1971 *The Dialectic of Sex: The Case for Feminist Revolution.* New York: Bantam Books.

Fleming, Charles and M. Ingrassia 1993 "The Heidi Chronicles" *Newsweek,* August 16.

Foner, Philip S. 1950 *The Life and Writings of Frederick Douglass, Vol. II: Pre-Civil War Decade 1850-1860.* New York: International Publishers.

Foster, John Bellemy 1995 "Ecology and Human Freedom" *Monthly Review,* 47:6.

Frank, Andre Gunder 1973 "The Development of Underdevelopment" in Charles K. Wilber, ed. *The Political Economy of Development and Underdevelopment.* New York: Random House.

Friedman, Robert I. 1996 "India's Shame: Sexual Slavery and Political Corruption Are Leading to an AIDS Catastrophe" *The Nation,* April 8.

Fürer-Haimendorf, C. von 1975 *Himalayan Traders.* London: Murray.

Fyfe, Christopher 1992 "Race, Empire and the Historians" *Race and Class,* 33:4.

Gaige, F. H. 1975 *Regionalism and National Unity in Nepal.* Berkeley: University of California Press.

George, Susan 1992 *The Debt Boomerang: How Third World Debt Harms Us All.* Boulder: Westview Press.

Ghimire, Krishna 1992 *Forest or Farm? The Politics of Poverty and Land Hunger in Nepal.* Delhi: Oxford University Press.

Graham, Ellen 1996 "How to Sell More to Those Who Think It's Cool to Be Frugal" *The Wall Street Journal,* September 30.

Griffin, Keith 1974 *The Political Economy of Agrarian Change.* Cambridge: Harvard University Press.

Guha, Ramachandran 1996 "Using and Abusing Gandhi" *Himal,* April.

___ 1989 *The Unquiet Woods: Ecological Change and Peasant Resistance in the Himalaya.* Berkeley: University of California Press.

Gyawali, Dipak 1996 "High Dams for Asia: Neo-Gandhian Maoists vs. Nehruvian Stalinists" *Himal,* March.

___ 1994a "A Fate Other Than Marginality" *Himal,* May-June.

___ 1994b "Buddhijibi: Intelligentsia Has No Clothes" *Himal,* September-October.

Hancock, Graham 1989 *Lords of Poverty: The Power, Prestige, and Corruption of the International Aid Business.* New York: Atlantic Monthly Press.

Harrison, P. 1984 *Inside the Third World.* Middlesex: Penguin Books.

Hayami, Y. and V.W. Ruttan 1971 *Agricultural Development.* Baltimore: Johns Hopkins University Press.

225

Hecht, Susanna and Alexander Cockburn 1990 *The Fate of the Forest: Developers, Destroyers, and Defenders of the Amazon.* New York: Harper-Collins.

Himal, "Voices" November-December.

___ "Limits to Growth: The Weakening Spirit of Kathmandu Valley" (Special Issue), January-February.

Hinds, John 1989 *Faces of the Night.* Bangkok: Duang Kamol.

Hinton, W. 1994 "Mao, Rural Development, and Two-line Struggle" *Monthly Review*, 45:9.

___ 1993 "Can the Chinese Dragon Match Pearls with the Dragon God of the Sea? A Response to Zongli Tang" *Monthly Review*, 45:3.

Hornblower, Margot 1993 "The Skin Trade" *Time,* June 21.

Hsu, D.Y. and P.Y. Ching 1991 "Worker-Peasant Alliance as a Rural Development Strategy for China" *Monthly Review*, 42:10.

Huntington, Samuel P. 1993 "The Clash of Civilizations?" *Foreign Affairs*, 72:3.

Illich, Ivan 1992 "Needs" in Wolfgang Sachs, ed. *The Development Dictionary: A Guide to Knowledge as Power.* London: Zed Books.

Ives, Jack D. and Bruno Messerli 1989 *The Himalayan Dilemma.* London: Routledge.

Jain, S.C. 1981 *Poverty to Prosperity in Nepal.* Delhi: Development Publishers.

Jameson, Fredric 1996 "Five Theses on Actually Existing Marxism" *Monthly Review*, 47:11.

Joshi, Bhuwan L. and Leo E. Rose 1966 *Democratic Innovations in Nepal.* Berkeley: University of California Press.

Kama Sutra of Vatsyayana 1963 (ed.) Translated by Sir Richard Burton. New York: G.P. Putnam's Sons

Kaplan, Paul F. and Nanda R. Shrestha 1982 "The Sukumbasi Movement in Nepal: The Fire from Below. *The Journal of Contemporary Asia*, 12:2.

Karan, P.P. and Hiroshi Ishii 1994 Nepal: *Development and Change in a Landlocked Himalayan Kingdom*. Tokyo: Tokyo University of Foreign Studies.

Kauffman, L.A. 1994 "Virgins for Christ: Young, Hot and Herded to Purity in a Pop Evangelical Extravaganza" *The Nation*, September 26.

Kenny, Judith T. 1995 "Climate, Race, and Imperial Authority: The Symbolic British Hill Stations in India" *Annals of the Association of American Geographers*, 85:4.

Lambers, H.W. 1973 "Foreword" in A. Beenhakker, *A Kaleidoscopic Circumspection of Development Planning with a Contextual Reference to Nepal*. Rotterdam: Rotterdam University Press.

Larmer, Brook and Patricia Roberts 1994 "With Courage and Condoms" *Newsweek* (International Edition), August 1.

Lenin, V.I. 1969 *Imperialism: The Highest Stage of Capitalism*. Peking: Foreign Language Press.

Levitt, Kari Polyani 1995 "Toward Alternatives: Re-reading *The Great Transformation*" *Monthly Review*, 47:2.

Lewis, W.A. 1954 "Economic Development with Unlimited Supply of Labour" *The Manchester School of Economics and Social Studies,* May.

Linden, Eugene 1991 "Lost Tribes, Lost Knowledge" (Cover Story) *Time*, September 23.

Lindorff, Dave 1994 "China's Economic Miracle Runs Out" *The Nation*, May 30.

Macfarlane, Alan 1976 *Resources and Population: A Study of the Gurungs of Nepal*. London: Cambridge University Press.

Majupuria, Indra 1985 *Nepalese Women* (Chapter 15: Sati Custom). Kathmandu: M. Devi.

Malthus, Thomas R. 1959 *Population: The First Essay*. Ann Arbor: University of Michigan Press.

Marx, Karl and Friedrich Engels 1996 *Basic Writings on Politics and Philosophy*. Garden City, NJ: Anchor Books

Matsui, Yayori 1983 "Why I Oppose Kisaeng Tours" in Kathleen Barry et. al., *International Feminism: Networking Against Female Sexual Slavery*. New York: International Women's Tribune Center.

Mazumdar, Sucheta 1992 "Women, Culture and Politics: Engendering the Hindu Nation" *South Asia Bulletin*, 12:2.

Mellor, John 1968 "Toward a Theory of Agricultural Development" in H.M. Southworth and B.F. Johnston, eds. *Agricultural Development and Economic Growth*. Ithaca: Cornell University Press.

Memmi, Albert 1965 *The Colonizer and the Colonized*. Boston: Beacon Press.

Metz, John 1989 "A Framework for Classifying Subsistence Production Types of Nepal" *Human Ecology*, 17:2.

Miliband, Ralph 1991 "Socialism in Question" *Monthly Review*, 42:10.

Mishan, E.J. 1970 *Technology and Growth: The Price We Pay*. New York: Praeger Publishers.

Moore, Barrington, Jr. 1987 *Authority and Inequality under Capitalism and Socialism*. Oxford: Clarendon Press.

Myrdal, Gunnar 1970 *An Approach to the Asian Drama: Methodological and Theoretical (Selections from Asian Drama: An Inquiry into the Poverty of Nations)*. New York: Vintage Books.

Nandy, Ashis 1992 "State" in Wolfgang Sachs, ed. *The Development Dictionary: A Guide to Knowledge as Power*. London: Zed Books.

The New Paper 1993 "No Way Out?" October 9 (published in Singapore).

Newsweek 1993 "Sex and the Church" August 16.

___ 1995 "More Bang for the Buck: Foreign Aid" May 29.

Olivelle, Patrick 1993 *The Āśrama System: The History and Hermeneutics of a Religious System*. New York: Oxford university Press.

Onta, Pratyous 1994 "Dukha During the World Wars" *Himal*, November-December.

Pahari, Anup 1991 "Ties That Bind: Gurkhas in History" *Himal,* July-August.

Panday, Devendra R. 1992 "The Enigma of Aid" *Himal,* March-April.

Pandey, Surendra 1993 "The Vadi Community and Prostitution" *South Asia Bulletin,* 13:1.

Patterson, John G. and Nanda R. Shrestha 1988 "Population Growth and Development in the Third World: The Neocolonial Context" *Studies in Comparative International Development,* 23:2.

Patterson, Orlando 1994 "Ecumenical America: Global Culture and the American Cosmos" *World Policy Institute,* 11:2.

Peet, Richard 1985 "The Social Origins of Environmental Determinism" *Annals of the Association of American Geographers,* 75.

_____ and Michael Watts 1993 "Introduction: Development Theory and Environment in an Age of Market Triumphalism" *Economic Geography,* 69:3.

Peluso, Nancy L. 1992 *Rich Forests, Poor People: Resource Control and Resistance in Java.* Berkeley: University of California Press.

Piel, Gerard 1993 "The West is Best" *Foreign Affairs,* 72:4.

Polyani, Karl 1957 *The Great Transformation.* Boston: Beacon Press.

Regmi, M. C. 1971 *A Study of Nepali Economic History.* Delhi: Manjushri.

Robinson, Lillian S. 1993 "Touring Thailand's Sex Industry" *The Nation,* November 1.

Rodney, Walter 1974 *How Europe Underdeveloped Africa.* Washington, DC: Howard University Press.

Rostow, Walter 1962 *The Stages of Economic Growth: A Non-Communist Manifesto.* Cambridge: Cambridge University Press.

Rubinstein, Annette 1992 "Shakespeare and the Subaltern" *Monthly Review,* 44:4.

Said, Edward W. 1993 *Culture and Imperialism.* New York: Alfred A. Knoff.

Schmetzer, Uli 1991 "Slavery Thrives in Asia: 1 Million a Year Sold" *Madison State Journal,* December 8.

Schram, Stuart, ed. 1974 *Chairman Mao Talks to the People: Talks and Letters, 1956-1971*. New York: Pantheon Books.

Schultz, T.W. 1953 *The Economic Organization of Agriculture*. New York: McGraw-Hill.

Schumacher, E.F. 1973 *Small Is Beautiful: Economics as if People Mattered*. New York: Perennial Library.

Seddon, David et. al. 1979 *Peasants and Workers in Nepal*. Warminster: Aris and Phillips.

Seers, Dudley 1973 "The Meaning of Development" in Charles K. Wilber, ed. *The Political Economy of Development and Underdevelopment*. New York: Random House.

Shah, Saubhagya 1993 "The Gospel Comes to the Hindu Kingdom" *Himal*, September-October.

Sharma, Gopi N. 1990 "The Impact of Education during the Rana Period in Nepal" *Himalayan Research Bulletin*, 10:2.

Sheldrake, Rupert 1991 *The Rebirth of Nature*. New York: Bantom Books.

Shiva, Vandana 1988 *Staying Alive: Women, Ecology and Development*. London: Zed Books.

Shrestha, Bihari K. 1993 *A Himalayan Enclave in Transition*. Kathmandu: ICIMOD.

___ 1992 "Rural Development Projects: Programmed to Forget the Poor" *Himal*, March-April.

Shrestha, B. L. "Valley Tourism: The Shine is Off" *Himal*, January-February.

Shrestha, Nanda R. 1993 "Enchanted by the Mantra of Bikas: A Self-reflective Perspective on Nepalese Elites and Development" *South Asia Bulletin*, 13:1.

___ 1990 *Landlessness and Migration in Nepal*. Boulder: Westview Press.

___ 1989 "Frontier Settlement and Landlessness among Hill Migrants in Nepal Tarai" *Annals of the Association of American Geographers*, 79:3.

___ 1985 "The Political Economy of Economic Underdevelopment and External Migration in Nepal" *Political Geography Quarterly* 4:4.

___ and Dennis Conway 1996 "Ecopolitical Battles at the Tarai Frontier of Nepal" *The International Journal of Population Geography* (forthcoming).

___ and Dennis Conway 1985 "Issues in Population Pressure, Land Resettlement, and Development: The Case of Nepal" *Studies in Comparative International Development,* 20.

___, Raja Velu, and Dennis Conway 1993 "Frontier Migration and Upward Mobility: The Case of Nepal" *Economic Development and Cultural Change,* 41:4.

Stevenson, Michael 1992 "Columbus and the War on Indigenous Peoples" *Race and Class,* 33:3.

Sutcliffe, R. B. 1973 "Introduction" Paul A. Baran, *The Political Economy of Growth.* Middlesex: Penguin.

Swasthani 2028 (Nepali Year) Version by Budhi Sagar Parajuli. Kathmandu: Ratna Pustak Bhandar

Sweezy, Paul M. 1994 "The Triumph of Financial Capital" *Monthly Review,* 46:2.

Tang, Zongli 1991 "Is China Returning to Semi-colonial Status?" *Monthly Review,* 45:3.

Tanzer, Michael 1995 "Globalizing the Economy: The Influence of the International Monetary Fund and the World Bank" *Monthly Review* 47:4.

Tiwari, Ashutosh 1992 "Planning: Never without Aid" *Himal,* March-April.

Toporowski, Jan 1995 "The Contradictions of Market Socialism" *Monthly Review,* 46:11.

Truong, Thanh-dam 1990 *Sex, Money and Morality: Prostitution and Tourism in South-East Asia.* London: Zed Books.

Ullrich, Otto 1992 "Technology" in Wolfgang Sachs, ed. *The Development Dictionary: A Guide to Knowledge as Power.* London: Zed Books.

Upreti, Aruna 1994 "Bombay, Byapar ra AIDS" (Bombay, Business and AIDS) *Gorkhapatra,* Saun 1, 2051 (A Nepali daily; date given in Nepali year).

Wagner, Thomas 1994 "Nepal Gambles on Casinos: Himalayan Kingdom Has Become Southeast Asia's Los Vegas" *The Milwaukee Journal*, January 30.

Wallerstein, Immanuele 1992 *Geopolitics and Geoculture*. Cambridge: Cambridge University Press.

Wallis, Victor 1996 "Socialism under Siege" *Monthly Review*, 47:8.

___ 1992 "Socialism, Ecology, and Democracy: Toward a Strategy of Conversion" *Monthly Review*, 44:2.

Washington, Booker T. 1986 *Up from Slavery*. New York: Penguin Books.

Weeks, Jeffrey 1991 *Sexuality*. London: Routledge.

Weil, Robert 1994, 1995 "China at the Brink: Class Contradictions of `Market Socialism' Part I and Part II" *Monthly Review*, 46:7 and 46:8.

Wells, Richard 1994 "Civilization and Its Discontents" *In These Times*, May 16.

The Worker 1996 (Organ of the Communist Party of Nepal—Maoist), June.

World Bank 1992 *World Development Report 1992*. New York: Oxford University Press.

___ 1988 *Nepal: Policies for Improving Growth and Alleviating Poverty, Report No. 7418-NEP*. Washington, DC: World Bank.

Yapa, Lakshman 1993 "What Are Improved Seeds? An Epistemology of the Green Revolution" *Economic Geography*, 69:3.

___ 1977 "The Green Revolution: A Diffusion Model" *Annals of the Association of American Geographers*, 67.

Zaman, M.A. 1973 *Evaluation of Land Reform in Nepal*. Kathmandu: Ministry of Land Reform.

Zurick, David 1992 "Adventure Travel and Sustainable Tourism in the Peripheral Economy of Nepal" *Annals of the Association of American Geographers*, 82:4.